THE SILENT COUP

Praise for *A Feast of Vultures: The Hidden Business of Democracy in India*

'This is a book about the truth about our nation. It confirms what we already suspect and shocks us further by unravelling the workings of the Indian system.' – Crossword Book Award Jury, 2017, for the best book in the non-fiction category

'This is an irritatingly brilliant book. Too sweeping, too condemnatory, and, perhaps, too true. This is not the kind of book Indians write. Such books are mostly written by foreign correspondents who after a stay of two or three years presumptuously do their obligatory "India book".' – Harish Khare, *The Tribune*

'Corruption emerges from a poorly regulated, unfree economy; personalities are irrelevant. Parties still need to be funded; allies still need inducements. I will not repeat all of what he has revealed and collated about the manner in which crony capitalism continues in the Modi era; buy *A Feast of Vultures* and be convinced yourself.' – Mihir Sharma, *Business Standard*

'This is a book that will depress you. It won't be an overstatement to say that it is a pessimistic take on today's India, but at the same time, it is a must-read for every Indian. The book paints a realistic picture of the country, which, sadly, never gets depicted in the works of our academicians or even journalists.' – Rishi Raj, *The Financial Express*

'Josy Joseph's *A Feast of Vultures* is an important, if sobering read, meticulously researched and intelligently written. India is a rich nation of poor people, and the vultures that prey on the common person are the everyday fixers, the multimillion-dollar-deal middlemen, and the billion-siphoning crony capitalists. The book starts with India's poorest and ends with the richest, leaving no doubt that the departure of the venal United Progressive Alliance (UPA) has made no difference to business as usual.' – Aditya Sinha, *Mint*

'Award-winning investigative journalist Josy Joseph's book, *A Feast of Vultures*, brings to the surface a narrative that calls for the cry of change in India. Exposing how our democratic system has been hijacked long ago, the book is explosive and frightening. It contains damning evidence against some of the largest businesses in India and highly-established politicians.' – Iftikhar Gillani, *DNA*

'Part memoir, part reportage and part polemic, Joseph's book is a cautionary tale of a nation losing its way because of an unchecked breakdown of some of its critical institutions. Rage seeps through the pages, and there is little hope. But there is some modest redemption ... When Joseph shines a light on the dark corners and the frayed edges and the decaying heart of the world's biggest democracy, it's a good time to ask: when will Indians confront their realities head on?' – Soutik Biswas, *Open*

'*A Feast of Vultures* is lending voice to millions of Indians, simmering with anger over huge corruptions ... Joseph's book is a big hope if not for changing, then at least for challenging the prevailing development discourse and pervasive corruption and rivalry in the upper echelons of power. A compelling multi-layered inquiry of deep corruption at the highest level of business and politics which must be read by activists, writers, teachers, students and public intellectuals to check the claims of transparency in governance and integrity in delivery of public promises.' – Manzar Imam, *The Criterion Journal*

'Every Indian citizen should read this book. It would perhaps even be advisable to translate this book into various Indian languages to ensure that it reaches everyone.' – Karthik Venkatesh, *Café Dissensus*

'In a time of strong charismatic leadership and whooping political changes, Josy Joseph's *A Feast of Vultures* reveals the truth about democracy in India ... The book comes up as a reality check for all those who believe in the efficacy of post-socialist India. The sad truth about democracy in India is that politicians come and go, the filthiness does not. It stays there, poisoning the entire system and laying down a path for systematic exploitation and destruction of a nation.' – Tejas Vasani, LegalBites.in

'Award winning journalist Josy Joseph wrote this book feeling anguished by the sheer scale of corruption in India, its dilapidated institutions and the deep immorality at the heart of its democracy. This is a fascinating study of an ugly India, a must read for those who care for the country and its future.' – *IANS*

Praise for *The Silent Coup*

'In this compelling book by the award-winning Indian journalist Josy Joseph, it is not India's political leaders who are under the spotlight but the murky workings of India's deep state, from the police to the federal investigative and intelligence agencies.' – Hannah Ellis-Petersen, *The Guardian*

'As you leaf through *The Silent Coup*, you are reminded of all those denied bail under UAPA. For instance, those accused of scripting the 2018 Bhima Koregaon violence and the 2020 Delhi riots. Judges must read the book to mull what they can do to prevent the deep state from engulfing the nation in darkness.' – Ajaz Ashraf, *Mid-Day*

'*The Silent Coup* is an eminently readable account peppered with such stories of characters like Ali and the good and bad men—they are mostly men—of India's sprawling security machinery. It is a scathing indictment of the police and internal intelligence professions, and of the profession that both Joseph and I belong to, the media.' – Samrat Choudhury, *Hindustan Times*

'A scathing indictment of the police, intelligence agencies and the submissive media, this well-researched book is a must read for everyone who is concerned about threats to Indian democracy.' – M.K. Chandra Bose, *Deccan Herald*

'Joseph's canvas is vast—from the Mumbai train blasts and the 26/11 terror attack to the Kashmir insurgency, turmoil in the Northeast, the Indian Peace-Keeping Force's debacles in Sri Lanka, and the "Gujarat model" of the war on terror whose central tenet seems to be the perpetual rediscovery of plots to assassinate Narendra Modi.' – G. Sampath, *The Hindu*

'Over the course of the book, Joseph recounts the remarkable lengths to which India's police-intelligence complex goes to do the bidding of political masters, including knowingly arresting and torturing ordinary Muslims to cover up their failure to prevent terror attacks, the seeding of fake narratives and involvement in terror conspiracies to advance communal agendas and the stubborn refusal to hold anyone in the security world accountable.' – Rohan Venkataramakrishnan, *Scroll.in*

'[T]his book by Joseph is an essential read to understand that recognised threats to democracy go beyond military coups and foreign invasions. They can take place through the whims and fancies of the ruling elites.' – Shaileshwar Yadav, *Leaflet.in*

'Joseph's has been a national service for outing India's deep state and mainstreamising a thought that has been present in the minds of India's Muslims and its alternative strategic community for long. India's strategic community will be judged on how it assimilates Joseph's findings, interpretations and conclusions.' – Ali Ahmed, *The Milli Gazette*

JOSY JOSEPH

context

THE SILENT COUP

A HISTORY OF INDIA'S DEEP STATE

cntxt

First published by Context, an imprint of Westland Publications Private Limited, in 2021

Published by Context, an imprint of Westland Books, a division of Nasadiya Technologies Private Limited, in 2022

No. 269/2B, First Floor, 'Irai Arul', Vimalraj Street, Nethaji Nagar, Allappakkam Main Road, Maduravoyal, Chennai 600095

Westland, the Westland logo, Context and the Context logo are the trademarks of Nasadiya Technologies Private Limited, or its affiliates.

ISBN: 9789395073035

10 9 8 7 6 5 4 3 2 1

Typeset in Scala Regular by SÜRYA, New Delhi

Printed at Manipal Technologies Limited, Manipal

Dedicated to my parents Annamma and Joseph and other children of independence,
In defiant hope that your greatest celebration won't turn into our worst nightmare.

'Real Swaraj will come not by the acquisition of authority by a few but by the acquisition of the capacity by all to resist authority when it is abused. In other words, Swaraj is to be obtained by educating the masses to a sense of their capacity to regulate and control authority.'

– M.K. Gandhi

Contents

Prologue

The message arrived on a winter morning as the year was winding up. I thought 2020 could hold no more surprises after the Covid-19 pandemic and the unravelling that followed. In my privileged seclusion, I was working on the last chapters of this book when the phone beeped: 'When I highlighted this ten years ago, no one bothered.'

Attached was a newspaper report about the latest Indian business family to flee the country after taking massive loans against non-existent businesses. The sender of this message, a successful petrochemical trader, had walked into my life more than a decade ago after a distress call detailing harassment at the hands of this business family. If I am to be honest, it took me a while to fully trust him. I had to hear his story a few times over, read hundreds of documents and meet other victims of the harassment. To begin with, I had thought he was hallucinating.

He claimed that he was hired to expand the petrochemical trading business of a Delhi-based company, owned by the business family, only to discover that the business was expanding into nowhere. Then he stumbled upon the company's dark secrets: its true business was money laundering, the circular trade of diamonds and other shady dealings. He wrote detailed whistle-blower accounts to Indian investigation agencies and banks. All of these complaints soon landed up with his company management or were ignored. Then began the harassment.

He, his extended family, his house help, his deputy in the

company who refused to file a fake case, all of them were hounded, harassed and tortured by the Punjab police. After our story[I] was published, partial normalcy was restored in their lives. During this period, the company tried its utmost to silence me through threats and inducements of a magnitude that was surprising even to a seasoned reporter like me. But stranger things were to come.

A decade later, here was my contact again, drawing my attention to another twist in the drama. The business family, like several others, disappeared from India after taking out hundreds of crores from Indian banks in loans that had been secured through political influence. When the family's questionable deals were exposed a decade ago by my contact, the police and other investigation agencies rushed to its rescue. Eventually, the family ran out of all options and quietly slipped away to safer shores. The Indian security establishment, and many banking officials, were enablers of the family's corrupt and criminal enterprise, and its final escape.

In many ways, this story is the essence of what this book documents.

At the heart of democratic India—protecting its borders, watching for subversions, maintaining law and order, investigating crimes and ensuring that the democracy does not slip into chaos—is the security establishment: a loose network of organisations such as the military, state police forces, paramilitaries, and the intelligence and investigation agencies. This sprawling establishment is constantly modernised and upgraded by the government through the taxes it collects from Indian citizens, just as the state maintains other national essentials like healthcare or roads.

A professional security establishment is at the core of the modern state. It is the state's best protection. But, if not managed well, it could turn into a nation's worst nightmare. The possibility that the military, the strongest arm of the security establishment, might take over governance has always been a real concern all over the world.

Some estimates[2] suggest that, since 1950, there have been over 460 coup attempts around the world, of which some 233 were successful. A ready example of such a threat materialising is our immediate neighbour Pakistan. Within years of its birth, the country's military became an active participant in its national politics, and by 1958, had carried out the first coup. Since then, the Pakistani military has executed several successful coups, subverted democracy repeatedly, crippled the country's social progress and assisted in imposing regressive religious beliefs. In short, it has established itself as not only Pakistan's most powerful institution but also its most menacing one. Similarly, soon after its formation in 1971, Bangladesh witnessed a coup in which its first president, Sheikh Mujibur Rehman, the 'Father of the Nation', was assassinated, along with his family and personal staff.

In contrast, the Indian military became a professional outfit that got down to the task of building a democracy. It was deployed in taking on insurgents and protecting the country's borders, and it joined international peacekeeping forces. Importantly, it became the frontline responder to natural disasters. Despite aberrations, the Indian military remains a fine professional institution to date. Many Indians draw solace from the fact that their military will never subvert the nation's democracy. I am one of them.

The founding fathers, and mothers, of India were acutely aware of the need for civilian control over the military. From the symbolic move of its first prime minister, Jawaharlal Nehru, into the residence of the commander-in-chief of the military to staffing the core of the entire Ministry of Defence (MoD) with civil servants, the principle of civilian control was firmly put in place. Even though civilian control could at times be overbearing, even occasionally immature, India was lucky to have very fine officers of high standing that would come to lead its military. This continues to remain true, mostly.

However, a military coup is not the only way to subvert a democracy. An invasion by a foreign power, the ouster of a regime by a rebel force, or assassinations, all of these are recognised threats.

But there is increasing evidence of a new threat—which I examine in this book—and this one comes from within: the subversion of democracy by the ruling elite of the country. Across the world, this is the most common reason that democracies descend into autocracies, as was seen in Singapore when Lee Kuan Yew imposed a one-party rule, or in Venezuela when President Nicolas Maduro won through a disputed election. India saw a similar subversion of democracy between 1975 and 1977, when Indira Gandhi declared the Emergency.

While analysing the reasons for such subversions, a critical question remains inadequately addressed: how can a person or a small coterie of influential people, stationed mostly in a single city, unsettle democratic institutions, intimidate millions into silence across hundreds of thousands of square kilometres, send thousands to jail, terrorise its business class into supporting it, smear its rivals and critics, bully the media into becoming its propaganda arm, convert the judiciary into a timid institution and silence even the most courageous of civil servants? Just a handful of people sitting in a city?

Through this book, I attempt to show—through real-life examples, characters and data—how a small set of such elites use the legitimate arms of the state to destabilise a large democracy of hundreds of millions of people.

How do they achieve this, especially, as is the case in India, when the military is not an active participant in it? And when every government servant is sworn to uphold the Constitution, rather than follow the diktats of an individual? This is where the non-military arm of the security establishment comes into play. The state's police forces, intelligence agencies, federal investigation agencies, tax departments and the like become the tools of the ruling elite. These agencies are empowered by labyrinthine laws, many of which were thoughtlessly passed by the political executive in a knee-jerk reaction to major historical developments, to make it easier for the authorities to haunt and harass their adversary of the moment, or indeed to deal with a real threat. Over time, through law and practice, there grew a parallel power structure—one that bolstered, not challenged, the executive. Most of these shadowy agencies stay out of the spotlight, and coerce the rest of the government machinery, including the civil services and judiciary, into actions favourable to the ruling regime. They raid, harass, eavesdrop, torture and kill. They malign, intellectually torture and create fake monsters out of ordinarily good people.

It was through the non-military arm of the Indian security establishment that Indira Gandhi and her coterie ran India during the Emergency. Police forces rounded up thousands of her opponents and threw them in jails; tax authorities raided the homes and offices of anyone the ruling elite did not like; laws were twisted to suit her office. And there were thousands of members of the non-military security establishment—from police constables to income tax officers—who were willing to be vassals of the ruling regime, rather than be protectors of the Constitution, which is what they are hired and paid for by the state. When Prime Minister Gandhi wanted to reconstitute the trust that ran the Vishwa Yuvak Kendra in Chanakyapuri, New Delhi, the lieutenant governor cited an obscure rule to requisition the building.[3] Coercive measures were used. In Haryana, when the people of Uttawar village refused to undergo the sterilisation programme, the district administration disconnected their electricity supply before the police raided the village and rounded up all the men into trucks and took them in to surgery.[4] When Haryana Chief Minister Bansi Lal wanted to settle a score with a family, the chief secretary acted to satisfy him.[5] The administration created fake claims to go after three generations of the family, detaining them under a draconian law. The youngest of them was denied a job in the judicial services. His father, uncle and grandfather were among those arrested. Similarly, in the national capital, a set of civil servants and police personnel were at Sanjay Gandhi's command to demolish the slums that were home to hundreds but eyesores to him, to forcibly sterilise thousands, and to round up politicians, journalists and activists. Sometimes, in their desperation to satisfy the masters, they also arrested the wrong guys.

The very same unaccounted part of the administration is also what the ruling elite uses to bestow favours. When Dhirendra Brahmachari, a close associate of the prime minister, wanted to import an aircraft during the Emergency and lied that it was a gift, officials showed great alacrity in clearing red tape to facilitate his outlandish purchase.[6]

The Shah Commission, which enquired into the excesses of the Emergency, said four decades ago: 'It is a matter of concern to the Commission that the prevailing acts of impropriety and immorality came to be accepted as a concept of a new propriety and a new morality.'[7] If another judicial commission were to investigate what is underway in the country today, without the fear of the stormtroopers of the ruling elite, it would reach the same verdict.

One of the finest judges of recent times said as much recently. Citing several instances of misconduct by officials, retired Supreme Court Justice Madan Lokur argues that the time has come to 'introduce an accountability jurisprudence and equal treatment under the law in respect of officers of the state acting not in good faith'.[8] Just a law may not be enough. A comprehensive, multi-level accountability and audit, and firm oversight by Parliament and state legislatures is the way forward for reining in the Indian security establishment, especially the non-military parts of it. There already exists a roadmap for such accountability, such as comprehensive police reforms, but those steps have been delayed by the political leadership.

What became of the officials who were indicted by the Shah Commission? Except for a few, very few, all of them went on to have flourishing careers. They became secretaries, ministers, police chiefs and heads of intelligence agencies. The big takeaway from the Indian experience of the Emergency period was that government-salaried stormtroopers were not accountable at all. Although the Congress party paid a price for its excesses in the 1977 elections, the faceless members of those agencies and forces who became willing slaves to the autocratic regime had learnt an important lesson: that serving political masters is an easy path to professional success and material benefits, and that there would be no consequences—unlike the difficult task of upholding the Constitution and the trust of the taxpayers. This book is about those willing slaves and their masters.

I have had a ringside view of this security establishment for over three decades. I did most of my schooling at a Sainik School, which has contributed hundreds of officers to the military. During our free time and even class hours in school, we were retold stories of their valour, and we basked in their glory. As a reporter, I mostly wrote about the security establishment. This includes the three military arms—army, navy, air force—and the coast guard; investigation agencies like the Central Bureau of Investigation (CBI), Enforcement Directorate (ED), Directorate of Revenue Intelligence (DRI), Customs, Income Tax Department; and intelligence agencies such as the Intelligence Bureau (IB), Research and Analysis Wing (R&AW), National Technical Research Organisation (NTRO), the intelligence arms of other agencies; state police forces and the paramilitary forces. I was very often overwhelmed by the courage and professionalism that I witnessed or heard of: the injured man who went back to the battlefield only to be killed; a young soldier who fell off an icy cliff as he fought on; a pilot who risked his life to save a city; an uncompromising eccentric who repeatedly challenged the lies of an entire establishment; a soft-spoken leader who tried to usher in grand reforms in the darkest corners of the intelligence network; an investigator whose obsession with detail unearthed some of India's biggest unsolved crimes. I spent the first two decades of my professional career among some of those inspiring professionals—military officers, spies, police officers, tax men and others.

However, these individuals are part of a larger whole. There is, equally, a dangerously unprofessional part of the security establishment that is willing to do the bidding of the political executive—and it is the role of these sections that we need to understand better if we are to save and protect this democracy.

There are about four million members in the non-military security establishment distributed across the country—from state police to tax collectors. In the seven decades since Independence, millions have suffered at the hands of the police; several families have been destroyed by intelligence agencies or fallen victim to motivated tax raids; thousands of undertrials await their turn at justice, many of them youngsters who are thrown behind bars for dreaming of a better tomorrow; and rival politicians are caught in the crosshairs of a ruling regime's ambitions. It is an endless vicious cycle.

It would be academically shallow and analytically incomplete if one were to blame only Indira Gandhi for the Emergency, or Narendra Modi for the present and dramatic decline in India's democratic standards or, indeed, a Western conspiracy to downgrade India's ranking as a free country. Throughout history, men and women who have been blinded by their pursuit of power have been not the exceptions but rather the norm. Occasionally, some of them benefit from the cracks in a society, latch on to emotional voids, deploy massive resources, build an aura and rise to power. They then proceed to destroy institutions built and nurtured over decades.

However, in mature democracies, such leaders are stopped in their tracks by robust institutions capable of the administration of justice. It is when democratic institutions give up their single-minded pursuit of justice that such men and women walk straight into the hallowed portals of a nation. India has been witnessing that reality for decades now. Rioters, murders, cheats, rapists are all climbing the ladder of power in this democracy.[9]

Indian democracy is at a crossroads today. Decades of repeated abuse have eroded much of the professional aura of the security establishment and permanent executive, and reduced these institutions to mere intimidatory arms of the political executive. Except in the rhetoric of the ruling elite, India no longer feels like a democracy. The contract of trust between citizens and law enforcers is permanently broken. In most parts, the Indian society is adrift in lawless waters.

This is a book about the gravest threat to the Indian state. It is, ultimately, an incomplete documentation of the vicious attack on the world's largest democracy by those who are duty-bound to protect it. This is the saga of the brownshirts who terrorise the sweaty masses who pay for them; these are the stories of those who wrap our ghettos in the silence of graveyards and snatch the dreams and voices of the next generation.

Corrective measures are urgently needed if future generations are to know what it means to live in a democratic state.

PART ONE

A TALE OF MUMBAI

'We must make our political democracy a social democracy as well. Political democracy cannot last unless there lies at the base of it social democracy. What does social democracy mean? It means a way of life which recognizes liberty, equality and fraternity as the principles of life. These principles of liberty, equality and fraternity are not to be treated as separate items in a trinity. They form a union of trinity in the sense that to divorce one from the other is to defeat the very purpose of democracy ... In politics we will have equality and in social and economic life we will have inequality. In politics we will be recognizing the principle of one man one vote and one vote one value. In our social and economic life, we shall, by reason of our social and economic structure, continue to deny the principle of one man one value. How long shall we continue to live this life of contradictions? How long shall we continue to deny equality in our social and economic life? If we continue to deny it for long, we will do so only by putting our political democracy in peril.'

– Dr B.R. Ambedkar

1

A Distant Echo

Cataclysmic events snake across oceans, over gardens in bloom, mountains bereft of snow and teeming cities, and sneak into our own homes. And in a tiny, unventilated home in Mumbai, such a thing can sit around uncomfortably, poking the residents every now and then, until suddenly, and without warning, it might engulf every inch of space in it.

The attacks on 11 September 2001 in the US reached Wahid Deen Mohammed Sheikh's[1] slum cluster home in Mumbai about two weeks later. Then twenty-one, Wahid taught at a government-aided school run by a trust, and had a future to look forward to. He was among the most educated in that corner of the Ghatkopar slums, on the eastern fringes of the city, and his steady monthly income could now ward off the persistent assault of poverty on the family.

Poverty was the pivot of their family history, and even of the religion that Wahid was born into. His father had run away as an eight-year-old from an impoverished Hindu family in Uttar Pradesh after his own father beat him up badly. The angry boy made his way to the local railway station and got on a train that brought him to Bombay. In this bewildering metropolis, he was adrift without a penny to his name or any place to call home.

After a few days of wandering, the child ended up at a dargah. Here, he met a tall woman dressed in a wrap-around skirt and kurta, with windblown open hair, furiously smoking cigarettes when she was not praying. She gave the famished boy water and food, and asked him to go back home. The boy said he would not. 'Do you want to stay with me?' she asked. He readily agreed, and moved into her home in a slum in Kalyan. She fed him and took care of him like her own child. Over time, she adopted two more orphans, and their family grew. One day, a man also moved in—together, they became parents to the three children, but the two never married. Eventually, the family shifted to a bigger slum in Ghatkopar.

When I first got to know Wahid, I asked him what his father's Hindu name was as a child. He did not know, and had to make enquiries to figure it out. His adoptive mother gave Wahid's father a new name, Deen Mohammed, which is the only name anyone remembers and the one he wanted to be known by. 'My father was given the freedom by Dadi to decide which religion he wanted to follow. He chose to become Muslim like the kind new mother he found,' Wahid explained. We were discussing the twists and turns of his life, including how he came to be a Muslim.

'Look at them,' Wahid says of his parents. 'I still find it surprising that they got married. My mother is tall (unlike him). Her name is Mumtaz.' He smiles. Mumtaz was just thirteen when she got married in 1977. A year later, their eldest was born, and they named him Wahid, one of the ninety-nine names of the Allah, meaning unique, peerless. Wahid and his siblings called their adoptive grandparents Dada and Dadi. Years later, when Wahid watched actress Pooja Bhatt in the song *Mainu Ishq Da Lagya Rog*, she reminded him of a photo back home—his grandmother in wrap-around skirt and kurta, her open hair flying in the wind. Dadi passed away a few months after Wahid was born. However, the big framed photo of her remained in the house. Before setting out for exams or any important events, Wahid and his brothers took her blessings at the photo.

While his own family holds liberal Sufi beliefs, Wahid grew up to be an orthodox and religious man. He has no real explanation for this choice, simply saying that he did not believe in the Sufi concepts of worshipping in dargahs or organising feasts for the public. Occasionally, he reprimanded his mother and brothers for doing what he believed Islam did not permit. He was also a regular at the local mosque.

One humid day, as Wahid stepped out of the mosque after his evening prayer, a stranger walked up to him and asked, 'Wahid?' It was 27 September 2001. When the young teacher confirmed his identity, the man said he was a policeman. A few more people joined him, and told Wahid to accompany them to the local police station. They gave him no reason, and assured him that it was for a short interaction with their senior officer. Unbeknownst to Wahid, the 9/11 attacks in the US were entering his own life, forever changing it.

In the course of time, it would become clear that the 2001 attack on New York would change the lives of millions of Muslims around the world—from misguided youth who went on to become terrorists to children who were bombed to death by the American desire for revenge; from rulers who became autocrats to militaries that got blinded; from mindless intelligence that killed innocents to hardboiled information that got deadly terrorists.

Those nineteen terrorists who staged the televised attacks, one of the deadliest in modern history on American soil, changed the world dramatically. Suddenly, there were no freedom fighters, insurgents or militants. Anyone who took up arms against the state was now a terrorist. US President George W. Bush told a joint session of Congress on 20 September that year: 'Every nation, in every region, now has a decision to make. Either you are with us, or you are with the terrorists.' The global response was instant, and most countries declared support for US actions. Over the next few years, more than 140 countries passed stringent counterterrorism legislations, according to estimates by the Human Rights Watch. The US war on terror gave cover to many illiberal democracies and autocracies for a brutal crackdown on those inconvenient to them. The world witnessed one of the largest burials of dissent in modern times.

For India, it was an easy decision to make. It was still chafing from the humiliation of the IC-814 hijack of 1999 and other high-profile terrorist attacks, such as the one on the Jammu and Kashmir (J&K) Legislative Assembly. New Delhi opened its deep intelligence archives to the Americans, and even toyed with the idea of joining the American war on terror by sending troops to Afghanistan. It was quick to move on the domestic side too. India declared the Students' Islamic Movement of India (SIMI) a terrorist organisation and banned it under the Unlawful Activities (Prevention) Act, 1967 (UAPA). Orders went out to state police forces to round up any and all members of SIMI—not an easy task in Mumbai or elsewhere. The order was ill thought out. To begin with, SIMI had not been proven to be a terrorist organisation. Complicating the situation was the near absence of Muslims in the ranks of the security establishment.

Besides, it was hard to deny the erosion in the establishment's professional standards. Over the years, police reforms had been mostly stalled by the political parties in power, both at the Centre and in the states. Many aspects of this are well documented. I know from the barrage of anecdotes that I have collected during reporting trips around India that the political executive and corrupt police officers had made a lucrative business out of transfers and postings.[2] Politicians in power tended to micromanage the police.[3] Now, India's participation in the war on terror worsened a fragile system. The numbers of fake encounters, custodial torture and killings, fake narratives, framing of innocents as terrorists, all went up under the cover of this crackdown on terrorism.

Human rights agencies were reporting a worrying systemic rot even in the pre-9/11 era. In 2000–01, the army alone registered 120 complaints of alleged excesses by its personnel in Kashmir and the Northeast, the National Human Rights Commission (NHRC) noted in its annual report.[4] Other than the Border Security Force (BSF), no other paramilitary force bothered to even reply to its queries regarding complaints of atrocities. NHRC received at least fifty-two complaints of human rights violations from the Northeast in

2000–01. In Kashmir, a team of army and police officers staged a fake encounter to kill five innocents, and claimed they were terrorists. Such brutal acts were not limited to militancy-hit areas. In 1999–2000, NHRC reported 1,093 cases of custodial deaths.[5] The same account said almost every second state reported police brutality, irrespective of the party in power. These trends sharpened after the Kandahar hijack of IC-814 in 1999.

When the ban on SIMI came, less than 1 per cent of Muslims made up the ranks of the Maharashtra state police,[6] far below India's embarrassingly low 4 per cent Muslim representation in the Indian Police Service (IPS). The story was not very different in other states: in Uttar Pradesh, just 2.3 per cent of sub-inspectors are Muslims, and a little over 3 per cent head constables and just over 4 per cent constables are Muslims, an RTI query revealed in 2014.[7] The High-Level Committee on Social, Economic and Educational Status of the Muslim Community of India, headed by Justice Rajinder Sachar, found that just over 3 per cent of the paramilitary force was Muslim. Only 3 per cent of the Indian Administrative Service was Muslim.[8]

With a history of communal riots and the general lack of trust between Muslims and the police in Maharashtra, reliable active intelligence was non-existent from within the Muslim communities.

The policemen began their search for suspected SIMI members from Parksite police station in Mumbai, not far from Wahid's mosque and chawl. It emerged later that they had an informant, the president of the local masjid. The police rounded up eight Muslims, Wahid among them. The eight spent a quiet evening in the police station.

Then, around 11 p.m., some policemen began mercilessly beating up a petty criminal who was in detention. Against the background noise of the man screaming and pleading, the head of the station, a senior inspector, made his dramatic entry and began his investigation into what he said were terror conspiracies. Despite the eight men's insistence that they were innocent, the inspector forced them to spend that night in the station, on newspapers spread on the cold cement floors, next to a stinking toilet. In the morning, they were taken to the local court, which granted the police custody of them.

The station head now changed gears. As soon as the eight were brought back to the station, physical torture began.

The inspector asked Wahid, 'You are a SIMI member?'

'No, who said that?' the teacher asked.

'Your masjid president.'

The questioning and torture continued in this vein: Did Wahid have a passport? Had he gone to Pakistan for training? What subversive activities had he learnt there? Could he make a bomb? One of the policemen pulled out a portrait of Osama bin Laden, the founder of the Al Qaeda, who had masterminded the 9/11 attacks, and asked Wahid: 'Do you know him?'

'Yes, it is bin Laden.'

'We got it from your office.'

'Which office?' Wahid asked.

'SIMI office,' the policeman responded. They had clearly concluded that he was a SIMI member, lack of proof notwithstanding.

Wahid was shown a file allegedly recovered from the SIMI office, with 'CP' scribbled on it. The policemen asked him to explain what 'CP' meant. When he continued to deny any association with SIMI or knowledge of what 'CP' might mean, one of the policemen made a written entry in the records, claiming 'CP' stood for 'Current Publication'. Then they showed him an *India Today* magazine with bin Laden on the cover, also purportedly recovered from the SIMI office.

The failure to make a breakthrough was making the policemen even angrier, Wahid recalled. The frenzied torture claimed its first casualty: one of those in custody suffered a heart attack and had to be rushed to the hospital. Those still in police custody were faced with a new routine of torture, bad food and communally charged invective. 'One day, the senior inspector called me to his room. A couple of people sat facing him. I stood behind them. He asked the men if I was Wahid. One of them turned to look at me, and confirmed my identity,' Wahid recalled. 'It was the president of the masjid.'

Wahid explained what the masjid president's motive might have been: 'He was upset with me for my religious line, for not accepting niyaz [offerings made to strangers, which many believers say can only be done in Allah's name]. He had heard of my orthodox position from my brothers, because I often argued at home with them.' The mosque had its own rules, and the president once told Wahid that, since he was not a Sunni Muslim, he should pray somewhere else. Wahid also related an unconnected anecdote—that, years later, this man was arrested on rape charges filed by his wife.

The then young schoolteacher was getting a peek into the incredibly opaque, mostly unverified and often bogus industry of informants that flourish across the Indian security establishment network. This industry of informants around the world, cumulatively, could well be bigger than the biggest multinational corporations, because, in the world of intelligence, information is the most valuable commodity. From senior intelligence officers to beat constables, everyone is desperate for information, and thus it is a legitimate function to cultivate sources: from street urchins to well-placed corporate honchos, from retired officers to journalists, from petty criminals to gangsters, anyone could have vital information. For each piece of information, there is a price that the security forces and intelligence agencies are ready to pay. Thousands of people across the country, whether your next-door neighbour or a high-flying journalist, could be retainers earning handsome fees as informants.

During my stint with the *Times of India* group's online division, I was designated, among other things, to look into India–Pakistan affairs. Within days, an acquaintance of mine from the IB reached out with word from a senior official, offering me a monthly retainer. 'Why would you pay me?' I asked him. He said the senior wanted me to ensure that 'our perspective is reflected in your efforts'. A few years later, when I had obtained admission to a master's degree course at the Fletcher School of Law and Diplomacy, a senior R&AW

official said they could sponsor my studies. But then he paused, took a sip of his drink, and said, 'Actually, you should not take our support, find your own resources.' He was genuinely fond of me.

Another time, when I had just returned from Nepal, after interviewing Jamim Shah, a media baron in Kathmandu suspected by Indian agencies of being Dawood Ibrahim's operative in Nepal, a senior IB official asked to meet. As we sipped tea in his North Block office, he asked if I could go back to Nepal. 'My boys will accompany you, just show them where you met Shah.' I turned down the request. A few years later, in 2010, Shah was gunned down in Kathmandu. In Nepal, it was widely speculated that the murder was an operation by the Indian intelligence. In my decades as a journalist, I have received several offers, some of considerable monetary benefit, for exclusive information. Most reporters have similar tales to tell. Some have enjoyed these benefits too.

Many informants have vested interests, either to earn a quick buck or tarnish a rival, sometimes even to deliberately mislead agencies. If information is not collected with such biases factored in, and not analysed with academic rigour, the whole system could get muddled. This is what the world saw in 2003, when the US invaded Iraq.

The US National Intelligence Estimate concluded that Iraq President Saddam Hussein was stockpiling chemical and biological weapons and was in league with the Al Qaeda. This intelligence was used to persuade the Congress to authorise war, and it formed the basis of the US Secretary of State Colin Powell's address to the United Nations in February 2003 arguing for the same. Later, it was found that the Estimate relied on misleading or incorrect information, much of it from a single source: a chemical engineer who was last in his class and drove a taxi in Baghdad before fleeing Iraq because of theft cases against him. Rafid Ahmed Alwan, better known to the world as 'Curveball', was probably an alcoholic, was definitely a pathological liar and was playing the system. He told the German and US intelligence operatives elaborate stories about how Saddam's regime was building mobile weapons laboratories. In March 2003, an international coalition, led by the US, invaded Iraq based on his information. It was an action that destabilised the country, caused the deaths of over 200,000 Iraqi citizens, and resulted in immense violence and cruelty.

However, this was an aberration. In most professional intelligence agencies, including in the US, sources are well accounted for and their information is constantly audited. If an informant is found to be providing false information, he or she is struck off the rolls and entertained no more. My research and reporting inform me that the Indian security establishment, however, has a very loose system of auditing, one without any critical supervision. As a result, Indian agencies have fake information pouring in through their vast network, which has dramatically and adversely impacted India's war on terror. Occasionally, it leads to comic situations. One time, central intelligence agencies received, and issued an alert for, a terror threat on the pilgrimage site of Sabarimala in Kerala, creating a public furore. Soon enough, though, a vigilant IB official established that a police inspector of the state Special Branch had received the information from one of his relatives, who also happened to be his paid informant. The IB official got the informant's number and called him. The surprise call gave the man no time to prepare, and he blurted out: 'I saw the threat in my dreams.'

Many intelligence operatives talk off the record about the absurdity of information collection along the Pakistan border. A Pakistani informant might be deliberately allowed to cross the border into India, where Indian agents pounce on him. He goes from agency to agency, feeding information, collecting his payments and liquor, if available. No one knows if those Pakistanis are genuine informants, or deliberately sent to mislead Indians. But no one dares to audit or question their information.

In the Kashmir Valley, several deaths of military personnel, especially officers, can be mapped to misleading inputs from informants, according to one veteran intelligence officer who has studied the pattern in recent years. When a military officer leaves the Valley on transfer, one of the truly valuable things he hands over to his successor are his sources. In the valley's hostile environment, there is little the forces can do to verify the credibility of their sources. Informants are rare and precious, and so kept a secret. The informant is a VVIP in the military compound, the officer's special guest. He establishes his credentials with the incoming officer early by providing accurate information about militant movements. Once he wins the officer's trust, the informant could well play him at a crucial time, feeding him information about a high-profile militant's presence someplace. Based on that information, the officer and his team might walk into a trap. In recent years, this is how several sensational killings of security officers have been carried out, the veteran told me as he enumerated the names of the senior army officers who have died in this manner.

Outside of conflict zones, one of the weakest spots for the Indian security establishment is its lack of credible information from Muslim communities. Given the fact that Pakistan has been actively trying to foment trouble across the country using its own agents and by recruiting Indian Muslims, the need to cover this gap has always been an intelligence priority. However, so deep-rooted and systemic are anti-Muslim biases in the security establishment that, in the two decades or so that I have reported on the security establishment, I have not come across an instance of R&AW appointing even a single Muslim to a senior position. In fact, at least a couple of senior officers who were in favour of appointing Muslim officers have told me how the system frustrated their efforts. The handling of the three-decade-old Kashmir crisis has further injected serious biases against Muslims into the system, according to officers who have watched these developments warily.

A member of the Indian security establishment is often brought up on fake narratives about Islam, half-baked analyses and an environment that is actively hostile to Muslims. More often than not, it is the most Islamophobic voices that jump in with twisted narratives, eager to find Muslim perpetrators to a crime at hand. There is such a build-up of false narratives and fake stories that the security establishment and mainstream media are floating in fake information, wrong claims and a frightening level of Islamophobia.

Petty criminals or other anti-social elements form a bulk of the informant network, and this is as true among Muslims as other communities. With their vested interest in making a fast buck from the agencies, these informants are not the best source if one wishes to impartially understand a community. So, that's the first step: cultivating criminal elements as informants. The second step is: since you don't know too many Muslims, arrest the ones you know. A broad analysis of several alleged terror cases in recent memory[9] indicates that Muslim informants are often nurtured so that they can be sacrificed in the future as alleged terrorists. A few years ago, when the National Investigation Agency (NIA) arrested several Kashmiris in connection with a few different cases, a contact of mine from the IB told me that most of these men were actually IB informants until then.

Such was the experience of Delhi resident Irshad Ali over a decade ago. In the 1990s, Ali lived in a single-room slum house in Rithala, on the northern fringes of Delhi. He had six sisters, and a brother who was a murderer and had been incarcerated. Ali took to driving a taxi to support his large family, but the income was not enough to meet even their bare expenses. Ali was a regular visitor to the jail where his brother was being held, and got to know some policemen. They suggested a way that he could earn more money: become their informant.[10] He readily agreed. His brother in jail would steal letters and collect other details of the inmates that the cops wanted to keep a close watch on and pass it all to Ali, who, in turn, gave it to the police. The reward was significant: Rs 7,000 per month. Besides the money, proximity to the police gave the poor man an immense sense of security. From working with ordinary constables, Ali graduated to assisting the IB and the Special Cell of the Delhi police. He also helped them recruit a few other informants, all of them poor Muslims, including his cousin Qamran.

On 12 December 2005, Ali went to a Delhi hotel for a routine meeting with his IB handler, who asked him to accompany him in his car. As he climbed in to the rear seat, two others jumped in from both sides, sandwiching Ali between them. The car sped towards Red Fort, even as the two blindfolded him. A stunned Ali could make no sense of what was happening to him. Meanwhile, the IB and Special Cell operatives were scripting a story to tie him to. It was a difficult time for the agencies. Over a month ago, on 29 October 2005, two days before Diwali, bombs had gone off in three crowded markets in the national capital, killing sixty-two people and injuring over 200. The security establishment was under immense pressure to solve the crime, with no information or leads on the real terrorists. So, they produced their own fake narrative.

For two months, Ali was kept in various hideouts, and finally produced before the media along with his cousin Qamran. The police said that they were dreaded Al-Badr terrorists caught from the northern fringes of the city, and were responsible for the Diwali bombings. The two cousins ended up in Tihar Jail for the next four years. Fortunately, they got effective legal assistance, and an efficient CBI investigation established their innocence. The duo was acquitted in 2016, after sacrificing more than a decade of their lives—years during which their families suffered immensely. Ali lost his young daughter while he was in jail.

In Ali's media interviews, well after he had been released, he had a further explanation for why he was picked up. He says that, in the months running up to his detention, he was being pressured by his handlers to indoctrinate local Muslims into taking up arms and then to pass on their details.[11] It was a simple plan—create a fake terrorist and arrest him, ruin his life and show him off to the public as a success of the war on terror. This model, of creating a fake incident or a fake terrorist, is among the dirty secrets of the Indian security establishment.[12]

Some of the most sensational terrorist attacks in India have fallen under the suspicion that they were orchestrated by the security establishment. The attack on the Indian Parliament on 13 December 2001 stands out in this regard—Afzal Guru was arrested for the attack and put on trial. He was accused of providing logistical support to the attackers. However, in an interview to the editor of *Caravan* magazine, Vinod K. Jose, in 2006, after he was sentenced to be hanged, Guru said that he had been tasked by a J&K police officer, Davinder Singh, with a small errand. 'He told me that I had to take one man to Delhi. I was supposed to find a rented house for him in Delhi. I was seeing the man for the first time, but since he did not speak Kashmiri, I suspected he was an outsider. He told his name was Mohammad,' Guru said.[13] Mohammad led the five gunmen who stormed Parliament on 13 December. Guru claimed that the five men used to get calls from Davinder Singh when they were in Delhi.

Meanwhile, he returned to Kashmir, and was arrested for the attack from the Srinagar bus stand. In the custody of the Delhi police Special Cell, Afzal Guru was forced to implicate several others, including a Delhi University professor, Syed Abdul Rahman Geelani, he claimed. When he was presented before the media to speak about his role, he deviated from the script, and ACP Rajbir Singh shouted at him in front of the media personnel who were taping him.

In a letter he wrote to his lawyer, Guru repeated these claims, and no one denied them.[14] He was hanged on 9 February 2013.

Rajbir Singh, who was leading the Delhi police investigations into the attack, did not live to see Guru's hanging. On 24 March 2008, he was shot dead by a property dealer in Gurgaon with a pistol that was issued to a Haryana police officer, who himself was accused of murder once.[15] The murky world of the security establishment was on display in Singh's murder. The CBI court said Singh was investing money in his killer Vijay Bharadwaj's property business. On his final day, he walked into the property dealer's office, asking his Z-plus security team to wait outside. One may argue that, by the time he died, Singh had scripted a rise that is an exemplar of the sinister side of the security establishment that this book explores.

Rajbir Singh had an unbelievable career, claiming over fifty encounter killings, most of them controversial. He led the controversial encounter at Delhi's Ansal Plaza shopping mall in 2002, was caught on tape dealing with a drug trafficker and was accused of manhandling some people in Delhi's Kirti Nagar while dealing with a property dispute. But none of it affected his professional life. He was the mainstay of the Delhi police Special Cell.[16]

What about DSP Davinder Singh of J&K police, the man who had been in touch with Guru? On 11 January 2020, he was arrested by his own police while travelling with two terrorists to Delhi. The police suspected that he was going to Delhi to organise another attack. But no one talks about the Parliament attack anymore, because every member of the security establishment resists transparency.

In interviews with the media after his acquittal, Irshad Ali had also said he was being pressured by the handlers to cross over to Pakistan, probably to infiltrate terror groups. However, he was growing tired of all this pressure, and had told his handlers that he would not be able to carry out their tasks anymore. In fact, Ali says he was waiting to meet his handler outside the hotel to collect his last payment. Despite the CBI's indictment of the Special Cell and the IB, not one official was punished, not one disciplined. In the secretive world of security agencies, failures are routine, mistakes are allowed and a crime is usually pardoned.

After about ten days in police custody, Wahid and the seven other suspected SIMI members were sent to Thane Jail. Some months later, the police filed charge sheets against them, saying that, on the day SIMI was banned, they met at its office late at night and planned to carry out a terror attack. The police had been alerted by an informant, the charge sheet claimed. Further, it alleged that when the police came to arrest them, the group resisted and had to be overpowered. In 2013, a court dismissed the entire case, discharged all eight men, and said the police could not even prove that they were

SIMI members, let alone a terror conspiracy. But by then, they were accused of the Mumbai train blasts, and in jail, according to Wahid.

The twelve-year-long path from detention in 2001 to acquittal in 2013 was one of years of turmoil, harassment, midnight knocks on the door, and repeated encounters with the deep biases and ignorance in the Indian security establishment. In this time, he lost his father, his mother's schizophrenia worsened, he suffered repeated torture and developed severe glaucoma.

Just before Wahid's detention, his family had finally begun to hope for a more stable life in the chaotic metropolis. When Wahid was still in school, his father had lost his job and had been ill most of the time since. Ammi, as he called his mother, was the family's anchor and breadwinner. She worked in middle-class houses nearby, cleaning and washing utensils, even as she braved schizophrenia with little professional help. Growing up, Wahid would often accompany Ammi to work after school hours.

Wahid's job as a teacher could have been a new beginning for his family. But his arrest spun it into turmoil. Within days of his detention, his father suffered a heart attack. When the news of it reached the jail, the police brought Wahid to the hospital. 'This is not for us, police, court, all this. You get out of it all,' the ailing father whispered from his hospital bed, almost innocently believing that his son had a choice. Wahid held his hand, and they both started weeping. As the trial got underway two months later, Wahid was released from jail.

The family elders decided that marriage might provide him with some kind of protection from police harassment. They decided to approach the family of Sajida, a teacher who was distantly related to their neighbour, and whose family stayed in Andheri before shifting to the Mira Road area. Wahid's grandmother travelled to Mumbai from Pune, so that the two of them could go and see the girl.

'How much dowry will you give your daughter?' the old woman asked the girl's family. Wahid pressed his grandmother's hand to silence her, because he firmly believed in the Islamic preaching of 'mahr', which obligates the groom to pay money or gift other possessions to the girl. The grandmother asked Wahid to shut up. The girl's side started laughing.

Though the old woman insisted that they would take gifts, before she could make any demands on the size of the celebrations, Wahid said firmly that only five people would be present from their side for the marriage. His grandmother was very angry, but Wahid was able to ensure a simple ceremony.

The in-laws gifted him with a Titan watch during the marriage. 'It was stolen on the second day,' Wahid said dryly. Such was the seamless existence of ordinary people, alleged terrorists, police informants and petty thieves in the crowded slum they called home. Some weeks later, the young couple rented a flat in Mumbra area, and started enjoying their freedom and planning a future together. Sajida quit her job in a private school, and Wahid went back to teaching. I asked Wahid if he had forced Sajida to quit, because I had sensed by then that he did not have very progressive views on women's rights, not unusual in an Indian man. He replied that she went back to work when he was in jail to support the family.

Amidst his personal struggles and the happiness of a new life as a married man, Wahid was aware of the communal tension that had been sweeping through India after the Babri Masjid was demolished by Hindu fanatics in 1992. Many years ago, on a summer night, when Wahid and his brothers were sleeping outside their cramped house, they were woken by a clamour. Soon, a group of people jumped over them and ran down the narrow lane. Before they could make sense of what was happening, their parents pulled the three brothers indoors. In the morning, they learnt that there were communal riots close by. Between December 1992 and January 1993, over 900 people were killed in riots across Mumbai. On 12 March 1993, in the deadliest terrorist attack in India, orchestrated by criminals with Pakistani state support, thirteen bombs were blasted in the city. About 260 people were killed and hundreds more injured.

Now, as Wahid settled down to married life, a series of events began to unfurl in western India that would rip his life apart.

The Sabarmati Express pulled into Godhra station on 27 February 2002, several hours behind schedule. As it did, there was a fire in coach S6, in which fifty-nine karsevaks, Hindu pilgrims returning from Ayodhya, were burnt to death. There were primarily two narratives about the Godhra carnage. One, propounded by then Gujarat chief minister, Narendra Modi, and the state's police, was that it was a planned conspiracy. Those who favoured this conspiracy theory claimed that a group of Muslims had planned the whole affair; they had organised petrol and other items the previous night and carried out the attack when the train arrived. Modi was the first one to say that there had been a conspiracy,[17] contradicting the then current version of local officials.

The second narrative was that the karsevaks in the train were unruly, got into a fight with Muslim vendors on the platform and tried to kidnap a Muslim girl at the station, resulting in stone-pelting by Muslims as the train left the station. Just outside the station, someone pulled a chain to stop the train. People continued pelting stones even as the jam-packed S6 witnessed an accident resulting in the spilling of inflammable material inside the coach, causing the fire to erupt. Those who favoured this conclusion argued that there was no evidence of anyone entering the crowded coach, and that all its windows and two doors were shut.

Addressing the Parliament at noon that day, Prime Minister Atal Behari Vajpayee said, 'An inquiry is being held and it will ascertain facts—what happened and why did it happen? But, from the preliminary reports, it appears that the train was stopped maybe because slogans were being shouted in the train and clashes took place. The Gujarat government has ordered an inquiry.' Godhra's district collector, Jayanthi Ravi, said after the accident that 'the incident was not pre-planned, it was an accident'.

The narrative and administrative attitude changed after the chief minister and some of his cabinet colleagues landed in Godhra around 2 p.m. By 5.30 p.m., while the town was under curfew, the administration had demolished forty illegal shops belonging to Muslims in the Signal Falia area.[18] At 7.30 p.m., Modi made a public broadcast claiming that the hand of Pakistan's Inter-Services Intelligence (ISI) was behind the incident. In a press release on the same day, the state government claimed that the incident was a 'pre-planned inhuman collective violent act of terrorism'. It was a premature statement, made before enquiries had been carried out, but the chief minister too had already made the same claim. Modi also announced a bandh the next day, joining the Vishwa Hindu Parishad (VHP) and Bajrang Dal, who had already called their own strikes.

The impact of Godhra and the 2002 riots in Gujarat that followed continues to reverberate, not just in the state but all of India. What was said in official circles in hushed tones was recorded in the report of a Concerned Citizens' Tribunal, headed by Justice V.R. Krishna Iyer, a man whom Modi called an 'icon in Indian public life' and 'an inspiration to all of us'. The eight-member tribunal said:

> It was the chief minister who decided that the charred, unidentifiable dead bodies be taken from Godhra to Ahmedabad in a motor cavalcade. As the cavalcade headed for Ahmedabad, senior members of his party and organisations affiliated to it shouted slogans and incited mobs to retaliate. The CM's role in condoning this behaviour, and in using official machinery to propagate the unsubstantiated view that the Godhra tragedy was a sinister conspiracy, is condemnable. Thus, it was the chief minister who was primarily responsible for the spread of violence, post-Godhra, in the rest of Gujarat.[19]

The tribunal went on to say that Modi then called a meeting of senior police officers, and gave instructions in the presence of cabinet colleagues on how the police should deal with the situation the next day. 'On the day of the bandh, there was absolutely no police bandobast [arrangements]. The state and city [Ahmedabad] police control rooms were taken over by two ministers, i.e., Shri Ashok Bhatt and Shri Jadeja. Repeated pleas for help from people were blatantly turned down.'[20]

Before the Godhra tragedy, Modi was going through a lacklustre phase, even though he had become the chief minister a few months earlier, in October 2001. In February 2002, a few days before the Godhra tragedy, he contested elections, for the first time in his life, to the state assembly from the Bharatiya Janata Party (BJP) stronghold of Rajkot II constituency. His victory was unimpressive, securing a significantly lower margin than his predecessor, from his own party, got in the previous election.

As the bodies of the karsevaks reached Ahmedabad, so did violence. During those tense days after Godhra, Chief Minister Modi made several misleading claims. On 2 March, he said that Gujarat was on the road to peace, though violence was spreading through the state.[21] On 3 March, he claimed that the army had been called in on the evening of 28 February, and had started operations from the very next day. However, Lt Gen. Zameer Uddin Shah, who was in charge of army deployment in Gujarat in response to the riots, would later accuse the Gujarat government of wasting precious time, and not providing assistance to the army for quick deployment on the night of 28 February. 'The crucial periods was the night of 28th February and the 1st of March. This is when the maximum damage was done. I met the chief minister at 2 a.m. on the 1st morning. The troops sat on the airfield all through the 1st of March and we got the transport only on the 2nd of March. By then the mayhem had already been done,' he said.[22]

Hindutva elements went on the rampage, and several hundred people were killed, a majority of them Muslims. In the first week of April, Vajpayee visited Gujarat, and made it a point to visit the camps of Muslim victims—something Modi had neglected to do—and at a press conference later, the prime minister told the Gujarat chief minister that he should follow 'rajdharma'.

The reason for this digression into the much-told story of the Gujarat riots is to examine the role of the security organisations in it, and in the aftermath. Modi appointed 1984 batch IPS officer Rakesh Asthana as the deputy inspector general (DIG) of police with the Criminal Investigation Department (CID) (Crime and Railways), which was already investigating the Godhra carnage. That would be the turning point in Asthana's career—the impact of which can be seen even in New Delhi in 2021, where he is now established as one of the most powerful IPS officers in the country, whether playing a crucial role in ousting a CBI chief or dictating the narrative for the TV drama that would follow the death of Bollywood actor Sushant Singh Rajput.

Despite allegations of corruption,[23] and the fact that his own agency filed an FIR against him,[24] Asthana has had a very robust professional life in Delhi. Among other things, he was appointed interim chief of the CBI for several weeks in December 2016 following a peculiar sequence of events. First, there was an unusual delay in the appointment of a new CBI chief, and then the most senior officer was shifted out after a position available in the Ministry of Home Affairs (MHA) was specially upgraded to accommodate him. In October that year, when the selection committee headed by Central Vigilance Commissioner K.V. Chowdary met to consider Asthana's promotion to the post of special director of the CBI, the agency's chief, Alok Verma, objected to it in writing. Among the information that Verma presented to the committee was a handwritten entry showing that Asthana was the recipient of a Rs 3.5-crore bribe from the Gujarat-based Sandesara group of companies. Asthana's friendship with the Sandesara family was no secret in Vadodara. In 2016, the family had even hosted a reception for Asthana's daughter's wedding in their lavish farmhouse.[25]

In June 2011, when the Income Tax Department and other agencies raided the premises of Sandesara group in various parts of India, they recovered hundreds of pages of evidence showing payment of bribes to various officials, and suspicious transactions to the US, Dubai, Nigeria and other countries. The documents revealed that the Sandesara group acted as a depository for bribes and kickbacks received by government officials, and that they moved the money around the world using over- and under-invoicing. The investigating agencies estimated that over Rs 5,000 crore had been moved abroad in this fraud. The group was also involved in a racket to raise Rs 5,383 crore from various banks. The total loss to Indian banks because of the Sandesara fraud is estimated at almost Rs 15,000 crore.[26]

In September 2020, invoking its powers under the Fugitive Economic Offenders Act, which was passed by the Modi government in 2018, a Delhi court declared the Sandesara brothers, Nitin and Chetan, and the latter's wife, Dipti, fugitives.[27] Only two others had until then been declared fugitives: Vijay Mallya and Nirav Modi.

The ED landed up at senior Congress leader Ahmed Patel's residence to question him about his links to the brothers and made a spectacle of it. On the other hand, the ED and the CBI have shown little enthusiasm for investigating Asthana and other Gujarat officials named in the Sandesara files.

None of this has slowed Asthana's rise in the Modi regime, where loyalty remains the first demand—not unlike other governments in the past.[28] But what marks out the security apparatus under the current establishment is its willingness to create false narratives that cater to the beliefs and agendas of the government.

The Godhra train tragedy laid the foundation for the security architecture that Modi shaped for Gujarat, one that he would carry to the national capital in 2014. He was not inventing something new, but only copying what had been actively used by many state and Union governments—only he was more efficient, more ruthless and less afraid of public opinion.[29] My reporting and investigations over the years have led me to believe that the Gujarat state police, other arms of the state and even the branch of the IB stationed in the state would all end up working for the political master, rather than fulfilling their constitutional and professional duties.

The criminal justice system in Gujarat was captured in ways that have rarely been seen before, except perhaps during the declared Emergency of the 1970s. In reports submitted by the Gujarat police itself, the CBI and official commissions, the state police is accused of staging encounters, cold-blooded murders and selective targeting of Muslims, among other things. These are not allegations levelled against the administration by activists, but captured in government files by government agencies when they were forced to act according to law.[30]

Rakesh Asthana's team went about their investigation on the presumption that the Godhra train burning was a pre-planned conspiracy, though the prime architect of it kept shifting—first the ISI, then SIMI, and for some time it was even blamed on narco-terrorism. The Godhra trial began in 2009 in a specially set up court inside the Sabarmati Jail in Ahmedabad. Terror charges were not pressed against the accused, but the conspiracy charges stayed. Though the trial court upheld the conspiracy claims, it acquitted sixty-three of the ninety-four accused, including the alleged mastermind, Maulvi Hussain Ibrahim Umarji.

By then, Umarji had spent eight years in jail, and had already filed some important documents in courts. They showed that he was not a fringe Muslim fanatic, but someone that the state administration had trusted in the wake of the riots. He was the only Muslim community leader that the district authorities had entrusted with running a relief camp for the victims of the Gujarat riots. He had also participated in peace meetings organised by the district collector, and even offered a public apology for the train-burning. Umarji was arrested in February 2003. In his bail application in the Supreme Court, Umarji claimed that he had been framed for embarrassing Modi during Vajpayee's visit to Godhra in April 2002, during which he had given a written representation to the prime minister about the persecution of Muslims in the area. When Vajpayee asked him for details, Umarji turned to Modi and said in a sarcastic tone that the chief minister would know better.[31]

With the mastermind acquitted, the conspiracy claim ought to have been called into question by the courts. This did not happen. In the judgement, two aspects stood out: the two Muslims who, according to Asthana's team, pulled the chain to stop the train outside Godhra station, were not among the accused; rather, they were prosecution witnesses. During the trial, they turned hostile, but the court relied on their pre-trial testimonies. The second disturbing aspect was that all nine VHP members who were prosecution witnesses, and made statements to support the state's claim that the attack was unprovoked, were rejected as unreliable by the court. All nine claimed that they had gone to the train station with garlands and food packets for the returning karsevaks. However, they had no answer when asked how they knew the train was reaching around 6 a.m. when it was originally scheduled to arrive at 2.55 a.m., and they had no way of knowing about the delay.

The Godhra investigation was a showcase of the decay that had set into the system. And what emerged in the post-Godhra riots in Gujarat was the political executive's capacity to manipulate the security establishment. 'There is no way that the debased levels of violence that were systematically carried out in Gujarat could have been allowed, had the police and district administration, the IPS and the IAS, stood by its constitutional obligation and followed Service Rules to prevent such crimes,' the Krishna Iyer tribunal said.[32] In many ways, the Gujarat riots of 2002 held up a mirror to Indian democracy.

It was, of course, the Congress party that had created the blueprint for manipulating the security establishment for political gains.[33] However, while the rest of the security establishment was being deployed for political ends, the Indian military was not, as its counterparts in Pakistan or Bangladesh were.[34] Maybe Indian politicians were smarter than their peers in those countries and realised that the military arm is capable of morphing into a demon that can ultimately devour everything. It has been apolitical and tightly controlled, even as the rest of the security network has been manipulated over these decades to subvert the Constitution, target adversaries, create false narratives and suppress dissent. That said, if the present rot in the security agencies is not reversed through accountability and systemic clean-up, it will eventually eat into India's great pride: its democratic and apolitical military.

Meanwhile, because the non-military security establishment is a multi-headed hydra that seems to operate without a unified command, it is not often studied as an interconnected and complex system.

The eight-member Krishna Iyer tribunal was set up by former judges and activists as the nation recoiled in horror at the fact that large-scale state-supported riots targeted at one community could take place in twenty-first-century India. What happened in Delhi against Sikhs in 1984, egged on and led by Congress leaders, was thought of as a wake-up call to the Indian soul, an outrage that would never again be repeated. The Iyer tribunal, comprising of several eminent people, including Justice P.B. Sawant and Justice Hosbet Suresh, spent a fortnight in Gujarat, recording 2,094 statements from sixteen affected districts of the state. They also visited several localities to speak to victims. Rumours soon emerged about a minister in the Modi government appearing before the tribunal, telling them about Modi's role in enabling the riots. When the tribunal report was released in November 2002, it said: 'Many senior government officials and police officers did agree to meet the Tribunal, responded to our queries, shared insightful observations and presented some valuable evidence to us. One minister also appeared and deposed before us. The Tribunal had assured this witness (minister) and other officials that their anonymity would be protected. Hence, while their valuable evidence is reflected in the Findings of the report, they have not been identified. Anonymity was urged especially because of the fear of reprisal from political bosses if names became known.'[35]

However, the rumour mill in Gujarat was abuzz with the minister's identity, because Haren Pandya was now Modi's biggest rival in the party. Pandya, the minister of state for revenue under Modi, was previously the state home minister. A lifelong RSS member, Pandya was mentored by L.K. Advani, and was seen as one of BJP's bright young leaders from Gujarat.

On 7 June 2002, P.K. Mishra, principal secretary to the chief minister, called in R.B. Sreekumar, the chief of Gujarat police's intelligence arm. The senior IPS officer had recorded—in a register that he used for keeping verbal instructions from higher officers, and which later became part of official proceedings—that Mishra asked him to find out which member of the Modi cabinet met with the Krishna Iyer Commission. The entry reads: 'Dr PK Mishra added that Shri Harenbhai Pandya, minister for revenue is suspected to be the minister involved in the matter. Thereafter, he gave one mobile number 9824030629 and asked for getting call details.'[36] It was Pandya's number.

P.K. Mishra joined the Prime Minister's Office (PMO) under Modi in 2014, and as this book goes to press, he is the country's most powerful bureaucrat: principal secretary to the prime minister.

Five days later, Sreekumar informed Mishra that the minister who met the commission was Haren Pandya. O.P. Mathur, the inspector general of police (IGP) (administration security), handed over the call details of Pandya's phone to Mishra. In August 2002, a few weeks before the tribunal report came out, Pandya resigned from the cabinet. By then, there were enough rumours and reports about a meeting that Modi chaired after the Godhra tragedy, in which he had asked the police to allow Hindus to take out their anger on Muslims.[37]

In December, the Gujarat state assembly elections were due. By several accounts, Modi did not want Pandya to be given the Ellisbridge seat, which the latter had represented for fifteen years. The RSS and BJP leadership resisted this demand, and the RSS sent an emissary to meet Modi. After refusing to listen to the emissary's suggestions, Modi got himself admitted to a local government hospital late at night, complaining of exhaustion and fatigue, and thus avoided any calls from the national leadership. He left the hospital only after Pandya had been refused the seat.[38]

In March 2003, Haren Pandya received orders from the BJP president to shift to Delhi. On 26 March 2003—some say this was the day after he had received that order—Pandya left for his regular morning walk at Law Garden. He drove there in his Maruti 800, which was found parked next to the garden, with Pandya in it, dead and riddled with bullets. After his body was discovered, it lay there for at least a couple of hours. According to the police, the killer pulled the trigger when Pandya was rolling up the window of his car. The killer would have fired down at him, they said. However, when the body was eventually removed from the car, there was almost no blood in it, and his bullet wounds did not fit the police's claims. It was as if he had been shot dead somewhere else, wiped clean and placed on the driver's seat.[39]

At the hospital where Pandya's body was kept, there were several dramatic scenes. His supporters heckled Modi when he arrived, and his father, Vitthalbhai Pandya, did not want the chief minister to garland his son's body, saying that the family did not want Modi's sympathy.[40]

Union Home Minister L.K. Advani blamed the Dawood gang for the killing, without any evidence. Advani would also say that denying a party ticket to Pandya will 'remain a burden on me'.[41]

Initial investigations into the Pandya killing were handled by the state Crime Branch under D.G. Vanzara, who played a key role in the Gujarat police over the next several years, and went on to become head of the Anti-Terrorism Squad (ATS). Under pressure, Modi handed over the investigation to a CBI team under Yogesh Chander Modi, a 1984 batch IPS officer. He wrapped up investigations quickly, mostly agreeing with the state police's claims. The trial court accepted this CBI report almost in its entirety and convicted twelve persons for the murder.[42]

However, the Gujarat High Court reversed the trial court findings and delivered a judgement that was a stinging indictment of both the

CBI and the trial court.[43] The high court said that the trial court, by ignoring experts and relying on CBI claims alone, 'only strengthened the argument for the appellants that the conclusions drawn by the trial court were perverse and illogical'. It was also scathing in its appraisal of the CBI's role. 'What clearly stands out from the record of the present case is that the investigation in the case of murder of Shri Haren Pandya has all throughout been botched up and blinkered and has left a lot to be desired. The investigating officers concerned ought to be held accountable for their inaptitude resulting into injustice, huge harassment of many persons concerned and enormous waste of public resources and public time of the Courts.'[44]

There were no repercussions either for the CBI team or Y.C. Modi. In 2010, Y.C. Modi was inducted into the Special Investigation Team (SIT) probing the Gujarat riots cases, and investigated the Gulberg Society, Naroda Patiya and Naroda Gam cases. Eventually the SIT too gave a clean chit to Narendra Modi. After Modi became prime minister, Y.C. Modi went on to become a special director in the CBI, and finally in October 2017, became the chief of the NIA, which is responsible for investigating terrorism cases across India.[45]

As for the Haren Pandya murder case, in July 2019, a Supreme Court bench comprising Justices Arun Mishra and Vineet Saran reversed[46] the Gujarat High Court order. The bench upheld the trial court verdict, while applauding the CBI for its thorough investigation because of which 'the conspiracy between accused persons has been found established'. The apex court went on to say that it 'cannot be said that investigation was unfair, lopsided, botched up or misdirected in any manner whatsoever, as had been observed by the high court in the judgement which we have set aside'.

The Supreme Court order dismissed the witness who saw the car window rolled up almost to the top, making it impossible to fire at Pandya at those angles. The Arun Mishra judgement said, 'Even if the witness had stated so, that would be merely his guesswork.' It ignored even the police photo of the incident site, which showed the car window just about three inches open, corroborating what the witness had said. The court ignored forensic evidence, as had the trial court, but which the high court had examined. Commenting on the bullet that entered Pandya's scrotum and went to his abdomen, the Supreme Court relied on the eyewitness—the same witness whose testimony about the car windows it disregarded—to say that, when Pandya was shot at, he must have immediately fallen in the car, his legs going up. All Indians who are familiar with the matchbox-sized Maruti 800, will no doubt wonder how such a thing was possible. In any case, when his body was finally found, Pandya was sitting up straight.

A writ petition filed by the Union for Public Interest Litigation (CPIL) in the Supreme Court was also clubbed with the CBI appeal against the acquittal of the accused by the Gujarat High Court. The writ petition pointed out revelations in the testimony that Mohammed Azam Khan—a prosecution witness in the trial of the fake encounter of Sohrabuddin Sheikh, his wife, Kausar Bi, and his associate Tulsiram Prajapati—had recorded on 3 November 2018. Khan's testimony stated that Sohrabuddin had told him that the contract to kill Haren Pandya was given to him by IPS officer D.G. Vanzara. 'Sohrabuddin's associate Tulsiram Prajapati, along with one Naeem Khan and Shahid Rampuri, murdered Haren Pandya,' the CPIL writ said.[47] Azam Khan had also revealed that he had given this information to the CBI in 2010, but the agency ignored it. Justice Arun Mishra's judgement brushed this evidence aside: 'In our opinion, the aforesaid statement made by Azam Khan was totally out of the context of a criminal case in which he had deposed.'

The Supreme Court also had a curious explanation for why the CBI did not examine Haren Pandya's wife, Jagrutiben: 'She was not an eyewitness to be examined in the case. Thus, it cannot be said that the prosecution has withheld her and she would have unfolded any part story which was material to the case.' The presumption appears to be that, beyond what happened at the moment of the murder, there could be no conspiracy. Pandya's family never accepted the CBI's claims. Their attempts at judicial appeals failed on various occasions.

The Supreme Court fined CPIL Rs 50,000 for wasting its time. A few months down the line, Justice Arun Mishra also held Prashant Bhushan, who had filed the CPIL petition in the Pandya case, guilty of contempt of court for a few tweets.[48]

Some months after the Pandya killing, the country plunged into general elections. Prime Minister Vajpayee suffered a shock defeat in the 2004 summer elections. In the second week of June, in Kullu for a week-long break after the polls, he told reporters, 'It is very difficult to say what are all the reasons ... but one impact of the (Gujarat) violence was we lost the elections.' Immediately, national media was abuzz with the news, quoting BJP sources, that Modi would be removed as the chief minister of Gujarat at the party's national executive meeting, to be held in Goa.

However, a dramatic twist occurred. A few days after Vajpayee's comments, the Gujarat police made a sensational claim: they had killed five terrorists, including Ishrat Jahan, a nineteen-year-old Mumbai student, who were on their way to assassinate Modi. A magisterial enquiry later established that cops commanded by the state's ATS chief Vanzara (whom Azam Khan had accused of contracting Pandya's murder) had staged the killings.[49] A few days later, at the national executive meeting of the BJP, Modi was triumphantly welcomed. And Vajpayee's leadership of the party was virtually finished.

In 2009, S.P. Tamang, a metropolitan magistrate of Gujarat, was ordered to conduct a magisterial enquiry into the killings of the alleged terrorists. He found that the police officers 'all associated together and in collusion with each other, for their personal interest which included to secure their promotion, to maintain his posting, so as to falsely show excellent performance, to get special appreciation form the Hon'ble Chief Minister and to gain popularity, hatched a systematic conspiracy'.[50] A CBI team too later found the encounter to be fake, and raised several questions about even the most basic claims of the state police. The bullets recovered from the victims' bodies did not match any of the weapons used during the encounter, a gun that fired 9mm bullets was never identified, and worst of all, the position of the car and bodies did not match the potential trajectory of the bullets fired.[51]

The Ishrat Jahan encounter has been a political hot potato, especially the question of whether the nineteen-year-old was a Lashkar-e-Taiba (LeT) terrorist. All arguments aside, there is one undisputed fact: that Jahan and the others were first kept in illegal custody, then killed in a staged encounter, and that both the Gujarat police and the IB's Gujarat branch were active participants in the killings.

Since the demolition of the Babri Masjid in 1992, several SIMI members had turned more radical, though they remained committed to peaceful protests. A small strand, however, had moved away, with some people even going to Pakistan for arms training and returning to carry out low-level terror attacks. According to some of the most reliable intelligence officers, the group that advocated violence was led by people like C.A.M. Basheer, a Keralite who worked at the Mumbai airport and was an active SIMI member. Basheer remains a mysterious figure, but one whom intelligence agencies suspect to be a key player in domestic terrorism in India.

The Gujarat riots led to a new call to arms among this fringe group. According to Indian agencies, this group of mostly former SIMI members finally ended up forming the Indian Mujahideen (IM) some time after 2002. Even today, there is no clarity about how many of these extremist groups exist and where all they operate. In part, this is because the police and intelligence agencies muddied the early investigations by trapping innocents like Wahid. Information on radicals was available in Kerala, Hyderabad, Mumbai and Azamgarh, among other places, but those investigations could go nowhere because the process was contaminated by fake narratives.

Sadiq Israr Sheikh, a Mumbai resident, was a key informant for the security establishment on the IM. In a detailed taped statement, Sadiq said that, in his early childhood, he was a nationalist because he grew up in a military area. Later, up until 1992, he was a communist. 'After Babri demolition and riots, my mentality changed and I turned towards my religion,' he said.[52] In 1996, he joined SIMI, where he stayed on till 1999. During this period, he also completed an Industrial Training Institute course in air-conditioning, and picked up a job with the Godrej group as a technician. Sheikh was a very aggressive youngster, who picked up fights, both within the home and outside. 'So, I thought I should try to change myself and get into the company of good people. I saw some people from SIMI and realised they were good people. They were Shafiq and Salim. These two were from Cheetah Camp in SIMI,' Sadiq recalled. For a youngster who grew up in a religious ghetto, with limited education and facing the rising tide of communal hatred, the choices he could think of were either SIMI or Tablighi Jamaat, a religious group committed to orthodox beliefs. 'They are not concerned about the world. So I joined SIMI to stay religious and change to become better.'

Before long, the angry, agitated Sadiq and a few others travelled to Pakistan for arms training. In the camp, they pretended to be from Karachi, and did not mingle with the other trainees. Over a short, month-long course designed especially for Indian recruits, they were taught how to use an AK-47 rifle, pistols and machine guns, and were also given training in explosives. Mixed with this was religious preaching that was intended to incite them. During the practical sessions, the trainees made charges and small bombs, and learnt how to create improvised explosives with chemicals that are available in the market.

Indian cities would soon witness dramatic terror attacks, and for a very long time, the security establishment would grope in the darkness. Even when they figured out the IM network, it only completed a part of the story. By the time the larger picture came into focus, they had messed up again.

2

Ripped Apart

The gaggle of children competed with the pitter-patter of rain as Wahid returned home from school in the evening. Munna, a neighbour, was just outside, and the two began chatting. Only the previous year, the downpour had claimed over a thousand lives in the city, and they spoke about this and other issues. Sajida had by now fully settled into the role of a homemaker, and the family had grown too—their son Umar was born in 2004 and daughter Umrah in 2006. As the neighbours spoke, the flashing news on a television set inside caught Wahid's attention. Several bombs had gone off in trains on the Western Line. His heart skipped a beat. It was 11 July 2006.

There was utter mayhem, the confusion evident in the constantly changing details of television news reports. A couple of hours into the evening, it became clear that seven bombs had ripped through the trains, killing over 189 people.[1] The explosives, placed in pressure cookers, went off between 6.24 p.m. and 6.35 p.m. in the first-class general compartments of trains running from Churchgate station.

The city had not seen anything of this scale since the 1993 serial blasts. But, by this time, Mumbai was used to the regular interruption of its frenzied pace by terrorists and criminals, and the hypocritical applause for the 'Mumbai Spirit' that followed. India's financial capital has paid a greater price for the inefficiencies of the security and intelligence agencies than any other Indian city. Following the 1993 blasts, the underworld battled it out with each other, businessmen organised hits against rivals using the chaos as a fig leaf, and police loyalties were more closely aligned with gangs than with the state. However, large-scale terrorists attacks appeared to have stopped for the time being.

Mumbai has always held a fatal attraction for all kinds of people—aspiring actors and terrorists, desperate poor from the hinterlands and multi-billionaires. There is a landmark around every corner. On that road, a billionaire has built an eyesore of a mansion, next to Cat Café is an indie filmmaker's office, this towering building is where terrorists planted a bomb in 1993, that glassed tower is called 'vertical Aram Nagar' because it has so many production house offices, behind those trees is that superstar's mansion, this hospital is where the first AK-47 was fired by the underworld, that is where you get the finest Parsi food. The lives of terrorists, superstars, strugglers and business magnates are all intertwined in this most storied of Indian cities. In this milieu, modern terrorism too thrives, as all other aspirations and perversions do.

Within months of the Gujarat riots, terrorism had resurfaced in Mumbai. On 2 December 2002, a bomb blast in a bus outside Ghatkopar railway station killed two people. A few days later, another went off in an air-conditioner duct in a food plaza. On 27 January 2003, a day after India celebrated its Republic Day, as Prime Minister Vajpayee landed in Mumbai, a bomb planted on a bicycle near Vile Parle railway station went off and killed one person. A little over a month later, on 13 March, a bomb blast in a ladies' compartment, near Mulund railway station, killed ten people, including four women, of them two police constables. Almost four months later, a bomb went off under a seat in a bus in Ghatkopar, killing four people and injuring over thirty. The ferocity of the terror attacks was picking up pace and scale. On 25 August 2003, two car bombs went off in Mumbai, killing fifty-four and injuring almost 250. One of the explosions took place next to the crowded Gateway of India by the sea. The other went off at Zaveri Bazaar, and both were during lunchtime, when the areas were busy.

Wahid grew uneasy as the rainy night drew on. A pattern had been established in his life by now. Ever since his detention as an alleged SIMI member in 2001, whenever a terror attack took place somewhere, especially in Mumbai, the police would call him in, and interrogate and harass him for several days. Even as the city was pulling out the last of the dead from the blasted trains, Wahid called his brother Zubair, who had news: the police had called for Wahid. 'I will go to the station tomorrow after school,' he replied.

As he began to narrate the new ordeal, Wahid paused and took off his sunglasses. His eyes twitched as he stared across the restaurant where we had been sitting for over an hour. 'Are your eyes okay?' I asked. He shook his head, but did not say much. A few meetings later, he would open up about what had happened—to his eyes, which developed glaucoma, and the rest of his body—because of the appalling levels of physical torture he endured at the hands of the police. For the moment, he focused on telling me about the day after the blasts.

After school, Wahid went to the Parksite police station. As he stepped in, a feeling of déjà vu swept through him. The seven others who had been rounded up along with him after SIMI was banned in 2001 were present too. There was a new senior inspector, but the questions were the same, xenophobic, communal and crude: 'You are all anti-social elements, you will all end up in camps ... Have you seen the plight of Palestinians?' After more of this rhetoric, the police took a detailed statement from him, then his fingerprints and, finally, photos from various angles. By evening, Wahid was let off, as were the other seven.

A few days later, it was the turn of the Mumbai Crime Branch. The other seven were there too, and visibly tense: 'The others asked me why was I so relaxed. Just tell the truth, I said. That was my big learning from the 2001 experience.' The truth, he falsely believed, would protect him. As was the routine, late into the night, the eight were allowed to go home. The rest of July was uneventful.

The ATS turned up on the eve of Indian Independence Day, on 14 August 2006. They drove to the school where Wahid taught, and called on the headmaster, who summoned Wahid to his room. The officers said that their boss, famed encounter specialist Vijay Salaskar, wanted to ask Wahid a few questions, and he would be let off in a few minutes. 'But I got suspicious, so I went to the staff room and requested a teacher to inform my brother-in-law, Mehmood.' Wahid returned, and climbed into the ATS jeep. 'As soon as I sat down, they started beating me, and started questioning me. Did you go to Pakistan? Which route did you take? You teach kids how to make bombs?' Wahid was driven to Byculla, and was put in a lock-up there. He would occasionally be taken out, beaten up and have his statement recorded in Marathi by an inspector. Then he was returned to the lock-up.

Salaskar arrived at about 9 p.m. 'Where is Riyaz?' he asked.

The inspector was referring to Riyaz Bhatkal, the man suspected of having founded the IM. Wahid readily admitted to knowing Riyaz—the wrong Riyaz, who lived in Kurla, and gave a detailed description of the acquaintance. As the questioning progressed, Wahid told Salaskar about his ordeals of the past few years, and professed his innocence.

'If you are innocent, then you help the police,' the inspector told him. Salaskar wrote down Wahid's address and phone number in his personal diary, and let him leave by 10 p.m.

The next morning, Wahid went to the school to celebrate Independence Day with flag-hoisting, sweets and patriotic songs. His own freedom added to the celebrations. He was relieved that the ordeal was finally over. Wahid, Sajida and their little children spent time together that day and the next.

But this normalcy was short-lived. On 17 August, around 2 a.m., Wahid was dozing off when there was a loud knock on the door.

'Wahid Sheikh?' asked a large contingent of ATS officers as they rushed into the second-floor apartment. They began searching his house. 'We are from the Mumbra police station, come with us, you can go in ten minutes,' one of them said, but Wahid knew what was coming. 'Shall I take my railway pass? Can I take a bath?' He was preparing for a long day. The police just forced him out.

As soon as Sajida closed the door, the police dragged him down. When they reached the ground floor, the kicking and beating began. They put Wahid into an SUV and drove to a nearby building, where they brought down a man wearing a burqa. In sensitive cases, informants are often dressed in a burqa, or other means are adopted to protect their identity. These informants are invariably men. The anonymous informant is an integral part of police operations, helping them identify suspects, hideouts, weapons and the like. The burqa-clad man sat in the other SUV, and the two vehicles drove into the night.

Over Thane Creek, the vehicles came to a halt, and Inspector Sachin Kadam asked Wahid to step out. The inspector held a revolver to Wahid's temple and told him that he would be killed and his body dumped in the creek. 'No one will even know,' Kadam said. Wahid started crying. The inspector landed a few blows on him and threw him back into the vehicle. At around 4 a.m., the two vehicles reached the ATS office in Kalachowki.

Almost immediately, Wahid was taken to a torture room, where an inspector removed his clothes and started beating him. After over two hours of torture, they handcuffed him and threw him in a lock-up. Police officers kept dropping in to meet Wahid, regularly beat him and asked him questions about the blasts. By the evening of 18 August, he was taken to a room and was handcuffed to a peg on the wall above his head. He could hear the sound of someone being tortured in the next room. A little while later, a group of officers approached Wahid, among them K.P. Raghuvanshi, who was heading the ATS.[2] 'Raghuvanshi slapped me and kicked me on my private parts and told the other officers to tie me strongly,' Wahid recalled in courts much later.[3] Unfortunately, this was not the last he would see of Raghuvanshi.

After shutting the door to her apartment on the police's instruction, Sajida did not go back to sleep. She tied one child to her back, picked up the other one in her arms and left the building. Some distance away, she found a rickshaw, and went to her parents' house in Vikhroli. From there, she alerted everyone possible. The family's trials were just beginning. Wahid had been banished into the blackhole of India's war on terror, where illegal custody is the order of the day and accountability is not.[4]

In New Delhi, since 2004, Prime Minister Manmohan Singh and his cabinet were reeling from some of the biggest security scandals to erupt in the country. Rabinder Singh, a former army officer who rose to become a joint secretary with R&AW, had staged a dramatic defection to the US in May 2004 after supplying the Central Intelligence Agency (CIA) with Indian secrets for years. Despite being under surveillance, Rabinder Singh was able to escape via Nepal to the US.

That was not the only challenge for the government, though. After a trail of unsolved attacks from Uttar Pradesh to Bengaluru, agencies had no true leads and only came up with the usual accusations against Pakistan. The Kargil conflict of 1999 had triggered a series of reforms in the security establishment, but they were not paying off.

On 15 August 2004, within weeks of the new government taking charge, Assam witnessed one of its deadliest terror strikes in recent memory. Eighteen people, many of them children, were killed when a bomb went off in the premises of a college during Independence Day celebrations. The next year was worse.

In July 2005, there were two bomb blasts in Uttar Pradesh. Then, two days before Diwali, the national capital was rocked by three explosions in markets crowded with shoppers—sixty-two people were killed and over 200 injured. On 28 December, terrorists stormed into the verdant campus of the Indian Institute of Science in Bengaluru, and fired on a group of academics attending a conference on operations research. The confusion in New Delhi was palpable. Those of us who reported on the national security beat were being fed a barrage of narratives about Pakistan-sponsored terrorists, ISI-trained modules and so on.

There are serious structural flaws in the way the security establishment deals with the media and other stakeholders. Confident that they are beyond accountability, these agencies feed journalists information that cannot be verified. Reporters are briefed in informal meetings and occasionally handed typed-out notes on A4 sheets without any file number notings or guarantees of authenticity. Instead of interrogating these officials and verifying the information through other means, reporters often carry that fog of secrecy back to their offices. Interactions with their anonymous sources also lead many journalists to believe that they are privileged members of some secret club, and carry a certain burden of saving the country. So they end up amplifying fake narratives and unverifiable information, which reduces them to pawns on a chessboard rather than respected members of a free media. What the security establishment gets out of this arrangement, apart from control over the narrative, is deniability.

Occasionally, the police would produce someone as a suspected terrorist. Even if no one actually believed their claims, faced with deadline challenges and the need to fill news columns, most of us had to run the propaganda. Media reporting during that phase was mostly disgraceful, and the editorial leadership at every media organisation, including the liberal media, failed the public.

In reality, the Indian security establishment was floundering. Its deep-seated biases, institutional decay and lack of accountability had forced it down a rabbit hole. Besides the profuse inflow of fake inputs into their mammoth of an information network, agencies were also engaged in turf battles, rather than cooperating in the hunt for the terrorists.

Although the next year began on a relatively peaceful note, it would not last. On 7 March 2006 three bombs went off in Varanasi, including in the Sankat Mochan temple, killing at least twenty-eight people. And then came the Mumbai train blasts.

As Mumbai scrambled to deal with the seven blasts that killed over 189 people, Manmohan Singh rushed one of his most trusted intelligence officers to the commercial capital to supervise the investigations. Known for his academic bent of mind, voracious reading habits, sharp analytical skills and soft-spoken nature, this officer was the classic spy of Western novels. He was stationed in Mumbai for several days to coordinate and oversee the investigations.

The Mumbai police had at least eighteen teams operating in the investigations, and every resource at its disposal was pressed into operation, including almost all its encounter specialists. As the 1990s encounters unravelled to show an ugly side of its policing—staged killings for corrupt purposes and a role in the underworld rivalry—most of the force's sharpshooters were either facing disciplinary action or had fallen out of favour. But the pressure to solve the train blasts overrode all moral and legal compulsions. Suspended officers like Daya Naik and Sachin Vaze were active in the investigations. In fact, as I was finalising this book, Vaze surfaced on familiar ground—caught up in a bizarre conspiracy to plant explosives outside Mukesh Ambani's house, a mystery in which the owner of the vehicle that was parked outside Antilia was later murdered, allegedly for not being willing to own up the act.

To return to the investigations into the 2006 serial blasts, Assistant Commissioner of Police (ACP) Vinod Bhatt—who was part of the team that investigated the 1993 serial blasts and was well versed in legal documentation—was brought in to supervise the investigation, especially documentation, for the court. Bhatt had the reputation of being an honest officer in a police force that was widely corrupt.

One day in August 2006, Bhatt summoned Wahid to his second-floor office at the ATS station in Bhoiwada. Ehtesham Siddiqui, another accused, was also present in the room. Wahid says Bhatt told them that he had been through all the documents and statements, and had come to the conclusion that they were innocent. Wahid recalled the conversation went as follows:

> Ehtesham: We have always said that we are innocent. Why were we arrested?
>
> Bhatt: Because we haven't found the real culprits.
>
> Ehtesham: Who is implicating us in this?

Wahid claims Bhatt told them that he was under pressure from Mumbai Police Commissioner A.N. Roy and ATS Chief K.P. Raghuvanshi to file charge sheets against them.

> Ehtesham: Will you do that?
>
> Bhatt: No, but they are planning to implicate my wife in a case.
>
> Ehtesham: Will we be released from this case?
>
> Bhatt: Have faith in Allah, I will die but not let innocent people fall.

Sometime after this conversation took place, the police filed an FIR in Santacruz police station against fourteen people, including Bhatt's wife, Seema, in a dispute involving a housing scheme for police families. Seema was a member of the society.[5]

On 28 August, Bhatt was late to office. He did not acknowledge his juniors, and shut himself in his own room, smoking his 555 cigarettes one after the other. At lunch, he ate nothing. At 4.30 p.m., he attended a meeting of senior officers involved in the investigations, where they discussed the progress thus far. Around 9 p.m., Bhatt asked his driver to drop him off at Tilak Bridge in Dadar. Before disembarking, the officer handed over most of his personal items, asking the driver to take them over to his wife, but kept his official identity card. Around 9.45 p.m., a motorman with a slow train informed the Dadar station master that his train had hit a man below the Tilak bridge. The railway police found Rs 30, a matchbox, a broken pair of spectacles and Bhatt's police identity card on the body. His superior, Raghuvanshi, told reporters that it was 'likely that he had been undergoing some difficulties of late'.[6]

Vinod Bhatt was not the only police officer who was empathetic to Wahid's plight. An inspector with the ATS, in whose custody Wahid was illegally kept for three months during the early part of investigation, had a penchant for photography. After a few days, as a new normalcy set in, the inspector asked Wahid to take a ride with him on his motorbike. So the 'dreaded terrorist' sat pillion as the inspector rode to the iconic Haji Ali dargah in the southern part of the city. There, the policeman clicked photographs of the structure against the setting sun. 'In his sunset pictures, you could only see the sun and everything else is in silhouette,' Wahid recalled. Once he was satisfied with the photos, the inspector and his charge drank a cup of tea and then returned to the ATS office to play their respective roles—officer and terrorist.

'Did he ever beat you?' I asked Wahid.

'Yes, initially. But later he figured out that I don't have anything on me, that I am neither criminal nor terrorist, and there is no evidence of my involvement, so he started behaving nicely with me,' he said.

The inspector sometimes even took him out for a meal. One day, Wahid told him that his students' studies were affected because he was being kept in illegal custody. The inspector gave Wahid a ride to the school. 'Go and teach the children. I will wait,' he said, and sat outside the school for a few hours until Wahid finished teaching.

Wahid was in illegal custody for several weeks. One of those days, a policeman told him: 'Your brother keeps sitting here outside. Tell him not to go to any politician. Tell him not to do that.' With this condition, Wahid was allowed to meet his brother. Javed broke down on seeing his sibling. A few days later, Wahid was released on several conditions: do not disclose what happened inside the ATS to anyone; do not go to a doctor; do not contact lawyers. Wahid told me that, for their records, the ATS officials made diary entries showing that he was always released on the same day that he was summoned, even though he was in their custody for three months.

Illegal arrests, especially of those from the vulnerable sections of society, are rampant across the country, despite the courts having laid down strict norms on arrests. The brutality of the police and jail authorities and their misuse of power is manifest in the data on people who die in custody. In 2019–20, on an average, five persons died per day while in custody, according to the MHA. From 1 April 2019 to 31 March 2020, a total of 1,697 people died in custody; many of these deaths would have been due to torture.[7] However, very few cases get investigated properly, because the system closes ranks to save its own. Police departments create fake documentation, medical certificates are often fabricated, and even the cases that are investigated do not go far.

Hundreds of people across India are denied their dignity and freedom, as Wahid was, and many are robbed of their very lives. Wahid emerged alive from ATS's custody. Relieved that his family's torment was over, he was willing to forget all that happened and attempt a return to normal life. The sweet monotony of life and work was back, or so they thought.

On 13 September 2006, Wahid was walking to the school canteen near the gate when he saw an ATS official outside. He signalled to Wahid. 'Raghuvanshi sahib wants to meet you,' he said. A 1980 batch IPS officer, who was brought in to lead and shape the Mumbai ATS when it was created in 2004, K.P. Raghuvanshi looked every bit the genial cop. A news article about him said he could pass off as 'an executive from a multi-national company in his trademark grey jackets and crisp cotton trousers'.[8] In fact, his appointment raised eyebrows because he was considered a 'gentleman cop'.[9]

Wahid already knew that this reputation was anything but true. From the school, he was taken to the ATS's Kalachowki office, and straight to a very odd room. He vividly recalls it, describing the room as looking like the set of a cheap Bollywood film. It had no windows, and its walls were painted white. Much later, he realised that the wall had two layers to make it soundproof. In the middle was a table and a chair, and a bright light was on. On the table were syringes, batons, coins, Iodex gel, electric wires and a water pipe. A large truck tyre hung at one end. There was a big belt, the kind used in factories, which are several inches broad, with slogans on it—'Sach-bol patta' (truth-speaking belt), 'Meri awaz suno' (hear my voice), 'Idhar goonga bhi bolta hai' (here even the dumb will speak). And then there were handcuffs and old newspapers.

Even before he could make sense of the lay of the room, Wahid was asked to strip naked. The AC was on full blast and the cement floor was freezing. As a naked Wahid stood shivering, Raghuvanshi walked in wearing civvies. It must have been around 12.30 p.m., Wahid estimates.

Pointing his finger at Wahid, Raghuvanshi asked: 'Who is this?'

'Wahid, sir,' a subordinate replied.

Raghuvanshi took a step forward, and kicked Wahid in his groin. Then he hit Wahid several times and threw him on the floor. Raghuvanshi thundered: 'Pakistanis came to your house on the ninth, tenth and eleventh. You gave them shelter, food and safe passage.'

Wahid stood up and murmured: 'This is a lie.'

'This is the truth,' Raghuvanshi replied. The ATS chief said Wahid would have to admit it. 'I am coming from Bangalore. You didn't tell me this, someone else told me.' He took out a diary from his briefcase and said that another accused, Ehtesham Siddiqui, who had been present in ACP Vinod Bhatt's office along with Wahid, had said this during the narco test in Bengaluru.

Wahid again replied, 'Sir, it is a lie.'

'My name is Raghuvanshi. I give you my word, I will save you, so admit it,' the ATS chief said. He had two options, Raghuvanshi said—become a state witness or be an accused.

Years later, as we sat sipping tea in a Mumbai restaurant, Wahid told me: 'Like a hypnotist, he stared at me and said: "You forgot it, I am reminding you."' Raghuvanshi said that four or five Pakistanis visited Wahid's house on 11 July and stayed with the family until 13 July, and that the schoolteacher had provided them with shelter and food, and finally helped them escape after they planted the bombs.

'Who's Wahid tailor?'

'I don't know.'

Raghuvanshi told Wahid that if ATS managed to get Wahid-the-tailor, they would let Wahid go. 'You want to be an accused or an approver?' Raghuvanshi asked rhetorically. After half an hour of the dramatic interrogation, the ATS chief left, issuing instructions: 'I want a photo of him jumping, so warm him up.' He slapped Wahid and said: 'I am not used to no.' The 'gentleman cop' walked out.

After their boss's departure, the other policemen told Wahid to accept everything. He refused. And then their torture shifted to a new gear.

The policemen pulled out a bottle of Surya Prakash oil—an Ayurvedic mix of oils extracted from eucalyptus, clove, mint and camphor—prescribed for pain relief. But in the interrogation rooms of the ATS, the oil was not being put to use as per the directions of D.M. Patel Pharma Pvt. Ltd, but as a tool in the war on terror.

The team thrust a tube into Wahid's rectum and injected the oil into his body. Within a few minutes, his body was on fire. He started jumping. What the ATS chief wanted, his subordinates and Surya Prakash oil had delivered in a few minutes.

The everyday din of Mumbai roared on outside, as Wahid fell silent after recalling this torture. His eyes rarely fill up. Wahid's nightmarish experiences have given him a stoic exterior and a matter-of-fact manner of talking. After a long pause, he looked away into the distance, and said, 'I still wake up in the middle of night in morbid fear and lie staring at the door. After some moments, I open the front door to see if someone is standing outside.'

Wahid was in ATS custody for over fifty days this time, of which only thirty were official. The other twenty were in clear violation of his constitutional rights. When he was released, the ATS officers had a specific instruction for him. His brother had been meeting a political leader named Arif Naseem Khan, who had called the ATS office to ask about Wahid. The family must stop meeting politicians.

On his return, Wahid's wife and brothers insisted that they complain about the illegal torture and intimidation. 'They were insisting, but I was reluctant. I think that was my mistake. Later, my lawyer told me that they detained you illegally for so many days, they took you around, but you did not complain even once. If you'd have done that, the situation would have been different. I told him that I didn't know anything,' Wahid recalled in 2019, almost a decade and a half after his nightmarish experiences began. By lying even to his lawyer, Wahid hoped he had a chance to resume a normal life.

'I could have gone to various authorities. I could have complained to the local police, political leaders at various levels, I could have told my lawyer, gone to human rights activists, media. All that is in hindsight,' Wahid said.

His conversations, I noticed, are peppered with legal jargon, a sharp awareness on how to fight injustices and a sense of constitutional values. When I pointed this out, Wahid drily replied: 'This knowledge is very expensive, it cost nine years of my life.'

After his release, Wahid was ordered to report to the ATS office every day to mark his attendance. Meanwhile, the squad struggled with political and media pressure to solve the case. In many ways, the creation of an ATS reflected the growing pressure on Mumbai's police forces to professionalise. The police was overburdened and mostly operated in silos. So, when sophisticated cross-border terrorist threats emerged, the city's police formed a temporary anti-terrorism squad sometime in 1990. As Punjab saw a widespread crackdown in the second half of the 1980s, many Khalistani terrorists moved to Mumbai.[10] Their AK-47s and brutal killings were evident in Bombay now. It was to deal with this new and emerging threat that the ATS was formed, only to be disbanded by 1993 because of serious allegations against the squad. Maharashtra formed an ATS again in 2004.

The senior intelligence officer sent by Prime Minister Singh to oversee the train blast investigations told me later that they mounted a massive surveillance in the city, listening in on phone calls and internet communications. He also accompanied ATS officers to various jails to interrogate suspected terrorists, including a Pakistani citizen in custody. 'It was a very challenging case, and the public pressure was severe,' he said. During his stay in Mumbai, the only hopeful lead they had was a call intercepted just after the blasts. It was from Mumbai to a border town in Bihar, speaking about a birthday celebration. 'It was a lead, just a lead, may have had nothing to do with the blasts,' he recalled. He returned to Delhi soon after, passing on broad instructions to the police chiefs about the need to conduct a professional investigation.

Around this time, Wahid was told to stop visiting the ATS office daily, but was advised to always carry some cash on him so that he could reach quickly if summoned. On one of his last daily trips to the ATS, Wahid saw a large media contingent and onlookers. Curious, he ordered a tea at the shop outside and watched the drama. Then a police constable came to the shop, and the two got talking. A 'big fish' was in the net, he told Wahid.

It was 22 August 2006, and it had been a dramatic early morning in the city, even if Wahid was oblivious to the developments. A few hours earlier, around midnight, the police stopped a car for a routine check at Wadala bus terminus and figured out that the driver, Mohammad Riyaz Nababuddin, was a Pakistani terrorist. According to Police Commissioner A.N. Roy, Nababuddin had told them that he was on his way to an abandoned building in Antop Hill to meet his partner, Mohammad Ali, known as Abu Osama in terror circles. The police rushed to the building, and Abu Osama challenged them with automatic gunfire. The neighbourhood woke up to the sound of bullets around 4 a.m. The firing went on for more than half an hour.

Raghuvanshi told the media later that they were still figuring out whether the terrorists belonged to Lashkar-e-Taiba or Jaish-e-Mohammed. The police said that they had recovered a diary containing several phone numbers from Bangladesh, and thus they were also probing the involvement of Bangladesh-based terror group Harkat-ul-Jihad-al-Islami. Among the items recovered from the Maruti car that Nababuddin was in were two kilograms of RDX, detonators, timer devices, US$ 50, a pistol and three maps—one each of the world, Maharashtra and Mumbai. Roy claimed that both the men had assumed Hindu identities and worked for a private company somewhere in northern India.

The prime minister's intelligence envoy was now back in New Delhi. He was flabbergasted at the television reports of the early-morning shootout. 'We had questioned that Pakistani when I was in Mumbai. He had been in their custody much before the blasts,' he told me later. 'He knew nothing about them.' It was a staged encounter by a desperate ATS.

Mohammad Riyaz Nababuddin, the alleged Pakistani terrorist captured from the Maruti car in Wadala, and who had purportedly tipped off the police about Abu Osama hiding in Antop Hill, was brought to Arthur Road Jail months after the encounter. By then he had been reduced to a vegetable, with severe damage to his scrotum.[11] After treatment at JJ Hospital, Nababuddin was shifted to jail, where Wahid, who was by now back in jail, and the other inmates took care of him. The Pakistani would not tell the others how he sustained the injuries because that was his one ticket to freedom. The ATS had promised to soft-pedal his case if he kept quiet about his injuries. The squad kept its promise. When they filed a charge sheet against him, the Pakistan citizen was accused only of illegal entry into India, not terrorism.[12] The dreaded terrorist was now a mere illegal resident, and was sentenced to a five-year jail term. At the end of that term, Nababuddin was brought to the ATS office, where for a while he was an informal attendant, serving tea and coffee to the officers.

In Nababuddin's version of events, he admits to being a Pakistani who had inadvertently crossed the border somewhere in Gujarat. He was detained by the BSF, and then handed over to the Gujarat ATS officer Vanzara, who has featured in our narrative before. It is understandable that the border guards handed over a Pakistani to the local state police. However, it is not clear why Vanzara sent him across to the Mumbai police.

Several trusted sources have pointed out to me that, in the last decade, counterterrorism operations involving the Gujarat state police have involved exchange and movement between Maharashtra and Gujarat, be it of suspects, alleged terrorists, phone calls or information.

It was not only the Maharashtra ATS that was groping in the dark, but the entire national security establishment. There was very little credible input on any terrorist movement, but unreliable information was aplenty. Anyone with access to the intelligence agencies could see the confusion.

On 8 September 2006, hundreds of Muslims had gathered in the afternoon in a cemetery next to a mosque in Malegaon to observe Shab-e-Barat, when two bombs went off. At least forty people were killed and over 125 injured.

I dialled some of my contacts in the intelligence establishment. While most of them were ready with the Pakistan-terror angle, two officials told me not to ignore Hindu extremists. A senior R&AW officer told me about a strange phone call they had intercepted a few days before the Mumbai blasts, on Friday, 6 June, after two explosives went off in the Jama Masjid complex just before it was time for the azaan, injuring thirteen people. 'There was a call to Indore, and we thought it suspicious. But the IB was not at all interested in pursuing that lead,' the officer said. He also asked me to look at the small but strange explosions reported in various parts of Maharashtra involving Hindutva elements.

I wrote an article for *DNA*, the newspaper I was then working for, saying: 'The crude bombs used and the timing and venues indicate that the Malegaon blasts may not be the handiwork of the usual suspects like the Lashkar-e-Tayiba, intelligence sources said.'[13] The article pointed out that the obsession with Islamist terror often misleads Indian investigators.

'We should keep a close watch on developments like the Nanded blast,' my source had said. In April that year, there had been an accidental bomb blast in Nanded in which two people were killed. The state CID blamed it on the Bajrang Dal. My editor R. Jagannathan, now editorial director of *Swarajya*, displayed the story prominently on the front page, below the ground report on the blast, with the headline: 'Malegaon blasts: It may not be the usual suspects.'

Next morning, I was out in the field when the staff officer of a senior IB officer called me: 'Boss wants to meet you. Can you come now?' I headed over to North Block, parked my car in the reserved parking behind the imposing building, took the lift up from the basement. The senior officer had always been warm and informal in the past, but this morning was different. Over a cup of tea, he admonished me, saying that it was irresponsible of me to write such a piece, raising doubts about possible Hindu terror groups. He insisted that the Malegaon blast was the result of an ongoing fight between two strands of Islam: Sunnis and Deobandis. The man looked visibly disturbed. 'You are such a seasoned reporter on national security matters. You cannot be so irresponsible,' he told me. I found his behaviour very out of sync with his usual self.

By the time I left the IB office, television channels were peddling the line I had just heard. National media dissected the simmering tensions between the two strands of Islam, and they found evidence in Malegaon. The town had witnessed tensions between orthodox Muslims and those who believed in reform, and the Indian media jumped on this theory to explain the blasts. Was the IB deliberately manufacturing a narrative? Or did it know more than we know even all these years later? Could it be that our premier intelligence agency was a victim of its own biases? I have no conclusive answers to the se questions.

As months passed, and the involvement of a Hindu terror group in the Malegaon blast and other big attacks emerged, there were several authoritative voices within the security establishment pointing accusatory fingers at the IB's conduct. A thorough investigation into what transpired at the bureau would have dramatically improved transparency in not only the IB but all security agencies. Instead, the Maharashtra ATS under Raghuvanshi took over the Malegaon blasts investigations.

On the day of the blasts, Wahid went to report at the ATS office. There, he found policemen distributing sweets, evidently celebrating the bombing. By the end of September, Wahid and most other suspects in the train blasts case were back in custody. By November, they had also been sent to jail.

Some time later, ATS officers visited the jail, seeking custody of two of the train blast accused, Asif Bashir Khan and Mohammed Ali, in connection with the Malegaon blasts. ATS claimed that they had supplied RDX and provided shelter to Pakistani terrorists. 'Asif cried a lot that day. He said he did not feel this bad even when he was accused in the 7/11 blasts. Accusing him of doing a blast in a mosque caused him unparalleled sorrow,' Wahid recalled. Khan and Ali were in ATS custody for a month as it constructed the claim that, just days after the Mumbai train blasts, explosives were taken to Malegaon. The theory had several gaps, but the police and state government did not seem to be paying attention to what the ATS was up to.

On 28 September, a couple of weeks after the Malegaon blasts, Wahid had gone to the ATS office to surrender his passport and the lease agreement for his Mumbra apartment on police instructions. Outside the station stood Dr Javed Ansari, Wahid's brother-in-law. Surprised, Wahid asked him why he was there, and discovered that Javed's younger brother, Sajid, had been in police custody for several days. The ATS's war on terror was reaching further into his family. After waiting for several hours, Wahid was taken to ACP Vinod Patil, who repeated what Raghuvanshi and other officers had been telling Wahid: that he had hosted the group of Pakistanis who bombed the city.

Wahid would not accept this. When he got home, Sajida insisted that the family should file a complaint against the police officers who were harassing him. Once more, he prevented her from going ahead, because the policemen had threatened to arrest him if he complained.

A day later, a police constable called Wahid, asking him to rush to the ATS office. Even as he was on a rickshaw, making his way there, the policeman called again and asked him to hurry. Some minutes later, the policeman called again, this time asking Wahid to meet him at a cinema hall near Ghatkopar. The constable was waiting in a car, and asked Wahid to get in, and drove him to the ATS office. There, Wahid was handcuffed without any explanation, and taken to KEM hospital. The inspector accompanying him threatened Wahid not to say anything to the doctor. After a routine medical check-up, he was taken to a court in Sewree. Again, before entering the courtroom, the inspector repeated his threat: do not tell the judge anything.

Wahid asked the inspector what was he being remanded in for, and was told it was a small case. He did not then realise that the police had already begun preparations to implicate him in the bomb blasts. While seeking the remand, the police produced a false witness testimony (panchnama) claiming that he was taken to his house for a search. 'The panchnama Exh. 1778 is entirely bogus,' Wahid told the court during the trial years later.

A day after he was produced in court, a constable came to the lock-up where Wahid was now legally detained and asked him to sign a paper. Wahid insisted on reading it, but the constable threatened harm if he did not sign. There was no option. On 2 October, Gandhi Jayanti, or perhaps a day later, he was taken to another ATS office. 'I was given third-degree torture during the police custody period in the torture room of the Bhoiwada office and the ATS Kalachowki,' Wahid told the court years later.[14]

While in police custody one day in October 2006, Wahid received a new instruction: don't eat or drink anything in the evening. The next day, he would have a brief encounter with India's VVIP culture. Around 5 a.m., ten or so jeeps arrived at the jail. Wahid and Naveed, another accused in the train blasts, were conveyed in one of these through the empty Mumbai roads to the airport. Their handcuffs were removed and they were escorted inside by policemen. Inspector Khanwelkar told the accused that they were not to deviate from the plan—no toilets, no other activities. The short-tempered Khanwelkar got into a loud argument with one of the attendants for not being provided enough special treatment, even though the security line had been emptied out for the high-security accused. After the security screening, Wahid told Khanwelkar that he needed to pee. Reluctantly, he took Wahid to the toilet. First, the inspector went inside and got everyone to leave, and once it was empty, Wahid was asked to enter.

As they walked to the aircraft, Wahid told Khanwelkar, 'I am very happy. I have never boarded a flight before.' And it was free. There was another reason for his happiness that Wahid did not tell the inspector: the truth would finally be established. 'He told me that I was mad to be thinking this way because my life is being spoilt,' Wahid said.

The party, comprising around ten to fifteen policemen and the two accused, moved to the rear of the SpiceJet aircraft and occupied the last four rows. Inspector Khanwelkar sat next to Wahid. As air hostesses came to serve food, Khanwelkar told Wahid to keep some of the food for later, and also passed on his own food items to Wahid. The air hostess who was serving food looked at Wahid with a great amount of curiosity. As she bent to put the food tray down in front of Wahid, she asked softly: 'Did you actually do the blasts?'

'Ma'am, can you see it written on my face? Am I a terrorist?'

Wahid asked her. She said no, and that is why she was asking him. Meanwhile, the other hostess was trying to appease the policemen and asking them if they needed anything more. Years later, when he recalled his flight to Bengaluru in October 2006, Wahid grinned.

As they alighted in Bengaluru, the local police formed a ring around and handcuffed the two accused, and took them to the Central Crime Bureau lock-up. Wahid says that there he met inmates who had been mercilessly tortured, some with fractured bones. One of them, though in severe pain, kept singing Mohammed Rafi songs, and between songs told the rest trivia about the legendary singer's life. 'Life is unpredictable and so don't waste it,' he said. During the day, the police contingent took Wahid and his co-accused to various hospitals for their narco tests. They were trying to get an appointment with Dr S. Malini, the celebrated narco-analyst at the Forensic Science Laboratory (FSL), better known as Dr Narco in the security establishment. She had a formidable reputation for having helped investigation agencies across India unravel many complex crimes. Dr Malini was almost a celebrity, and some of her interrogations, recorded on video, have been sensational news. After much chasing, she told the police team that the narco test would not be possible that day. So, Wahid and Naveed were to be brought back after the weekend.

While the duo were anxiously awaiting their narco test, some comfort came from another group of accused in the Malegaon blasts, all Muslims. They were in the same lock-up. 'They asked me not to worry. They said nothing would happen and that I would just feel a little drowsy,' Wahid recalled. All of them seemed to share Wahid and Naveed's sense of gratitude that the truth would finally be out.

On Monday, Wahid was eagerly looking forward to his narco test. 'We thought the narco test will prove the truth and we would be let off,' he recalled. ATS officers brought him to the hospital, where Malini was sitting outside the room, sipping tea with the hospital staff. By then, Wahid had developed the habit of talking to people, defending his innocence. He asked the doctor if he would be let off if he told the truth. She replied in the affirmative, and told the hospital attendants to take him away for the test.

In a large room, resembling an operation theatre, with a camera behind him, Wahid lay down. He was then administered an injection. Malini walked in, and began by asking him his name, his educational qualifications. It was mechanical and in Hindi—a question, its answer and the next question. Wahid was fully conscious.

Years later, Wahid recalled, almost verbatim, the exchange he had during the narco test. He recalled with a lot of amusement, and a sense of incredulity.

Wahid says that he had told her that once he was in a semi-consciousness state, he would tell the complete truth. 'I am telling you the truth even now.' This is how he remembers the conversation:

> 'No one says anything when unconscious, you will speak only when you are conscious,' Malini told him. Then, she switched pace. 'Who did the blasts?'
>
> 'I don't know.'
>
> 'Who is the SIMI president?'
>
> 'Pratibha Patil.' Wahid thought she was asking him who the Indian president was.
>
> Pat came a slap. 'Who is the SIMI president?' Malini raised her voice.
>
> This time Wahid did not have an answer. She took out a tweezer, gripped one of his ears with it and pulled. She asked again: 'Who is the SIMI president?'
>
> Wahid was silent.
>
> 'Say, Dr Shahid Badar Falahi.'
>
> Wahid repeated after her, like an obedient student following the instructions of a tough teacher.
>
> Malini was now warming up. She asked about the bomb blasts. 'How many people came and stayed with you?'
>
> Wahid said, no one.
>
> She asked him to say that four people stayed with him.
>
> Wahid was silent.
>
> 'What comes after three?' she asked.

> Wahid replied, four.
>
> 'Did Pakistanis stay in your house?' Malini asked.
>
> Wahid said no.
>
> The next question was, name India's neighbouring countries.
>
> Wahid started saying, Nepal, Bangladesh, Pakistan and so on.
>
> Throughout the narco test, a senior police officer from the ATS stood next to Malini, instructing her on what to ask him, and then prompting the answers expected.

Wahid was still entirely conscious. 'I remember every question they asked me. It is a little blurred, but I remember everything,' he told me.

As the narco test came to an end, one of the attendants bandaged Wahid's bleeding ear. The next day, Wahid and a co-accused underwent a polygraph test. After the procedures, during the team's return journey to Mumbai, Wahid recalled in court later.

In a complaint before the court during the trial, Wahid's team claimed that the recordings of the narco tests had been edited to show Wahid indicting himself and others. When he listed 'Pakistan' among India's neighbouring countries, it had been edited into another part of the conversation; when he recited numbers, as he was asked to, 'four' was taken out of context.

What Wahid went through, and complained about to the court, was yet another dark secret of India's criminal justice system. There are several questions over the scientific accuracy of deception-detection tests—polygraph, narco-analysis and brain-mapping—and the debate continues. Given the manner in which these tests are administered in India, the NHRC, on 11 January 2000, wrote to the states with a set of guidelines.[15] There had been several complaints about the violation of constitutional guarantees against invasiveness and self-incrimination in the way these tests were conducted. The guidelines said: 'No Lie Detector Test should be administered without the consent of the accused. Option should be given to the accused as to whether he wishes to avail the test.' Wahid neither gave consent, nor was he given an option. According to NHRC guidelines, the consent of the accused should be recorded before a judicial magistrate. Further, if the accused volunteers for the tests, he should be given access to his lawyer, and the police and lawyer should explain to him all the implications of the tests.

Even in normal circumstances, investigation agencies routinely breach these guidelines. This was no ordinary circumstance, and Wahid was a 'dreaded terrorist'.

Malini's narco tests have played a critical role in solving many a sensational crime during that period. According to her own estimates, she has conducted the tests on about 130 suspected terrorists and fifteen Naxalites, among others. In the narco test she conducted on Abdul Karim Telgi, who made almost Rs 10,000 crore selling counterfeit stamp papers, he purportedly named several top Maharashtra politicians, setting off a political storm that had few legal outcomes.

In the murder case of Sister Abhaya in Kerala, in which two priests and a nun were accused, the court received a doctored CD of the narco tests that had been prepared by Malini. A Kerala High Court judge said that the editing was 'clearly visible to the naked eye and to find out the evident editing even an expert may not be necessary'.[16] So crudely was it done. Yet, this middle-rung official of a regional forensic lab was one of the most decisive players in some of the biggest terrorist cases in India: the Mumbai train blasts, the Malegaon blasts and the terrorist bombings in Hyderabad, among other cases.

However, Dr Narco's run did not last. In the first decade of the twenty-first century, courts found that Malini had repeatedly misled India's already shaky war on terror.[17] On 25 February 2009, the Karnataka government sacked her for forging her educational certificates to secure her position.[18] A few months earlier, a confidential police investigation had found that Malini had changed her year of birth from 1960 to 1964 so that she could qualify for the powerful position of assistant director of the FSL, deciding the fate of sensational cases. The report also accused her of submitting fake certificates issued by the University of Calgary, claiming that she had undergone basic and advanced hypnotherapy courses. The investigation found that the forged certificates had silly spelling errors, and the Karnataka police termed her a 'security risk'.

By the time she was sacked, India's most famous narco-analyst had conducted over 1,000 narco tests, some 3,000 lie-detection tests and 1,500 brain-mapping tests, according to a report in the *Bangalore Mirror*.[19] No one cared to go back to her findings and tests, or assess their impact on the many criminals and innocents she had indicted through them. In 2010, the Supreme Court held that narco analysis, brain-mapping and polygraph tests conducted without the consent of an individual were illegal and a violation of personal liberty.[20]

Almost everyone produced before a magistrate in India pleads to be sent to a jail, rather than be held in police custody, for fear of police brutality. Most importantly, it is almost the norm for suspects to fear that the police will force them to give fake statements that suit a predetermined narrative. Of course, jails are naturally violent places, but most of those arrested still prefer them to the alternative.

For Wahid and the other train blasts accused, there was no escaping the police, even in jail. Wahid says that the jail authorities actively assisted the ATS as it continued to coerce them to admit to their alleged terror activities.

On 28 June 2008, according to a writ petition filed in Mumbai High Court by some of the accused in the train blasts, forty-odd prisoners were brutally beaten up in the Arthur Road Jail. Superintendent Swati Madhav Sathe told the court that after the Supreme Court stayed the trial of the case, and because of over-crowding in her jail, she had sought the judge's permission to transfer thirty-seven of the undertrial prisoners, many of them accused in the train blasts, to different prisons in the state. On 28 June, when the police-escort squad arrived at the prison, an announcement was made, asking thirty-two undertrials to gather near Lal Gate. Seven of them were sent to Ratnagiri Special Jail at 11.40 a.m. Another nineteen were sitting outside. In her written filings before the court, Sathe claimed that this was when the commotion began. Some of the undertrials used abusive language and misbehaved with the jail officials. The twenty-one undertrials charged at the officials, attacking them with bricks and stones. Alarm was sounded in the jail and 'after using reasonable and required force', the situation was brought under control, she claimed. After the situation cooled off, fifteen undertrials were sent to Kolhapur Central Prison, and ten to Nagpur Central Prison. The high court ordered an enquiry by the principal judge of the city and sessions court. What this judge found was not in line with Sathe's filings.

Ruling on a bunch of criminal writ petitions about the violence, the high court said on 21 July 2009 that the jail superintendent and her staff used 'force excessively and for the reasons extraneous and not for the reasons to maintain discipline in the jail'.[21]

The sessions court judge 'found that the bricks and stones were not available as contended by the jail authority and story of jail authority was not true'. The judge also recorded that the prisoners were all severely injured but did not get any medical attention. Besides, the jail doctor also colluded with the superintendent.

'The injuries recorded in the medical certificate of the jail authority were manipulated in order to help the jail authority because the injuries were found by the Government Doctors even after 20 to 23 days after the prisoners were shifted to other jail,' the high court pointed out.[22]

Jail Superintendent Sathe filed her statement before the high court, objecting to the findings of the judge, and quoted from something called 'lesson eighteen', apparently some Al Qaeda manual. She did not care to prove that the inmates knew of it, nor dispute the findings of the judge.

Why was there so much violence? What was the motive for targeting the alleged terrorists?

The enquiry finally got to the crux of the matter, and found that it was all part of a desperate effort by the ATS, with active assistance from the jail authorities, to turn some of the accused into approvers.[23] When they refused, the torture began.

The high court concluded that, instead of being the custodians and protectors of the inmates, the jail authorities had acted to support the illegal actions of the police. In its order, the court reminded the jail authorities that convicts and undertrials must be treated like human beings. It said the superintendent's conduct could not be condoned, and that other officers must have acted under her command. Her conduct 'was shameful', the court said.

The judgement also found other serious procedural violations by the jail authorities. A sessions court, and not the trial court, had responded to the transfer request from the jail, allowing authorities to take appropriate action 'as per rules and regulations', and not bothering to send a copy of the order to the affected parties. 'The transfer itself was illegal, improper and bad as the Jail authority had no power at all to transfer the prisoner, who had been confined to a particular jail by the trial court,' the high court said. The judgement also found that the transfers were made over a weekend, so that inmates could get no immediate legal help. The high court directed the chief secretary of the state to 'initiate disciplinary inquiry against all the Officers involved in the incident for using excessive force and for using force for extraneous reason'. It also ordered an enquiry into the conduct of the jail doctors for 'fudging the record'.

When the officials filed an appeal in the Supreme Court against the high court order, the apex court said some of the observations of the high court which gives the impression that 'the misdemeanour of the jail officials had been proved, do not appear justified', because the officials indicted should have been given the opportunity by the sessions court judge to cross-examine those who alleged misconduct against them. The Supreme Court it left it to the state government to decide whether to hold further enquiry.[24]

It is not known what action the state government took against Sathe and the others who were indicted. From public records, we know that, in 2017, an inmate named Manjula Shetye died under suspicious circumstances in Arthur Road Jail, and Sathe was among those who figured in the episode.[25] In June 2020, she was transferred to a less important post.[26] The detailed documentation of violence inside the jail and the high court's indictment of the authorities were important milestones in recording the reality of Indian jails.

But, for Wahid and the others who were tortured in Arthur Road Jail in June 2008, there has been no justice so far. No part of India's complex democracy is bothered about them.

3

Meet the Bombers

In the last days of August 2008, a private vehicle wove through Mumbai traffic towards a secret location, racing against time. As the five passengers sat silently, the tension inside was palpable. The Indian security establishment's hopes that the terrorists behind the deadly blasts across India would be caught were contained in that vehicle. The five men inside were a strange group: three policemen and two car thieves. They were rushing to seize a Maruti Zen that had been hidden away.

Smart police investigation and some sheer luck had brought the five together. A series of bombs had gone off in Ahmedabad on the evening of 26 July that year. City buses were torn apart, crowded markets shaken up, and as the injured were being taken to hospitals, two bombs went off there as well. In a little over an hour, twenty-one bombs had killed fifty-six people and injured a few hundred. A day earlier, Bangalore had witnessed nine bomb blasts, which killed a woman waiting at a bus shelter. The group that bombed Bangalore could not have reached Ahmedabad to carry out the bombings the next day. However, there were great similarities between the two series of blasts. They were set off by low-intensity bombs of very similar design, and raised the possibility that a pan-Indian terror group with multiple modules was in operation.

A few minutes before the Ahmedabad blasts, several media houses had received a fourteen-page email from an organisation calling itself the 'Indian Mujahideen'. The subject line of the email was 'await 5 minutes for the revenge of Gujarat'. It contained threats to various people, a reference to Mukesh Ambani building his house 'Antilia' on Muslim wakf land, and to the Maharashtra chief minister and his deputy for framing the wrong people in the serial train blasts of July 2006 (Wahid numbered among the wronged).

As the dead and injured were rushed to hospitals, the Gujarat police searched cities across the state for unexploded bombs. They recovered two cars in Surat packed with explosives, and also evidence regarding two other cars used in the Ahmedabad bombings. It soon emerged that all four cars had been stolen from Navi Mumbai in the first week of July.

The Mumbai Crime Branch, now led by Rakesh Maria, did some on-the-ground investigation and found a link between two car thieves from Indore, who were sitting in that speeding car, and the theft of the cars used in the blasts.[1] Irfan and Amin, the thieves, had established their careers in Mumbai, and in recent years, their primary business was stealing cars from Mumbai and selling them to agents around the country. Irfan had started out snatching people's bags in Mumbai trains and moved to car theft by 2001. Amin was a school dropout, and had several cases registered against him in Mumbai for stealing vehicles as well as other items.

Their sources told the Mumbai Crime Branch that Irfan and Amin would reach the city soon. As soon as they did, the duo was picked up and questioned through the day and late into the night. According to Maria, around 3 a.m., both thieves confessed that they had stolen the four vehicles and sold them to a man called Afzal Mutalib Usmani, who had placed the orders for them. One of the duo had spent eighteen months in jail, where he had become friends with Usmani. They told the police that there was a stolen Maruti Zen in a city hideout that all three of them used for moving around.

That was the secret location the police car was headed to now. However, the vehicle broke down while navigating the traffic at Chunabhatti, a Mumbai suburb. When the policemen could not fix the problem, the car thieves offered their expertise. The two got into the front seat and began fiddling with the levers there, and asked the three policemen to push the car. As the car kicked into life, the thieves sped away with it, leaving the three outsmarted policemen behind. Rakesh Maria admits in his autobiography, *Let Me Say it Now*, that the scene was 'straight out of a Charlie Chaplin slapstick comedy, funny in a bleak, black-and-white way'.[2]

Although that first attempt at cracking the IM fell through, the Crime Branch now had a name: Afzal Mutalib Usmani. They discovered that he was part of an extortion racket run by the gangster Fazl-ur-Rehman, who operated from the Gulf.[3] Maria writes that Usmani was known to open fire indiscriminately to terrorise his targets. Once, he fired at someone in a shop selling firecrackers, another time in Hotel Sea Princess in Juhu. He had been arrested for murder in the past, for killing the wrong guy, not the target of his extortion.

Even as the Crime Branch began its hunt for Usmani, yet another email popped up in the inboxes of several media houses on the evening of 13 September 2008. With rambling allegations and political claims, it warned of blasts in Delhi in the next few minutes. In fact, even before the email had reached most media houses, the first of the bombs had gone off in Ghaffar Market in Karol Bagh. Four more blasts followed. At least twenty people were killed and almost a hundred were injured.

The Mumbai Crime Branch, meanwhile, had a new lead: Usmani was in Dhilai Ferozepur of Mau district, Uttar Pradesh. Maria ordered a police party to secretly go to Mau to pick him up. The team reached Varanasi late in the evening, and was in the Dhilai Ferozepur area later that night for the top-secret operation. What greeted them in the morning was yet another comic episode. The local newspapers carried front-page news saying that a Mumbai police team was in Dhilai Ferozepur to probe the Ahmedabad blasts. The police team quietly retreated to Varanasi. Luckily, they got information that

Usmani was to board a train to Mumbai from Belthara Road railway station. When he boarded the train, a police party in disguise also got on. Usmani figured out that something was wrong, got off the train and began to run. The police chased him, and after a long pursuit, nabbed him.

After several days of interrogation, Usmani admitted to the Crime Branch that he was working for the IM. He gave the names of two leaders—Riyaz Bhatkal and Sadiq Israr Sheikh. Soon after, the police captured Sheikh, a resident of Cheetah Camp in Mumbai. His interrogation threw up new information on the group, and the names of many cadres. Sadiq also led the police to a garment factory in Sewri, Mumbai, where they recovered arms and ammunition that the IM had stored.

According to details that emerged later in investigations by the NIA and state police, Indian Mujahideen was not the name that the organisation had settled upon for itself. After the bombing of an Uttar Pradesh court in 2007, when they sent out an email claiming responsibility for it, the media picked up on the term 'Indian Mujahideen' in the letter, and the group decided to adopt the nomenclature. IM had begun to take shape sometime in early 2004, when a preacher from Uttar Pradesh visited Bhatkal, a seaside locality in Karnataka, and motivated some militant-minded activists to come together. They called themselves 'Usaba', and elected Iqbal Bhatkal as the group's 'amir'. The earliest Usaba gatherings were in Bhatkal, usually on Fridays, and most often in the home of Iqbal Bhatkal. That house became the seeding ground for the deadliest domestic terrorist group to take shape in India, outside of Kashmir and the Northeast. The group sent some of its members to Pakistan for arms training, reached out to like-minded people across the country, and brought men like Sadiq Sheikh from Mumbai and Atif Ameen from Uttar Pradesh into the fold. As the group's violent intentions were firmed up, it leased a three-acre farm near Udupi, where its members reared cows and goats and kept dogs, and planted 1,200 banana plants.

'Sadiq owned up responsibility for the Dashashwamedh Ghat blasts, the Shramjeevi Express blasts, the Diwali-eve Delhi blasts, the Sankat Mochan temple blasts, the Gorakhpur Market blasts, the Lumbini Park and Gokul Chaat Bhandar blasts in Hyderabad, the UP courts blasts, the Jaipur serial blasts, the unexploded bombs found in Bangalore, the Ahmedabad serial blasts and the unexploded bombs found in Surat,' Maria writes in his autobiography.[4]

I was startled by Maria's omission of the 2006 Mumbai train blasts from the list, because Sadiq himself told the police in elaborate detail how they bombed the trains.[5] With information he provided, they were able to track down key members of the IM as well as recover explosives.

Maria's book does not mention the train blasts among the attacks by the IM. It is to be noted that, while the Crime Branch under Maria unearthed the existence of the IM, it was the ATS under Raghuvanshi that had made the claims about Wahid and other bombers. There is a high likelihood that we may never know who really bombed the trains, despite Sadiq's statement, as well as the numerous statements[6] that emerged from IM terrorists and other sources.

Sadiq detailed the rise of the Pakistan-backed homegrown terror group, unlike any other in recent memory. A fair number of its members were educated Indian youngsters. Of the twenty-one people the Crime Branch arrested, ten were software engineers and one was an MBBS doctor. The politics of this group had been shaped by the communal frenzy kicked up by the right-wing Ram Janmabhoomi movement in the late 1980s, which culminated in the demolition of the Babri Masjid on 6 December 1992 and nationwide riots. After a few terrorist acts, which members of the latter-day IM had little to do with, the group was slowly dying out in the 1990s. That is when the Gujarat pogrom happened in 2002. This time, the group that began to take shape as IM was deadly, and far more violent. The group drew considerable strength from criminal elements, from car thieves to hardened kidnappers, and many of its members went to Pakistan for arms training. An angry network of disaffected youngsters quickly metamorphosed into a deadly terror group.

Among the details that the Mumbai Crime Branch had been able to gather about the IM was this: its fifty members operated in three independent groups based out of Pune, Mangalore and Delhi. Besides the apartment in Sewri that was used for the 2006 train blasts, IM had hired two apartments in Pune and one in Delhi. The Delhi group was operating from a flat in Batla House in Jamia Nagar in the southern part of Delhi, near a famed university. The Mumbai Crime Branch learnt of this hideout sometime in September 2008, and rushed a team of officers to Delhi on a late-night flight.[7]

The team carried out detailed reconnaissance in the Jamia Nagar area, and realised that, in that crowded locality, even more packed than usual because of Ramzan, it would be impossible to arrest the IM members from their apartment. They continued to listen in on the phone calls of one of the Batla House suspects, Atif Amin Shaikh, who was among those identified as a key member of the terror group. As their team in Delhi began an anxious stakeout, Shaikh dialled a number and told a girl that he would meet her on the afternoon of 19 September at an inter-state bus terminal. The team decided to arrest him when he ventured out to meet her. On the evening of 18 September, they began planning the details of the big operation the next afternoon.

However, on the morning of 19 September, they were in for a nasty surprise. Television news channels began to flash the news that a Delhi police team had carried out a raid on Batla House. The chaotic raid resulted in the death of a police officer, Mohan Chand Sharma, but also the killing of two terrorists and the arrest of two others. Among those killed was Atif Amin Shaikh. The Mumbai team returned quietly. A few years later, one of the senior officers involved in the Mumbai police operation told me that he suspected that the IB had done a one-upmanship on the Mumbai team, and roped in the Special Cell of the Delhi police to carry out a hurried raid so that the Mumbai Crime Branch would not walk away with all the glory for exposing the IM.

The encounter also left behind a trail of questions, about the conduct of the Delhi police, the exact way in which the police inspector was killed, bullet injuries mostly on the head of those killed, other injury marks on the alleged terrorists, and so on. At the very least, such discrepancies prove the core argument of this book—the urgent need to hold police and intelligence agencies accountable.[8]

We may never know the full details of what happened on the morning of 19 September, but the raid showed once again that turf battles between the agencies, and the resultant mess, is a reality that the security establishment must contend with.

Just after the Batla House encounter, the police recovered seventeen crude bombs in Ahmedabad, and another was recovered near a temple in Faridabad. Rumours and false alerts were the order of the day. Then, on 29 September 2008, ten days after the encounter, three bombs went off in two different cities of western India—two in Malegaon, Maharashtra, where nine were killed, and one in Modasa, Gujarat, in which one person was killed. In Modasa, someone on a motorbike had dropped the bombs in a crowded marketplace where Muslims had gathered to break the Ramzan fast. In Malegaon, where two years previously thirty-one people were killed in an attack, seven people died when bombs tied to a motorcycle went off.

By now, the Maharashtra ATS had a new chief, Hemant Karkare, who was widely held to be a highly competent and professional officer. A former R&AW chief told me that Karkare voluntarily decided to go back to Maharashtra. 'I never understood him. Not many officers who come to R&AW would voluntarily go back to the state police. If he stayed back, he would have had a very comfortable life, and probably ended up heading the organisation one day,' he said. The day after the blast, Karkare landed in Malegaon, and spent a fair bit of time examining the mangled remains of a golden motorcycle on which the bomb was strapped. It was an LML Freedom made in 2003, with the number plate 'GJ 05 BR 1920'.[9] Within weeks, the ATS was able to identify its engine number, and that helped them trace the agency in Surat that sold the bike. The buyer was Pragya Singh Thakur, a former member of the Akhil Bharatiya Vidyarthi Parishad (ABVP), the student wing of the BJP. The ATS investigation quickly established the existence of a shadowy Hindutva terror group, which included a serving military intelligence officer, Lt Col. Prasad Purohit, and retired Major Ramesh Upadhyay, among others. The ATS investigation revealed that the group intended to retaliate against Islamic terrorism and thus specifically targeted Muslims localities.

Even as the ATS was closing in on the Hindutva terror group, hundreds of kilometres away in Haryana, a group of policemen had also picked up the trail of a secretive right-wing group of bombers. They were investigating the February 2007 bombing of Samjhauta Express, a train that perfectly captured the emotional swing of the subcontinent between animalistic hatred and the desperation for a peaceful future.

Around midnight of 18 February 2007, after the Samjhauta Express had passed through the historic town of Panipat, where some of the most defining battles were fought to decide the fate of the region, bombs went off in two carriages, lighting up the night sky. The train had just crossed the single-platform station of Diwana at the time of the blasts, which killed seventy people and injured many more. Most of the dead were Pakistanis.

The Samjhauta Express, its name meaning 'compromise', had signified the efforts of India and Pakistan to build a more civilised future after the Bangladesh War. The train service commenced in July 1976, and was a mirror to the see-saw relationship between the two nuclear powers. During peaceful periods, the train would be packed; when tensions rose, passengers began to thin out, and as tensions peaked, it would freeze. After a cooling-off period, the cycle would begin again. The train has helped thousands of ordinary people, mostly Muslim families, to meet their relatives across the border. The frenzy and confusion of the 1947 Partition had left hundreds of thousands of families divided, a sister here and brothers there, a brother who went away to Pakistan while everyone else stayed back in India, a child left behind, a father who abandoned the family, families split in every way imaginable. Even into the new millennium, some families were newly discovering the existence of relatives who had survived the massacres of 1947 and made a home across the border. Every time the Samjhauta Express left or arrived in Old Delhi railway station, it was packed with ordinary people and barely contained emotions.

The Haryana police formed an SIT headed by Vikash Narain Rai, an IPS officer of the 1977 batch, to investigate the blasts. The police had recovered an unexploded bomb, packed in a suitcase, and the SIT began to dismantle it. The team began by tracing the origins of each item recovered, and contacted their respective manufacturers to figure out where the items may have been procured from. The suitcase, it turned out, was bought from the Raghunandan Ataichi store in Indore.[10] That was the beginning of a series of surprising findings: almost every item they found in the bomb, whether the newspaper or battery, was from Indore, almost all bought from the same market. The team soon figured out that the bombs were assembled in Indore.

It was the second time that evidence pointed to Indore, but a section of the security establishment was actively disinterested in pursuing the lead, according to multiple sources I have met over the years. On an earlier occasion, on 6 June 2006, when two explosions took place in the courtyard of Jama Masjid in Old Delhi, R&AW intercepted a suspicious call to Indore soon after the blast. But the IB did not investigate the call, a R&AW official then told me.

Initially, the Haryana SIT suspected SIMI, which had an active presence in Indore. The team interrogated the group's activists, including Safdar Nagori, a policeman's son who had studied journalism but was radicalised in the wake of the Babri Masjid demolition and was now in jail with terror allegations against him. 'We investigated many Islamists in jail that time, including SIMI's head Safdar Nagori. We were pretty convinced after that it was a Hindu outfit [that carried out the blasts]. Indore was not only notorious for SIMI but also for Hindutva activists,' Vikash Rai recalled later.[11]

As the involvement of Hindutva elements became clear, the Madhya Pradesh police developed cold feet.[12] The state was now ruled by the BJP. However, the Haryana police carried on, and learnt about an RSS leader called Sunil Joshi, locally known as Guruji. Before they could reach him, though, Guruji was murdered on 29 December 2007. Joshi had been hiding in a single-room apartment in Chuna Khadan area of Dewas for some time. Apparently, he was wanted for the murder of Congress leader Pyarsingh Ninama.[13] Two people on a bike pumped bullets into him outside his hideout.

The Sunil Joshi murder case was full of twists and turns. In early 2017, a court in Dewas effectively said in its judgement that no one had killed Guruji.[14] It acquitted all the eight accused in the case. Among those acquitted was Pragya Singh Thakur, or Bharati, who was the BJP's candidate for the Lok Sabha from the Bhopal seat two years later, even though she was on trial for organising terror attacks.[15] She defeated former Madhya Pradesh chief minister Digvijay Singh.

Her nomination was a formal blessing for the fringe elements. They now run cow-vigilante groups with impunity, campaign against inter-religious marriages and terrorise anyone romancing in public spaces, and freely advocate unscientific, regressive practices. The mainstreaming of criminal elements automatically weakens the administration of justice, and also curtails the ability of professionals in the security establishment to discharge their duties. Further, an unholy nexus between the fringe elements of the Hindu Right and the unprofessional parts of the security establishment has taken deep roots—from federal agencies to the state polices, the connection is clear.[16]

This sledgehammering of the professional security establishment at the national level has a precedent: it is a governance architecture that was perfected in Gujarat and has an eerie parallel to the Emergency days. It is no more a rare sight to see the faceless members of the security establishment descending on a political opponent of the BJP on the eve of an election,[17] registering a criminal case against an airport operator so he is forced to sell off the assets to a regime favourite,[18] burying an activist under a heap of senseless claims,[19] jailing journalists who are critical[20] and deploying, in a number of other ways, the enormous resources of the security agencies in the service of the political executive. This was, in fact, the architecture of the Indian security establishment until the mid-1990s, when the Congress dominated national politics. In the era of coalition governments in the latter part of the 1990s, the grip of the political executive over these institutions began to loosen. In many ways, that is when India's security establishment slowly began to professionalise.

The Supreme Court, on 18 December 1997, issued its landmark judgement in *Vineet Narain & Others vs Union of India*, which concerned the Jain Hawala scandal, and had captured the imagination of the nation. Indians were horrified at how the CBI's investigation had collapsed. It had failed to professionally investigate politicians and other influential persons who had received through hawala routes money that was linked to the Kashmir militancy. In deciding the public interest litigation (PIL), the apex court agreed with the petitioners, and passed orders to ensure the autonomy and independence of the CBI and ED. It also provided the Central Vigilance Commission (CVC) with statutory powers and superintendence over the two investigation agencies. The Supreme Court laid out several steps—including the creation of an impartial committee to select the CVC, and timelines to speed up investigation and prosecution—to ring-fence the CBI and ED from the political executive.

After the judgement, the two agencies registered significant progress. Between 2010 and 2014, they displayed admirable professionalism and initiative by investigating and arresting many powerful ruling party associates, corporate czars and other influential persons. Of course, there were many loopholes in how they operated, and some innocents, including some very respected senior civil servants, suffered.[21] On the whole, however, there appeared to be a slow maturing of the Indian democracy.

Since 2014, the slow gains of that process have been fully scuttled. The handling of the Sunil Joshi murder case, and several cases linked to right-wing fanatics, is evidence that the security establishment is once more in the service of the political executive. It has been widely argued that the government's approach contains a strong tinge of religious bias and an active hatred for constitutional values.[22]

The investigation into Joshi's murder was first led by the local police. In 2011, however, the NIA took over the case, as it was linked to the terror attacks in Malegaon and in the Samjhauta Express. The police and the NIA had discovered that Joshi was a close aide of Pragya Singh Thakur's before the two fell out. In 2010, the Rajasthan ATS had arrested Harshad Solanki, an accused in the Samjhauta Express bombing. He, in turn, told them about Ramcharan Patel, a BJP corporator, whose interrogation then led the investigators to Pragya Thakur, who was by then in jail for her role in the Malegaon blasts of 2008. In June 2011, the NIA told the Mumbai High Court that the Joshi murder case was part of a larger Hindutva terror conspiracy, and must be included in its ambit. The court agreed.

By 2014, the NIA had produced a charge sheet against eight persons, further broadening the list of accused that the local police had already identified.

In August 2014, in its first charge sheet, NIA claimed that the murder was planned by Pragya Thakur and two others because Joshi had made sexual advances towards Thakur. According to that claim, she had visited Joshi's single-room accommodation and collected a briefcase, which contained material for bomb-making, on the night of the murder. This suitcase was later given to Ramji Kalsangara, who allegedly played a role in most of the Abhinav Bharat bomb blasts. A couple of hours after she left with the suitcase, Joshi was murdered.

However, a Bhopal-based NIA court ruled that it was a plain murder case and handed it back to the Madhya Pradesh police, which, in turn, filed a new charge sheet in September 2014. Eventually, in 2017, the court acquitted Thakur and seven others in the Joshi murder case, observing that 'the contradictory evidences by the police and NIA in the case raised serious doubts'. The investigation agencies acted out 'of prejudice or reasons best known to them', the court said.[23]

The Sunil Joshi case is not the only one that has not been resolved. The victims of a string of terror attacks have not yet found justice because the bombers were found to be Hindutva elements. The BJP's aggressive campaign[24] against the idea that there could be any Hindu terrorists appears to have been adopted by the investigation agencies as well. The fact is that every religious belief has, deep in its folds, the recipe for both peace and violence, and this has been misused by violent elements to launch attacks on followers of other religions throughout history.

Meanwhile, Wahid was in Arthur Road Jail's high-security section, called the 'anda cell'. To reach it, you would have to walk through twelve gates from the main entrance of the jail. This is where he received news of Karkare's appointment as ATS chief. He had heard of the officer's reputation, and his public statements assuring a fair and just investigation. Wahid sat down to write him a letter in Marathi. Even today, the schoolteacher has a copy of that letter in his meticulous collection of documents detailing the twists and turns of his life. While making a general appeal for unbiased investigations, he also explained that his case had been framed by the ATS under Raghuvanshi. 'I don't know if you will be able to do anything in our case and whether you have the power or jurisdiction to do anything, or if you can reopen or reinvestigate the case,' he wrote. Then he made a heartfelt appeal asking the new chief to ensure that no other innocent is framed in a terror case. 'If you are unable to find the actual culprit, please don't arrest any innocent just to save your own reputation. If you do it, just like it happened with us, just like K.P. Raghuvanshi did with us, the family of that accused suffers along with the accused himself. If it happens with a certain community, then the entire community is stigmatised,' Wahid wrote. Karkare did not respond to him.

Sometime after Wahid wrote the letter, a prominent resident of Vikhroli, Abdur Rahman, organised a feast at his home, and Karkare was the guest of honour there. In attendance were local political and social leaders. The group too spoke to Karkare about Wahid's case, assuring the officer that the man was innocent. Karkare told them that he had received several complaints regarding the train blast investigations, and specifically about Wahid too. He promised to look at the investigations again.

Wahid's hopes that Karkare might help him find justice soared further when he heard about the breakthrough that the ATS had made in unearthing the Hindutva group behind the bombings in Malegaon and Modasa. 'We were seeing something new. He was the first one to expose Hindu terror. He arrested Hindu religious leaders and even those in the army. This gave us some relief that now the arrests won't be limited to the Muslim community, and because of Hemant Karkare, the culprit, irrespective of his community, will be arrested. We were also a little hopeful that he would reopen our case or order for a fresh investigation. But our hopes did not last,' Wahid recalled.

Sometime in October 2008, Haryana IPS officer Rai, who was heading the SIT investigating the Samjhauta Express blasts, spoke to Karkare, and told him about the network that they had been able to crack open. Karkare promised to come back to Rai once he had managed to piece together all the evidence.[25] Karkare would not keep his promise.

A few weeks after Wahid wrote to Karkare, and a few days after Rai spoke to him about the Hindutva terror group, India's war on terror witnessed yet another unusual twist. Just as the 9/11 attacks in the US had rewritten the course of Wahid's life, this time, the Pakistan-backed LeT's terror raid on Mumbai snatched his hope. The Indian security establishment had received multiple warnings about the attack on Mumbai in November 2008, but it had not examined the repeated indications and acted on time.[26] The attack had been planned by Pakistan's flourishing terror factory, but it was the unprofessionalism of the Indian security establishment that brought it to the country's shores.[27] A key part of the blame must be laid at the door of the US intelligence agencies for not revealing everything they knew about the attack plan.[28] The US was selfish, Pakistan was deadly and India was unprofessional.

4

Raiding Mumbai

Even before ten uneducated, desperate men with deadly weapons sailed on the Arabian Sea towards Mumbai, there had been alarm bells that preparations were underway in Pakistan for such an operation. For several months before November 2008, the Maharashtra police had received a flurry of alerts from central intelligence agencies about an imminent attack. There were, in fact, eerie similarities between Kargil 1999 and Mumbai 2008. In both cases, there were credible intelligence inputs, and in both cases, that information was not analysed and acted upon.

In early 2008, intelligence trickled in, primarily from US agencies, that the LeT was planning to attack Mumbai. Unfortunately, this information flowed into a severely contaminated intelligence set-up, where it mixed with unreliable inputs, and often outrageous falsehoods, that were sending Indian agencies on wild-goose chases. The secretive world of intelligence, with almost no external accountability and minimal formal audit of the quality of its information and analysis, believed its own lies and falsehoods, amplified its own biases and justified its own mistakes. Many arms of the state police, meant to tackle organised crime and terrorism, were often mere killer squads, staging encounters based on false claims.[1]

It was not only this internal crisis that led to the Mumbai attacks, though. The US did not convey all the information it had on the preparations for the Mumbai attacks in a bid to protect a key US witness: David Coleman Headley. Even by the standards of international intelligence networks, Headley was an unusual informant, indeed an unusual terrorist. When caught smuggling drugs into the US, he became an informant for the country's Drug Enforcement Administration and ratted out his suppliers in Pakistan. He then went back to smuggling and graduated to becoming a CIA informant. Headley ended up becoming an important member of the LeT, but secured his own position by tempting the CIA with information on Osama bin Laden.

Even as he was busy with his criminal enterprise, Headley found time to marry three women and make several trips to Mumbai for reconnaissance on behalf of the LeT. In Mumbai, he even befriended some socialites as he worked to complete his preparations for the November attack. He was planning strikes in Europe, beginning with an attack on the Danish newspaper *Jyllands-Posten*, which had published cartoons of Prophet Mohammed, when the Americans finally decided to end his run. Meanwhile, terrorists had stormed and savaged Mumbai using the coordinates and information that Headley had gathered.

Born Daood Sayed Gilani, he changed his name in 2005 to David Coleman Headley. The man, with his heterochromic eyes and easy charm, was so good at his work that, in a few trips to Mumbai, he had dug out details about Nariman House in Colaba and the fact that a few Jews lived there. An official enquiry later noted that, when the first police officer reached Colaba market on hearing about the attack, he was unable to locate the target building 'since none in the locality knew anything about the significance of Nariman House. It was only after reaching the spot that he came to know that Jews were staying there'.[2]

To return to the ten terrorists, by the time they had set sail for India, the IB had received the coordinates of a satellite phone they were carrying. We will have to presume that the American agencies had passed this on. What I know for sure is that a joint director of the IB wrote a formal alert to the MoD, which, in turn, alerted the navy and the coast guard. As Mumbai was ravaged by the terrorists, a senior MoD official showed me the alert, railing against the IB, the navy and the coast guard. 'How much more specific can an alert get?' the official had asked in exasperation. Once again, no one was punished for the blunder.

The high-level commission of enquiry appointed by the Maharashtra government, comprising former Union home secretary R.D. Pradhan and former R&AW special secretary V. Balachandran, said that, starting 7 August 2006, there were several intelligence reports warning of preparations to infiltrate fidayeen into India by a sea route.[3] The state police sent copies of twenty intelligence inputs that arrived between December 2007 and October 2008, and a further five alerts received between August 2006 and February 2007 about this attack. The Mumbai commissioner had twenty-six intelligence alerts from various agencies.

'Six alerts were on the possibility of sea-borne attack, while eleven were on the possibility of multiple and simultaneous attacks and three were on the possibility of commando attack,' the enquiry committee said.[4] The alerts had even mentioned three specific dates, and listed targets such as the Taj and Oberoi hotels.

The committee said there was 'total confusion in the process of intelligence alerts at the level of state government and police'. The police, it pointed out, would mechanically forward alerts received to various operational units, via either the director general of police's (DGP's) office or the ATS. In the Home Department, the situation was no different.

The two most senior civil servants looking after the Home Department—the additional chief secretary and the principal secretary—wrote to the committee that they had not received any intelligence alerts from the MHA. However, the police chief of the state had submitted copies of several intelligence alerts issued by the MHA and addressed to the civil servants. When the committee asked about this, the principal secretary (Home) came back with circulars issued by a 'desk officer' in his department regarding the alerts. He told the committee that, according to the existing procedure, the lowly desk officer could receive and process such alerts without telling his senior officials. 'This is a shocking revelation of working of a system that does not enable the senior-most officials in Mantralaya to keep themselves briefed on the intelligence front,' the committee said.

The litany of blunders in this case had parallels with the IC-814 hijack. Crucial initial hours were wasted by indecisive leadership at various levels. A decade after the Kandahar hijack, it turned out that the security establishment had not really learnt the hard lessons it needed to.

The first call came at 9.48 p.m. It was from Leopold Cafe, telling the police control room that foreigners had been injured in a shootout. Between 9.50 p.m. and 9.55 p.m., the Colaba police and control room exchanged twenty-one messages regarding the attack. The floodgates were just opening. At 9.54 p.m. came the call about firing at the Taj Mahal Palace, and two minutes later, a call about shooting at the Oberoi Trident came in, and at 9.59 p.m., news about the carnage at the Chhatrapati Shivaji Terminus (CST) arrived. A few minutes earlier, at 9.56 p.m., there had been information about a taxi being blown up at Wadi Bunder.

The firings triggered panic across the city, and the air was thick with rumours. The control room received 1,365 calls between 9 p.m. and 2 a.m., almost 4.5 calls per minute. The wireless communication system was soon overloaded, and many police officers shifted to their personal mobiles to convey critical official messages. As the field units kept asking for more manpower, it resulted in the 'deployment of striking reserves in a haphazard and helter-skelter manner', the committee found.

'What we have found are instances of lack of: intelligent appreciation of threats, handling of intelligence, maintaining high degree of efficiency in instruments specifically set up to deal with terrorist attacks and certainly lack of overt and visible leadership in carrying out operations to face multi-targeted attacks,' it said.

That was the crux of the matter: the Mumbai police did indeed have a set-up specifically trained for dealing with terrorist attacks. The Quick Response Teams (QRTs) were summoned to the various locations of the attacks. However, once there, they were divided into smaller groups, which is against the very principles of how commando teams operate: as autonomous single units. When the QRTs reached the Taj and Oberoi, there was no one to lead them.

Though the teams had undergone the commando course at Pune and spent three months at the National Security Guard (NSG) centre, Manesar, they had not been trained 'in facing terrorist attacks and hostage rescue'. Worse, since 27 September 2007, no firing practice had been done due to shortage of ammunition. According to procedure, QRTs are expected to do firing practice every fourth day. The last supply of AK-47 rounds had been received in 2005, almost three years before the terrorists landed in Mumbai. The state police needs Rs 65 crores worth of ammunition annually so that each policeman, not just QRT members, can fire the mandatory forty rounds each year. In the five years running up to the attack, the police got a paltry Rs 3 crore annually. While the government was apathetic, the police leadership did not seem to have put up much of a fight to reverse this situation either.

The Pradhan committee also pointed out that the structure and operations of the ATS were in a confused state because of the duality of command: it reported in part to the state DGP and in part to the Mumbai police commissioner. The Assault Mobiles, an anti-terrorist unit under the ATS, was, in practice, ineffective. Many of the police mobile vehicles had only riot gear—lathis, gas guns and .303 rifles—which were no match for the terrorists' AK-47 assault rifles, pistols, hand grenades and bags of RDX, the committee pointed out.

That the police force is not well-equipped is not always a matter of funds shortage. Corruption and nepotism had seriously compromised the quality of procurement over the decades.[5] Being a manufacturer of military supplies or an arms dealer had long been among the most lucrative businesses in India. For all their nationalist chest-thumping, politicians continued to make a good deal of money out of arms deals, as did many senior officers. From the Siachen glacier to the lowest police station, the Indian security establishment has been a victim of, and a participant in, the destruction of its technological capabilities.

The committee also pointed to the fact that the commissioner of police had violated procedural guidelines. Mumbai police's standard operating procedure (SOP) in case of a terrorist attack is for the joint commissioner of police (law and order) (JCP (L&O)) to head the Crisis Management Command and be in charge of all control rooms. The JCP (Crime) is to work in close association with the ATS leadership. 'These instructions were not followed on 26/11/2008,' the enquiry committee found. The commissioner decided instead to direct JCP (Crime) Rakesh Maria to be in charge of the control room, instead of the JCP (L&O), who 'being in-charge of all police stations in Mumbai, was better suited to decide on marshalling of forces at various sites'. Maria did a commendable job, the committee noted. But laid-down norms were subverted in the process. With no systemic briefing, or a public face for the Mumbai police, the media went to town, and often ended up aiding the terrorists with their live telecasts.

The committee was describing the erosion of professional standards and democratic accountability that had crept into the Mumbai police over the decades—through staged encounters, political patronage for trigger-happy cops and politicisation of senior leadership—when it said that there was an 'increasing tendency' among senior officials to take liberties with established procedures.

In many ways, the Mumbai attacks were a showcase of both rare heroism from the police force as well as its politicised, unprofessional side. The police protection given to the Taj Mahal Hotel, based on alerts from the IB of a potential terrorist attack, had been withdrawn by a local inspector before the attacks without consulting anyone.

Though there were at least six warnings, starting August 2006, that the terrorists would come through the sea route, no specific steps had been taken to beef up coastal security or hold regular reviews with the Indian Coast Guard, which is responsible for security along the territorial waters. This was despite the fact that, during the last Pakistan-sponsored attack on the city, in 1993, explosives had been brought in via the sea route.

To understand how it was that the commissioner himself flouted procedural norms, how the police force could go without firing practice for months, how basic commando operation tactics could be ignored and how communication systems were so quickly overwhelmed, we must go a long way back—to 1857, the first war of independence. By the time the revolt had been suppressed, the British Empire had introduced sweeping reforms. It dissolved the East India Company, making India a formal part of the British Crown, and the governor general became the viceroy of India.

One of the most significant and lasting reforms triggered by the 1857 revolt was the promulgation of a new Police Act to establish a force that would be the agent of the Empire in crushing any uprising by Indians. For the British Empire, the police was its authoritarian presence on the ground to identify any brewing revolt and to deal with it in real time. The Act made the police fully dependent on the political executive, and thus open to manipulation by those in power. The police was not envisaged as the agent of the people, instituted to ensure peace and harmony, but as an arm of the Empire to suppress people.

The Police Act of 1861 continues to be in effect, either as it was or with some variations, in most states of India over a century and a half later. Some states have enacted their own Acts, but even they borrow heavily from the 1861 Act. As a result, the state police chief is in office only as long as the chief minister of the state pleases. The police chief's first loyalty, therefore, is to the chief minister and, by extension, to his political base—and not to the rule of law. And that goes all the way down to the last constable in line.

This colonial history—the accumulated baggage of the state's inability to carry out comprehensive police reforms—went some distance in causing the Mumbai police to make several strategic mistakes as terrorists stormed into the city. There had long been calls to reform the police, hold it accountable and make it work for the people rather than the political executive. In the wake of the Emergency, during which police atrocities had become routine, the Janata government had set up the National Police Commission, which produced eight reports, including a Model Police Act. This proposed bill recognised that, while superintendence of the police must vest with the state government, undue political influence must be avoided. It suggested the setting up of a State Security Commission, which would be headed by the minister looking after the police, a member each from the state legislature's ruling and opposition parties, and four members—retired high court judges, retired government servants, social scientists or academics of prominence—to be nominated by the chief minister with the approval of the state legislature. This forum would lay down broad guidelines for the functioning, performance and evaluation of the police. It also would have the power to hear the grievances of senior police officers against illegal orders. The model bill also laid down a professional way of selecting state police chiefs and ensuring the person has a fixed tenure.

Under the present Code of Criminal Procedure, without government sanction, courts cannot take up cases against police officers for offences committed while discharging their duties. Governments are often reluctant to grant permission to prosecute the police, and thus, even criminal acts go unpunished. Internal inquiries against policemen are often a sham. Without any external accountability under the Police Act of 1861, the Indian police has had a free run, routinely crushing the law and ordinary citizens. The police atrocities of the Emergency have been washed over by new memories in a land where there is no dearth of painful histories. Unsurprisingly, subsequent governments have shown little interest in the National Police Commission's recommendations.[6]

Frustrated by the apathy, two retired IPS officers—Prakash Singh and N.K. Singh—approached the Supreme Court with a PIL in 1996, asking that the apex court order state governments to implement the recommendations. The hearings went on for a decade, during which the court set up a committee under legendary IPS officer Julio Ribeiro, which submitted its reports in 1999. Then, a committee under the then home secretary, and later, another one under celebrated lawyer Soli Sorabjee, called the Police Act Drafting Committee, were set up. The Sorabjee committee drafted a new Police Act to replace the 1861 Act. A decade after the PIL hearing began, the Supreme Court delivered its judgement in 2006, directing states and union territories to implement seven binding directives. These were: constitute a State Security Commission to minimise undue political pressure on the police and to evaluate their performance; appoint DGPs through a merit-based system with a fixed two-year tenure; other police officers on operational duties such as head of a district or a police station must also have a minimum two-year tenure; separate investigations from the law-and-order functions of the police; Police Establishment Boards should decide on the transfers, postings, promotions and so on of junior officers; Police Complaints Authority should inquire into complaints against the police at both state and district levels; set up a National Security Commission for selection of chiefs of Central Police Organisations with a fixed two-year tenure.

In September 2020, an assessment by the non-profit organisation Commonwealth Human Rights Initiative found that, fourteen years after the landmark Supreme Court order, not a single state has fully implemented its seven directives. Why are states so adamantly against police reforms? Because when the the system is reformed, the police will become neutral to a great extent, no longer under the thumb of the political party in power.

As things stand, what the data shows is that the next time a terror group storms into a city, the police would still be largely incompetent and unprepared, with a politicised leadership that will likely ignore SOPs, and many innocents will pay for this state of affairs with their lives.

On the evening of 26 November, it was fast becoming clear that what was unfurling in Mumbai was an organised and unprecedented terrorist attack. By 11.30 p.m., the Maharashtra government had reached out to the Union for NSG to take on the terrorists. The terrorists had by then taken over the Taj Mahal Hotel, Nariman House and Oberoi Trident, and completed the massacre at CST.

As the attacks progressed, and as innocents dropped dead, the ghosts of the past came visiting. At every step, bureaucratic deliberations delayed the process, as was the case during 1999's IC-814 hijack. First, there was the question of how many commandos were required. The Union wanted Maharashtra to suggest how many were needed. The Mumbai police, overwhelmed and having lost many of its personnel, wanted as many as possible. The Union finally decided on 200 commandos.

By 1 a.m., the NSG chief received orders to rush his forces to Mumbai. Even though the NSG had begun organising its men in anticipation, organising 200 commandos was a challenge. Men were commandeered from social functions, from their sleep and anywhere else they could be found. Then came the process of mobilising arms and ammunition, and other equipment and provisions—every step added to the delay. The deployment of such a large contingent with heavy equipment required the IL-76 Russian transport aircraft. In the middle of the night, MoD woke up the air force machinery and discovered that no IL-76 was available in Delhi. The nearest such aircraft was in Chandigarh. Then the MHA contacted Air India, which offered its Airbus 320s, but did not have its crew ready. The plane, anyway, would not have sufficed for such a large load. Nobody seemed to have discussed the possibility of two or three Airbus 320s taking off for Mumbai. After discussing issues like the crew roster, and wasting crucial time and sacrificing several more lives, the officials had an epiphany. The R&AW's Aviation Research Centre has a fleet of aircraft—an IL-76 was sitting right there in the national capital. Sometime after midnight, the R&AW chief gave the orders to mobilise the aircraft. By this time, Hemant Karkare and his team had been mowed down, and terrorists were running amok in every location, killing diners and attacking marriage parties.

The 200 commandos, meanwhile, left the NSG's Manesar campus in buses for the hour-long journey to the Delhi airport. They loaded the equipment themselves and boarded the IL-76, which finally took off around 3 a.m. The giant transport aircraft landed in Mumbai three hours later. From the Mumbai airport, again, most of the commandos were taken by buses to the various locations. By the time the NSG began its operations, it was almost 9 a.m.

This failure of crisis management at the highest levels reflected an almost lethargic attitude to terror threats—and in it, some kind of assurance that everything will continue as it has always done, no matter what the outcome.

While the bureaucratic wrangling was on, Mumbai had been in the grip of horror and confusion. The world watched in horror as the live telecast of an improbable terror attack unfolded—the terrorists were now going around killing people in pairs. At CST, the Gothic Mumbai landmark that used to be called the Victoria Terminus, two men stormed into the crowded passenger hall around 9.30 p.m. They shot down fifty-eight people and injured over a hundred in the space of a little over an hour. A vigilant railway announcer turned out be an unlikely hero, alerting passengers about the terrorists. The two men left CST, and walked onto the streets, firing on people. They passed a police station, where the policemen were hiding in the premises with the lights switched off. They walked two kilometres to Cama Hospital, where a quick-thinking staff member had locked all the patient wards.

ATS Chief Hemant Karkare was at his residence in Dadar when he got a call about the attacks. With his driver and guards, he left for CST, where he put on a helmet and a bullet-proof vest—something that would come to be the lasting visual of his life. By the time he reached CST, the terrorists had moved on. There he received information that IPS officer Sadanand Date had been injured at Cama Hospital. So, Karkare and another IPS officer, Ashok Kamte, got into a Toyota Qualis, driven by controversial encounter specialist Inspector Vijay Salaskar, and packed with four constables in the back-row seats.

Constable Arun Jadhav, who was in the jeep and the only one in the group to survive, later said that, five minutes after they left CST, 'two persons carrying AK-47 rifles emerged from behind a tree and started firing at our vehicle'. The vehicle had just turned towards Rang Bhavan. The officers sitting in the front—Kamte and Salaskar—fired at the terrorists and injured at least one of them. But it was not enough to stop men carrying deadly weapons. Most of the policemen were dead in seconds. 'The two terrorists then came up to our vehicle and pulled out Karkare, Kamte and Salaskar's bodies out and threw them on to the road. Thinking that we (the constables) are also dead, the terrorists then got into the car and started driving towards Metro junction,' he told an *Indian Express* reporter later.[7] At the Metro junction, they fired at some journalists and police vans, and then drove towards Vidhan Bhawan, where too they opened random fire. A few seconds after that, one of the tyres of the Qualis burst and they abandoned the vehicle. It was then that Jadhav was able to call up the control room and report the killings.

Karkare's death was preceded and followed by much controversy. Only days earlier, his team had cracked the Hindutva terror case, challenging inherent biases in the security establishment. Violence by Hindutva elements, it had thus far been believed, would be low level and likely in the form of riots, not bombs and explosives. After he exposed the Hindutva terror groups, Karkare was under intense attack. BJP President Rajnath Singh said he was not willing to believe that Pragya Thakur could be a terrorist, and suggested that there was a conspiracy. BJP's then prime ministerial candidate, L.K. Advani, had demanded that the ATS be disbanded. Narendra Modi, then Gujarat chief minister, also pounced on Karkare and team. After Karkare was killed in the Mumbai attacks, Modi was quick to announce a Rs 1 crore compensation for his family, which it turned down. The chief minister was told at least three times that he should not visit them at their home. However, Modi turned up, and sat in the drawing room for some time and left.[8]

The BJP's irrational agitation over Karkare's exposé was prompted by the fact that it was not good PR for the Hindutva family. Hindu terror is, however, a reality. Many political movements around the world mainstream themselves by shedding their violent fringes, but the BJP and its larger ecosystem have failed to do that. In fact, under Modi, the party has actively encouraged such elements, most visibly in its nomination of Pragya Singh Thakur to the Bhopal Lok Sabha constituency. This reticence of the BJP to fully commit itself to peaceful, democratic means, and to shedding or disciplining its fringe elements, will cost both the party and Indian democracy dearly.

After Karkare was killed, his bulletproof jacket mysteriously disappeared from the hospital mortuary, and became the centre of a new controversy. Much later, a sweeper at the hospital claimed that he had disposed of it without realising its significance. There was a question mark over the quality of the jacket, and why it had been unable to protect the officer.

Karkare's death sparked speculation that the investigation into the Hindu terror group would slacken, and so it did. However, in January 2009, the ATS filed a charge sheet against fourteen Hindu terrorists, of whom three were absconding.

Many within the intelligence community were stunned by the emergence of a sophisticated Hindu terror network, and tried to find answers on their own. Was it a mere coincidence that a military intelligence officer was mixed up with a group of radicals? Where did he get the RDX and other ammunition that he gave the group? Why were indications about possible terror modules operating out of central India ignored all these years? Why did various agencies make desperate efforts to create false narratives, blaming Islamic groups for all the blasts, even when mosques had been attacked?

Over the years, I have been told by several credible sources, in both intelligence and investigation agencies, that they suspect that Abhinav Bharat was propped up by a section of the Indian security establishment, with political blessings, to send a warning to Muslim terror groups. One former chief of an intelligence agency, who had examined the group's activities, said the idea was born sometime in 2003, and was, almost certainly, a creation of one of the intelligence agencies. Importantly, he also believed that the strategy was prompted by a foreign nation with which the then government had a well-publicised affinity.

A former army chief told me that the RDX that Colonel Prasad Shrikant Purohit, the key conspirator in several terror attacks, supplied the group with did not come from army stores. So where did he get it from? Brigadier (retd) Rajkumar, who, as the deputy director general (DDG) of military intelligence was the nodal officer dealing with the Malegaon investigations, later told the media: 'I had written then to the Northern Command base in Udhampur to ascertain his postings and if he had any access to RDX. They had informed us that, though he was in Srinagar for a while, he was not involved in handling of RDX, it is given for a particular operation and not to everyone.'[9]

Many officials also noticed that there was effort by a section in the security establishment to discourage investigations into the Hindutva terror angle, despite specific leads being available. A veteran CBI officer told me that they had submitted a demand to the CBI chief to question three very high-profile Hindutva ideologues—senior RSS leader Indresh Kumar, a south India-based eminent person and a retired official—but they were shut out.

The Mumbai carnage that began on a Wednesday evening lasted until Saturday. At least 174 people were killed and several hundred were injured. Almost sixty people died in CST, over thirty in Taj Mahal Hotel and an equal number in Oberoi Trident. Among the dead were people from twenty-nine countries, many celebrities and several others who, in their last moments, carried out improbable heroic acts to save strangers. Also among the dead were nine attackers, the desperately poor killing machines who had been moulded in Pakistan's terror factories. The Union government showed a breathless urgency in the aftermath of the attacks. Union Home Minister Shivraj Patil resigned, taking moral responsibility for the attacks, so did the deputy chief minister of Maharashtra, R.R. Patil. Though the tradition of owning up political responsibility is a noble one, what was absent was an effort to hold individual officials to account in the security establishment, or to investigate who could have prevented the attack or how the system could have responded better. In fact, no one from the IB, R&AW, navy, coast guard or Maharashtra police faced any serious disciplinary action, though all of them were sitting on intelligence inputs about the attacks. It is a matter of speculation whether these agencies had become so powerful that the political establishment had lost the appetite to improve, or even discipline, them.

Instead, within days of the Mumbai terror assault, the Union government came up with a set of reforms to overhaul the security establishment, improve its response mechanism, sharpen the ability to fight terrorism and to secure coastal areas. It announced the setting up of NSG hubs in major cities, a coastal command to secure the shoreline and amendments to existing laws, among other steps. The most significant steps—and both with long-term implications—were stringent amendments to the UAPA, the country's primary federal act against terrorism, and the National Investigation Agency Act 2008 to set up a federal counterterrorism investigation agency. Both laws were passed in a hurry, with minimal scrutiny and debate.

Mumbai lay wrapped in mourning, but an unprecedented

determination swept through Raisina Hill, where the MHA had a new boss. The government was in informal consultations with the military leadership on action against Pakistan. Even mature elements within the establishment, including External Affairs Minister Pranab Mukherjee and Foreign Secretary Shiv Shankar Menon, were in favour of targeted attacks on Pakistan. It was not an easy decision to make. Any attack on Pakistan would unify that country, and more importantly, strengthen the hands of the military establishment. That was the last thing New Delhi wanted. Prime Minister Manmohan Singh was under tremendous pressure to mount military attacks, because this time there was unimpeachable proof of Pakistan's involvement. The militaries on both sides were on high alert.

Menon says that there were a series of informal discussions to consider India's responses. 'The then national security adviser, M.K. Narayanan, organized the review of our military and other kinetic options with the political leadership, and the military chiefs outlined their views to the prime minister. As foreign secretary, I saw my task as one of assessing the external and other implications and urged both External Affairs Minister Pranab Mukherjee and Prime Minister Manmohan Singh that we should retaliate, and be seen to retaliate, to deter further attacks, for reasons of international credibility and to assuage public sentiment,' he recalled in his book *Choices: Inside the Making of India's Foreign Policy*.

For Wahid and the others, 26/11 was not just another attack that would trigger fresh police harassment. It was a huge setback, because they had come to believe that Hemant Karkare would be the man to undo the injustice perpetrated by the ATS under its previous chief. Now Karkare was dead, and a new wave of Islamophobia was sweeping through the country.

5

Free at Last

The high-security 'anda' section of the Arthur Road Jail was so called because it was shaped like an egg. In single-person cells, five prisoners were packed in. A mesh screen ensured they could see the guards and jail officials. Wahid and his co-accused were now swinging between extreme optimism and intense fear. The optimism stemmed from the news that was trickling in about the arrest of IM members, who had confessed to, among others, the 2006 train bombings. The fear was because, after every major terrorist attack in the region, the police had come for them. Sometimes they were named as the accused, often they were tortured, at the very least they would be subject to long interrogations.

A few days after the Mumbai attacks, the jail lay wrapped in the mild winter afternoon sun. It was around 4 p.m. Wahid was walking in the small veranda outside the cell—the only open area accessible to high-security prisoners—as he did at this hour. It was his only opportunity to stretch and move around. At one end of the veranda, a handsome young man sat, eating his dinner. The jail dinner is served by 4 p.m., and typically consists of rice, lentils, roti and some vegetables.

Wahid said to him, 'You eat dinner so early.'

The young man replied that he suffered from bad acidity, and so had to eat warm food. The ice broken, they made introductions: Wahid and Sadiq. Wahid knew who this man was. A few days earlier, jail guards had told the inmates that a new prisoner was being moved into the anda jail, and that he was a member of the IM. From newspapers, Wahid knew that the IM may have carried out the 2006 train blasts. Information was sketchy, but it had lit new hope in the damp cells.

Once they got talking, Sadiq told him quite simply: 'We did the train blasts.' It was that one stroke of luck Wahid and his fellow accused had long desired. Sadiq had no regrets about the series of blasts they carried out across India. His list of grievances that had forced him to become a terrorist, from the Babri Masjid demolition to the Gujarat riots, was very long.

Sadiq often spoke of his trajectory from nationalism to terrorism. When Kashmir went up in flames, Muslims in the rest of India did not take up arms to support the Kashmiri cause—a sign of their belief in secular India. However, the Babri demolition was a seminal event. It altered communal equations in the country and probably created the first terrorists among Indian Muslims, such as C.A.M. Basheer, the former SIMI president from Kerala who was among the first Indians to go to Pakistan for arms training. Intelligence agencies believe that he is operating from Saudi Arabia, and may have partially funded the IM operations.

Sadiq said he turned religious after the Babri Masjid demolition. He was a member of the SIMI between 1996 and 1999, when he also did an Industrial Training Institute course in refrigeration and air-conditioning from an institute in Dongri, Mumbai. Sadiq landed a job with the Godrej group.

As political as he was, Sadiq was also quick to anger. He would pick fights both within the home and on the streets, and sought the support of two friends, also SIMI activists, to control his rage.

Sadiq had no regrets. What about innocent people who are in jail because of the IM's actions, Wahid asked. Sadiq declared that he was willing to depose in a court, give affidavits or whatever else was required to save them. 'We informed our lawyers that Sadiq had committed the crime and that he was ready to depose before a court.

They said that if he confesses to everything in court, you will all be acquitted,' Wahid said. In anda jail, happiness and excitement spread like a pandemic. There were thirteen of them on trial and in jail, and another fifteen listed as wanted.

Sajida, meanwhile, was struggling to stay afloat and look after her young family. Even though she went back to teaching, Wahid's young wife was finding it hard to keep up financially and emotionally. Sajida vacated their rented apartment, and with the two little children, she first shifted to her in-laws' home and then to her parents'. Wahid regularly wrote long and affectionate letters, updating her about developments, and noting down little anecdotes from the jail or some religious comments to comfort her.

According to Sadiq's statement, some IM members were in Sarai Mir, in Uttar Pradesh, a few days after they blasted bombs at the Sankat Mochan temple in Varanasi and the nearby railway station on 6 March 2006. Twenty-eight people were killed and over a hundred injured. Atif, who was killed in the Batla House encounter, and Sadiq were leisurely walking around the area when they decided on targeting Mumbai trains. They roped in two more people for the operation.

The group then went about getting logistics in place for the attack. One of them rented a flat in Sewri, and more men began to join the operation. Finally, they formed a group of five operatives. The IM founder, Riyaz Bhatkal, arranged explosives in Mangalore, which Atif collected. Others got passes for the first-class compartments of local trains, and they also began to study the time table to identify target trains. Then they bought bags and cookers. 'All of us readied the bombs in seven cookers on the morning of July 11, 2006. We had set a timer of four and half hours and our plan was to do the blasts at 6.30 p.m., so accordingly we set the timer at 2 p.m.,' Sadiq recalled in a videotaped confession to the Gujarat police.[1]

Sadiq was the first bomber to set out from their hideout. He left for Dadar railway station in a taxi with a bag containing the cooker bomb. From there, he took a local train to Churchgate. Atif followed him on the same route with two bombs. Abu Rashid and Sajid followed with a bag each. Finally, Shahnawaz left with two bags, according to Sadiq. The operatives planted bombs in trains in Churchgate, Dadar and other locations. By the time the terror module reassembled in their rented apartment in Sewri, the bombs had gone off during the rush hour, killing over 200 Mumbai residents. The bombers did not have a television to watch the carnage they had unleashed, and instead tuned in to the radio. A day after carrying out one of the world's deadliest terrorist acts, these misguided rebels left for their homes, intending to plan more bloodshed.

Back home, Sadiq slipped back into a normal life. Married a year earlier, he was now the father of a little girl. He was also reading newspapers and taking in the enormity of what they had done. 'Stories of sad backgrounds of the victims started appearing in the newspaper. I started putting myself in their shoes while reading the stories. By then, because I was married and had a wife and kid, I could feel their pain. I realised what we were doing was grossly wrong,' he said.[2]

The train-blasts hearings were underway in the special court. Sadiq, seated in one part of the court, pointed out Wahid and the other accused to an old man in a kurta-pyjama, who then approached Wahid. The old man was traumatised and crying. His son was a deadly terrorist. But Sadiq also had a young family that had become his father's burden. 'Do you want Sadiq to admit his guilt so that he can be hanged, and you people be set free?' the father asked Wahid. He had approached with one request: please do not summon Sadiq as a witness.

Wahid told the father that they had no desire to see anyone hang, because they were opposed to the death penalty. 'We were confused,' Wahid admits. The ATS lawyer was opposed to summoning Sadiq.

The court agreed with the ATS, and Wahid and the other twelve accused returned disappointed. However, the fight was not yet over. They moved the high court, and obtained permission to summon him.

The blasts accused and Sadiq, the man who held the key to their freedom, were taken to the sessions court in Cuffe Parade in separate vehicles. The accused were gathered outside the court, waiting anxiously, when the judge summoned them. They walked in and took their seats. Judge Y.D. Shinde began the proceedings.

Sadiq took an oath promising to tell only the truth. The defence lawyer began by asking the witness details like his name, age and address. Sadiq replied to each of the questions. He then went on to speak in great detail about his arrest, torture and how his confession was recorded, including the allegations of terror activities against him.

Sadiq concluded: This is according to the confession recorded under duress by the Crime Branch.

Wahid's lawyer asked: The DSP has signed your confessions?

Sadiq: Yes.

Lawyer: Was it recorded before the DSP?

Sadiq: No.

Lawyer: Did you do the 7/11 blasts?

Sadiq looked at the judge, the judge smiled, and said that if he did not want to answer, he could refuse to do so.

Lawyer: Your mobile number was located at Churchgate station on the day of the blast.

Sadiq refused to respond to that too.

The defence lawyers had several more questions for him—the fate of thirteen people depended on his answers. The court adjourned until the next day. Sadiq was not brought back to the anda cell, but moved to another location.

The lawyers also wanted the police officer who had recorded the statements of the other IM bombers, including Sadiq, to be summoned as a witness. The high court agreed, but the Supreme

Court did not. Many who have watched the trial of the train blasts believe that if the apex court had allowed the police officer to be summoned as a witness during the trial, the story would have been different.[3]

It was 11 September 2015. The thirteen men woke up early that day, took a bath and put on their best clothes. Some dyed their hair and beards, most wore perfume and they all congratulated each other. They ate a light breakfast, because it was going to be a day of great celebration. How would they refuse sweets on such a day?

The public announcement system reported that a police squad had arrived to escort the blasts accused to the court, and that they must gather at the main gate. The men had been waiting for a year now. Their trial had concluded in September 2014, with both the prosecution and defence filing closure proceedings. The court reserved its judgement, and set the next date for fifteen days later. The accused speculated that the judgement may not be ready that soon because it was a huge case. The judge had to peruse statements by 250 witnesses, thousands of pages of exhibits and articles, and then write the judgement. 'We guessed that he would take at least two–three months,' Wahid recalled. They would go to the jail's judicial department religiously to enquire if the court had issued a date for their appearance—the date came a year after arguments were concluded. They had been in jail for nine years by this time.

Wahid wore jeans and a T-shirt. He had never worn a pair of jeans before he went to jail, but because it was a hardy garment that could be worn for longer without washing, jeans suited life in jail. Whenever we have met, Wahid has worn jeans. It is now his favourite attire.

A massive police contingent waited outside. The thirteen men travelled in a convoy with a heavy security escort. When they reached the court, it too was crammed with police. The media was not allowed to enter, even though it was an open court proceeding, and so an argument ensued. Eventually, the media was permitted in. The accused were not allowed to speak to anyone. Their family members stood anxiously outside—another sizeable contingent.

The proceedings began around 11.30 a.m., and quickly turned grim. The judge read out that everyone, except accused number eight, was guilty of the bombings. Wahid was accused number eight. 'I was about to cry because people who were just as innocent as I was had been pronounced guilty. It was a painful day,' he recalled.

Wahid said that the police had made some fatal errors in his case. Most critically, they did not have a confession from him. This, he explained to me, was part of a police strategy to disprove the claims of the others accused that their confessions were obtained under torture. Besides, one of his brothers-in-law, a witness in the case, went into hiding in the run-up to Wahid's appearance to avoid pressure from the ATS. The brother-in-law turned hostile, the ATS claimed. He spoke the truth, Wahid said.

The accused were being tried under Maharashtra Control of Organised Crime Act (MCOCA), the UAPA and the Indian Penal Code.

'Luckily, the trial was not under POTA [Prevention of Terrorism Act 2002],' Wahid said one day. That stringent anti-terror legislation of the past would have provided very little space in a case like his.

Since Independence, India has struggled with insurgencies and, more recently, with terror. The result has been a state that reacted with increasingly draconian anti-terror laws. The list of such legislations is very long: the Prevention of Detention Act 1950 that expired in 1969, and was replaced by the Maintenance of Internal Security Act (MISA) 1971. Then there is the Terrorist and Disruptive Activities (Prevention) Act 1985 (and modified in 1987) (TADA), POTA, and laws such as the Disturbed Areas (Special Courts) Act 1976 (DAA), the Armed Forces (Special Powers) Act 1958 (AFSPA), the Assam Preventive Detention Act 1980, the National Security Act 1980, the Essential Services Maintenance Act 1968 and the Armed Forces

(Jammu and Kashmir) Special Powers Act 1990.

The collective output of these laws is staggering. For example, under TADA, at least 76,000 people were detained, and 25 per cent of them were freed without the police even filing charges. According to most reliable estimates, only in 35 per cent of the cases was trial completed. Wait for the final figure: 95 per cent of the trials under TADA ended in acquittals. Thus, the law had an overall conviction rate of less than 1.5 per cent.[4] In 1995, TADA was allowed to lapse.

After 9/11, India passed POTA, and the states discovered the political power it packed. In Tamil Nadu, Chief Minister J. Jayalalithaa arrested her political opponent Vaiko and detained a magazine editor under POTA.[5] In Jharkhand, a few hundred were detained under the law.[6] In Gujarat, the Modi government slapped POTA on Muslims who were allegedly involved in the Godhra train attack, but did not apply POTA to book rioters in the anti-Muslim riots that followed.[7] A POTA review committee found that 11,384 people booked under POTA should have been charged under regular law.[8]

Besides, there are British-era laws—such as sedition and criminal defamation—too that provide the security establishment with that extra bite. The UAPA 1967 is a legislation that has found great favour in recent years. According to data presented in the Rajya Sabha in February 2021, only 2.2 per cent cases filed under UAPA between 2016 and 2019 ended in convictions.[9] Almost 2,000 people were arrested under the law during this period.

As the judge read out his decision, the accused tried to pass on the news to their family members through gestures. Eventually, they asked one of the police escorts, a kind soul, if he could pass on the news to their families. He did. The dejected men were then packed into cars and driven back to Arthur Road Jail. Many journalists and family members followed the convoy. Even at the jail, no one was allowed to speak to them.

Sometime later, a hawaldar called for Wahid and took him to a senior jailer, who suggested he change his cell. In the case of such split verdicts, he was advised, the convicted usually blame everything on the one acquitted, and there could be ugly scenes. Wahid refused. He also had a request for the warden. Could he please visit jail number fifteen? Wahid walked into the premises of jail fifteen, where the IM members, including Sadiq Sheikh, were housed. When Wahid informed them of the court's verdict, they began crying. 'They must be crying thinking that innocents were being punished for what someone else did,' Wahid speculated.

Sajid, Wahid's brother-in-law, who was among those convicted, met him in the evening and requested him to stay back that night because he wanted to send some letters to his family and also needed to talk. Wahid told the wardens that he would like to stay another night, even though his bail formalities could have been completed that day. Sajid spoke till late into the night. He wrote letters to his wife, mother and his child. He then asked Wahid to try and organise some documents to bolster their case. It was a long night in anda jail.

As the full impact of the judgement began to dawn on them, the men began to see patterns. And the murder of advocate Shahid Azmi on 11 February 2010 was definitely part of the pattern—of suppressing anyone who wanted to defend their innocence, and of creating a certain narrative to implicate Muslims. In their decade-long struggle for justice, these thirteen men had accumulated a mountain of questions. From the way they were picked out to how their statements were recorded or the manner in which key pieces of evidence had been ignored, there was much that agitated them. But it was the murder of Azmi, who represented eight of them, during the trial that left the men most crushed. That night, stunned and grieving, they truly cursed the system.

Azmi was just sixteen during the Mumbai riots of 1992, and was among those arrested for violence. Though he was let off because he was a juvenile, he could not forget the naked communal bias that the police had displayed.[10] Like several angry young men at the time, he decided to take revenge, and went off to Kashmir to join the militancy. When he returned to Mumbai in 1994, Azmi was arrested once again by a Delhi police team, this time under TADA, for allegedly conspiring to murder some political leaders. He was later acquitted by the Supreme Court. By then, he had spent seven years in Delhi's Tihar Jail, and completed both his graduation and master's. Azmi decided he would work within the system. Back home in Mumbai, he completed a degree in law and began practising, with a focus on fighting for Muslims who were accused in terror cases. In his seven-year legal career, Azmi managed to prove the innocence of at least seventeen Muslim men who had been framed in terror cases.[11]

Around 7.30 p.m. on 11 February 2010, Azmi received a call from someone enquiring about his whereabouts. The man sounded like a prospective client. At around 9 p.m., the thirty-two-year-old sat down in his law chambers in Taximen's Colony, Kurla, to listen to the four people who had just arrived. Instead, the four of them pumped him with bullets and left. The case continues to drag on.

Wahid maintains that the judgement was seriously flawed. The confessional statements contained major errors, including the fact that not one of them mentioned pressure cookers, even though the bombs were placed in pressure cookers. Besides, the narco analysis test results were not produced in court, there was a lack of clarity about what timers were used to activate the bombs, two of the police witnesses had criminal records, the court refused to accept the request of the accused persons to retract the so-called confessional statements.[12]

There were any number of deeply disturbing anomalies. For instance, the prime accused, Kamal Ahmed Ansari, spent almost four hours in Nepal on the day of the train attacks, and was otherwise in his village of Basopatti in Madhubani, Bihar. This fact is borne out by his mobile records as well as the entry register at the Nepal border.[13] While I was investigating this story, a source informed me that the mobile records of another accused person showed that he was in his office from morning until 6.25 p.m. on the day of the bombing, when, according to the ATS, he was out planting bombs.

On Wahid's last night in anda jail with the other twelve men, they told him that he should start life afresh and forget them. But he assured them that he would do whatever was in his capacity to help them. Wahid took down their home addresses, phone numbers and other contact details. He also got them to sign a few blank pages for filing petitions with public figures.

After almost a decade in jail, Wahid returned home a free man. After meeting his mother and brothers in Vikhroli, he took a local train to Mira Road to meet his wife and children who were staying with his in-laws. 'I had a weird feeling. This was the same train in which the blasts had happened. The same case for which I was kept in jail for nine years. The same stations—Dadar, Matunga, Jogeshwari, Borivali, Mira Road, Mahim,' Wahid said to me. The next day, he brought his family back to Vikhroli.

And a day later, he went back to court, to hear the final arguments on the quantum of punishment. Wahid was allowed inside, since he had been one of the accused. But he was free, and so could take messages from the other accused to their family members outside, and bring tea and biscuits to those who were inside the court. The arguments went on for several days. Finally, on 30 September 2015, the judge released the 1,839-page judgement. He ordered five of them, the 'bombers', to 'be hanged by their necks till they are dead'. The other seven, who allegedly provided logistical support, were given life sentences. A few weeks later, the convicted were transferred to various jails in Maharashtra.

In the outside world, Wahid began to put his life together. He also visited the families of the convicted, and travelled to jails in Nagpur, Yerwada, Amravati and Nasik to meet the accused.

Wahid now has two lives. One, as an ordinary schoolteacher

and family man. The other, as an activist, a lawyer who is trying to secure freedom for those who have been framed by the security establishment. On top of his priority list are the twelve men convicted in the train blasts. But the wheels of justice move slowly. Although he has been slogging at it for five years, the appeal of the convicts is still stalled in the Bombay High Court, and no new dates have been given.[14]

Remember Kamal Ahmed Ansari? The man from Madhubani whose records, including mobile and border-entry register, showed that he had spent four hours in Nepal on the day of the blasts. In April 2021, the Covid-19 pandemic claimed his life, with family members not getting a clear answer from jail authorities about his last days.[15] Ansari had claimed in his statements to the court that he was tortured by the police and was offered Rs 4 lakh if he became an official witness. When he rejected the offer, they upped it with more money and a flat. When he refused, the ATS chief threatened to implicate his family members in the case, according to his statements recorded in the court.[16]

Wahid has expanded his activism with the Innocence Network,[17] which seeks out people who have been deliberately framed by the system. He has documented almost a hundred such cases. Wahid regularly organises lectures, seminars and discussions—one of them named after Shahid Azmi. He refuses to give up hope in a system that has been harshly unfair to him.

How did our police and intelligence agencies come to display such utter disrespect for the law, citizens and the state? This systemic corrosion is the outcome of a process that began decades ago, as India hurriedly went about the business of building the world's largest democracy and its security establishment spread out to protect the new nation's sovereignty. At that time, neither the political executive nor the courts paid attention to the accountability of the security establishment, especially its non-military arms—the police that was still governed by colonial laws, intelligence agencies that were growing by the day to deal with ever-increasing threats, the crime investigators and taxmen whose roles were not adequately legislated.

The rot that consumed more than a decade of Wahid's life also deprived the victims of the Mumbai train blasts of true justice. They do not know who the real terrorists are, even though hundreds of people, especially Muslims and other disadvantaged groups, have been framed.

What further enabled this degeneration was the failure of the state to shed colonial laws on sedition, the criminalisation of issues such as defamation and homosexuality, draconian laws like the Official Secrets Act, and most importantly, the influence of the British Empire's Police Act of 1861. The Indian deep state took shape amidst the cacophony of its democracy and the global rhetoric of India being the world's biggest democracy. Though we cannot put an exact date or place to it, a guesstimate would place the beginning of this slow degeneration somewhere in the stunning Kashmir Valley, some days after the bloody Partition of 1947.

PART TWO

MANY TALES OF INDIA

'My notion of democracy is that under it the weakest should have the same opportunity as the strongest.'

– M.K. Gandhi

6

A Valley in Flames

It had been another day of violence, rumours and barricades for me and everyone else in Srinagar. Most of the city had already turned in for the night when the old phone in my room began clanging. Throwing off the blanket, I rushed to pick up the call.

'Is that Joseph?'

'Yes, it is,' I said.

This was followed by a long silence, and the call was disconnected. As I turned back to the bed, the phone rang again. It was another person, with the same question, and then silence again and disconnection. This was repeated a couple of times, until the last caller instructed me: 'Come to the North Gate of Kashmir University at 7.30 a.m. tomorrow morning. Just you.'

The year 2001 was possibly the deadliest in Kashmir since the flare-up after the rigged 1987 state assembly elections. The violence claimed close to ten lives in the Valley every single day. One early morning, for instance, while riding the empty highway to Baramulla, my car was held up by an unruly crowd that burst onto the road, protesting the excesses of the security forces. Even as I watched, the forces opened fire on them. By the time we had managed to reverse our vehicle in an effort to get away, some protestors were dead and the agitation had turned more violent. Another evening, as I sauntered across the wooden Zero Bridge from Sonwar to Rajbagh, I heard the sound of something whizzing past. I fell to the ground in a panic. When I looked up, a few hundred metres ahead, a hotel that had been occupied by paramilitary forces was in flames. A rocket had flown overhead. Most of the time, the city was under a shutdown; when it opened, only the security forces and fear appeared to walk the streets.

Ever since I landed in Srinagar in early 2001, I had been awaiting that fateful phone call, which finally came in April. Meanwhile, I was living in a rented house near the headquarters of the All Party Hurriyat Conference in Rajbagh, and was equipped with an emergency telephone line and an old Kashmiri cook. All of this was inherited from a colleague at Rediff.com, whose term preceded mine in the Valley. One of my key agendas was to try and meet Abdul Majid Dar, the charismatic operations commander of Hizbul Mujahideen, the largest militant group in Kashmir. Dar had quite unexpectedly announced a ceasefire with the Indian forces in July 2000. The collapse of the ceasefire, less than two weeks later, was just as dramatic: from across the border in Pakistan, Hizbul leader Syed Salahuddin called it off. Dar vanished immediately after.

I wanted to understand what had driven Dar to announce the historic ceasefire, and what his plans were for the future of Kashmir. But it was not easy to meet a militant commander at the time. By the mid-1990s, the dynamics of the Kashmir militancy had completely changed, with foreign fighters from the Afghan war entering the theatre and Pakistan co-opting it. Kidnapping for ransom was rampant, and journalists no longer had easy access to militants.

In my attempt to establish contact with Dar, who was from Sopore, I had met with his old friends and associates. I frequently met Fazal-ul Haq Qureshi, whom the Hizb nominated as its negotiator with New Delhi during the July 2000 ceasefire. Qureshi was almost a decade older than Dar, and, in many ways, one of the progenitors of militancy in the state. A soft-spoken man, he freely discussed his role in fomenting local militancy as far back as the 1960s. But times had changed, and he was now fiercely committed to negotiating a peaceful future instead.

The lives and politics of these two friends, Dar and Qureshi, provide an unusual framework for understanding the complexity of the Kashmir issue. Qureshi was born in 1945, and commanded respect not just from other militants but also a broad section of locals and outsiders. A man of ordinary build, with a long, flowing white beard, Qureshi's appearance offered a contrast to the strapping Majid Dar's. While most of the Valley, including Dar, was initially drawn to the democratic protests of the 'Lion of Kashmir', Sheikh Abdullah, against the Union government, Qureshi was among a group of youngsters who took up arms.

The armed movement of the 1960s is a mere footnote in the modern narrative of the Kashmir conflict, but is critical to understanding its chaotic history. The sporadic and desperate violent efforts of the past allow us to fathom how the New Delhi leadership has repeatedly squandered opportunities for lasting peace in J&K, and failed ordinary Kashmiris, both Hindus and Muslims.

In the resultant tumult, there is another casualty: the erosion of the professional ethos of Indian security institutions, a decline that spreads beyond the borders of J&K and also to the non-military security establishment.

The raiders crossed into Kashmir on 22 October 1947, and swiftly progressed to Srinagar. At Baramulla, they plundered, murdered and possibly raped the locals. In St Joseph's, the first women's hospital in the Valley, are the modest tombs of six people who were killed by these assailants, grieving reminders of that history. In the summer of 2001, I visited the hospital mission to meet Sister Emilia Montavani, the last survivor of the 1947 attack, who would stay on in the Valley until her death. The frail nun took me around the compound and to the tombs of her friends and colleagues. With few words and many long silences, she spoke of the ordeal that she had lived through. The Afridi and other Pathan tribesmen killed six people at the hospital, she recalled—a British colonel and his wife, a nurse, a patient, the husband of the hospital doctor and Sister Teresalina. St Joseph's Hospital was run by a small group of foreign nuns, including Sister Teresalina and Sister Emilia, who had crossed over to Baramulla from present-day Pakistan a few years previously. The last survivor of that group died a few years after I met her, and was buried next to Sister Teresalina.

The raiders from the North-West Frontier Province (NFWP) were freedom fighters to some, mere thugs to others. In a small pamphlet produced by Montavani's colleagues a few decades after the attack, a Pakistan Army officer is credited with saving the hospital. He came riding on horseback and forced the raiders out of the campus. The officer had studied in a missionary school, the pamphlet noted. The tribal raiders vanished as swiftly as they arrived. What they left behind was warning of a monstrous military establishment being nurtured in Pakistan.

The history of Pakistan can be seen through the prism of Kashmir. The country was visualised as a utopian homeland for Muslims, but fell well short of that ideal. Kashmir then became its moral cause. Pakistani leaders believed in freeing Kashmir from India's clutches, but also feared a military reprisal from its larger neighbour. Thus, a strong armed forces and intelligence set-up became crucial to the very idea of the Pakistan nation state. Unsurprisingly, the military behemoth took over the state by 1958, in the first of many military coups. The Kashmir dispute turned out to be a boon for the Pakistan military. It became a justification for the military's running of the country, building its own businesses, nurturing a deadly intelligence apparatus, and executing and torturing those who dissented. The first of its victims was democracy itself. Seven decades later, the Pakistan Army continues to be the country's most powerful institution. When observers say that most countries have an army but the Pakistan Army has a country, they do not exaggerate.

When the tribesmen rode into Kashmir in 1947, ISI was not yet in the picture. Set up in 1948, Pakistan's premier intelligence agency was the brainchild of Major General Sir Walter J. Cawthorn, a veteran

British-Australian intelligence officer, and Brigadier Shahid Hamid, a former personal secretary to Field Marshal Claude Auchinleck, the last commander of the British Indian Army. The ISI's first major statement on Kashmir was an assessment titled 'The Expansion of the Indian Armed Forces since 15 August 1947', which predicted that India would not invade Pakistan.

ISI presented to the US security establishment exaggerated threats of communist influence in Pakistan. Initially, the US provided counter-propaganda support, later stepping it up to a strategic partnership between the CIA and ISI. A small group of US Special Forces personnel and CIA officials helped Pakistan create the Special Services Group (SSG), which became ISI's action arm. According to Owen L. Sirrs, who published a detailed study of ISI in 2017, the first anti-India insurgency that the agency actively engaged in was in the state of Nagaland, not Kashmir.[1] In 1956, ISI helped Angami Zapu Phizo, the founder of the Naga rebellion, to flee India through East Pakistan (present-day Bangladesh) and reach London. In 1958, SSG began training a group of Naga warriors under rebel commander Kaito Sema in Sylhet, in the northeastern part of East Pakistan. (Kaito was later murdered in 1968 during a factional feud among Naga rebels.)

In Kashmir, Pakistan began working to wean leaders and organisations away from India's embrace. One of the first groups to receive active Pakistani backing was the Kashmir Political Conference, which staged a major pro-Pakistani demonstration in the Valley on 19 June 1953, points out journalist Iftikhar Gilani in his unpublished paper, 'Genesis of Insurgency in Kashmir: 1947–1989', tracing the Kashmir insurgency. Indian agencies also claimed that they had intercepted a Pakistani agent in Bombay while he was handing over Rs 100,000 to a prominent leader of the National Conference (NC), Iftikhar says, citing Muhammad Yusuf Saraf's book *Kashmiris Fight for Freedom (1947–78): Vol-2.*[2]

The IB and other Indian agencies moved quickly too. The bureau set up its base in J&K soon after Independence, aggressively making its own moves in the Valley. The initial euphoria for Sheikh Abdullah among Indian agencies had started to wane. In the early 1950s, divisions started emerging between the pro-India and pro-Independence factions within the NC. The result of this stand-off was that, in August 1952, rumours began circulating that Abdullah would declare independence in Kashmir on 21 August, the day of Eid. So, two weeks before Eid, twenty-one-year-old Karan Singh—who had replaced his father as the regent, and was later made the first, and last, president of J&K—dismissed Abdullah's government.

The Indian intelligence and defence arms expanded their operations in Kashmir over the next several decades. Those who set up base never left. R&AW began with monitoring the troubled border with Pakistan, but over the years, it has established a considerable presence in Srinagar. The Indian Army consistently grew its operations in the region, as did the paramilitary forces. Today, Kashmir is one of the world's most militarised zones,[3] brimming with all kinds of intelligence operatives and interception stations. Everyone is listening in on everyone else. One agency's rat is another's terrorist.

The shadow game amongst intelligence agencies in Kashmir is a story that will never be fully known, but much can be gleaned from the occasional glimpses that we do gain of its workings.

Sheikh Abdullah was a seasoned politician courted by two countries, and stood astride the fault-lines of nation-making in South Asia. In October 1951, when elections to the Kashmir Constituent Assembly were held, he ensured that the nomination papers of several leaders of Praja Parishad, a party of Jammu Hindus that was opposed to him, were rejected on mere technicalities. NC won all seventy-five seats. Abdullah went on to jail over 10,000 people on political charges, and in many instances, his detractors were expelled to Pakistan. In short, he manipulated the state machinery to meet his own political ambitions. Thinking back, it is not surprising that J&K, which has witnessed some of the worst tragedies of state machinations, should have been one of the first Indian states where the political and permanent executive manipulated the security apparatus.

Even as Abdullah was settling down to the task of running the state, and manipulating its security arms to his advantage, the global community was also getting entangled in Kashmir. International engagement in Kashmir began in January 1948, when the United Nations Security Council (UNSC) adopted Resolution 39, establishing the United Nations Commission for India and Pakistan (UNCIP).[4] The UN secretary general appointed a military advisor to support this commission, and in January 1949, the first unarmed military observers arrived in the region: the United Nations Military Observer Group in India and Pakistan (UNMOGIP).

Among the visiting commission members was Josef Korbel, later to be chairperson of UNCIP. Korbel had just returned home to Czechoslovakia after the collapse of the Nazi regime in the Second World War. It would turn out to be a brief interlude of calm, and he would flee his homeland a second time because of the rise of communist oppression. Months after the Kashmir mission, Korbel sought refuge in the US where, a few decades later, his daughter Madeleine K. Albright became the first female secretary of state. Drawing from his experiences, Korbel wrote the rigorously documented *Danger in Kashmir*,[5] one of the earliest books on the dispute.

The UN intervention resulted in the Karachi agreement of 1949, in which military representatives of both sides agreed to establish a ceasefire line in Kashmir. UN military observers assisted in verifying the line on the ground. In July 1972, a few months after Bangladesh was liberated, India and Pakistan signed the Shimla Agreement defining the Line of Control that exists to this day. India now had a new position as far as the UNMOGIP was concerned: it was of the opinion that the group's mandate had lapsed, as it was specifically meant for the ceasefire line under the Karachi Agreement. The UN insisted that the mandate could only be terminated by a decision of the Security Council, which never came. So, like many outsiders who came in, the UN observers too stayed on.

Today, the UNMOGIP office in Srinagar—an old bungalow in a prominent location in the city, with a permanently closed front gate, with a few staff members inside—is where residents march to when they protest against Indian crackdowns and violations. The military observer group has an annual budget of US$ 20 million,[6] and enjoys great accommodation from Pakistani authorities, who regularly file complaints of ceasefire violations against India. In India, which is where the group's physical office is located, the government pays it no heed.

Many argue that the impossible attraction Kashmir appears to exert on every party that comes into contact with it is due to its scenic beauty, and not necessarily the profits of mayhem. The Valley itself is to blame, if you would believe that—a stunning landscape that seduces every visitor, glorious mountains wrapping around a chain of lakes and every view a mesmerising vista. Add to that its strategic location, bordering several nations. For the world's great powers, it is an enticing springboard deep into Asia's interiors.

On 27 December 1963, it was reported that a holy relic of the Prophet Mohammad, the *Moi-e-Muqqadas,* believed to be a strand of hair from the Prophet's beard, had been stolen from the Hazratbal dargah in Srinagar. Though the relic was found and restored within days—the thief turned out to be one of the custodians of the shrine—it led to serious rioting in the subcontinent. The ensuing turmoil became fertile ground for anti-India forces in Kashmir, especially Pakistan.

India's arch-foe across the border was reaping the benefits of the Cold War and American desperation in the region. By end-July or early-August 1965, a group of Pakistani commandos from the SSG, trained by the Americans, and insurgents trained by the Pakistan military crossed over to the Indian side and occupied key heights in Kashmir. The 1965 conflict blew up into a full-fledged war across the entire India–Pakistan land border beyond Kashmir, with some dramatic tank battles and gruesome standoffs that resulted in the death of thousands. There were also strong rumours that foreigners were coming to free Kashmir; for many youngsters, it was a call for rebellion.

Fazal-ul Haq Qureshi, the militant-turned-peacenik, was among those who heeded that call. Born in politically sensitive old Srinagar's Nawa Kadal area, he had been baptised early on in the fiery politics of South Asia. In the 1960s, he had a secure government job but also led a secret life. Along with a few friends, Qureshi had joined a nascent underground movement that provided logistical support to the Pakistani forces in the 1965 war. They called the movement Al Fatah (Victory), and established liberation cells in various parts of J&K. The group's first operation, which is also believed to be the first local militant attack in the Valley, was on 13 February 1967. They killed a BSF constable, Charan Das, on a bridge in Nawa Kadal.

'We were clear that we would not be taking any foreign money, so we had to raise our resources locally, both weapons and money,' Qureshi said, as he steadied himself on a bed in his modest house on the fringes of Srinagar in the winter of 2018. He looked like a Sufi preacher, not someone with a violent past. Now and again, he stared up at the cartoon playing on a television mounted on the wall, fiddling with a blanket that covered his frail legs. Outside, policemen had secured the area. While the Indian state was no longer wary of him, he posed a threat to militancy now. His peace activism was seen as pro-India.

On 1 April 1970, Qureshi's group carried out its second big operation: a raid on the educational office of Pulwama Tehsil, from where they looted Rs 72,000. With that money and donations from some members, Al Fatah established its first safe house in Bazroo village, about fourteen kilometres out of Srinagar. The youngsters told locals they were setting up a fruit concentrate and juice manufacturing plant. Three of them lived in the compound, Qureshi among them, as their book-keeper. Their third operation was in police uniform; the gang took hostage the manager and clerk of a bank in Hazratbal, and carried away Rs 97,000 on 2 January 1971. While the operation was successful, it gave the police its initial leads on the mysterious militants. Sensing the police closing in on them, the group decided to vacate the Bazroo hideout and relocate to the Dal Gate area of Srinagar.

Late in January 1971, on returning from a short walk, Qureshi had some surprise visitors. 'Shall we go?' The young man quietly raised his hands in surrender. The police contingent had been waiting at the house in Bazroo village since that morning. It was not Qureshi's first encounter with the police—he had been arrested in 1967, but he was not yet a militant then. Now, he was part of the Al Fatah leadership.

Over the next few days, the police arrested twenty-two members of the group. At one of these locations, insurgents fired back at the police, prompting an aggressive state-wide crackdown, which led to the detaining of 250 Kashmiris, including two serving magistrates of the state, three doctors, six professors and several other educated young men. They were all sent to various interrogation centres, as Qureshi was.

For several years to come, Qureshi would spend his life in and out of interrogation centres, all the while being part of the underground and continuing to be agitated about the treatment meted out to Kashmir by all sides. Many of his friends fell to bullets, some betrayed the group, others surrendered, but a few soldiered on. Their efforts, however, were mostly futile.

'Violence won't solve Kashmir's problem. But the problem with violence is that it gets more complex and graver with each generation. We were careful and did not want to die then, but today the youth are ready to die,' Qureshi said.

From Bazroo, Qureshi was taken to a location not very far from the UNMOGIP office—Red-16 in Talia Manzil of Sonawar, Srinagar, possibly the police's first interrogation centre in Kashmir. A two-storey, red-brick building with arched windows and a chimney, it was once the house of the second wife of a powerful bureaucrat. Over the next few decades, as militancy flared up, a number of interrogation centres would come up—in a palace, in a house by a busy city road, in an anonymous plantation, on a hilltop bungalow, in buildings by the river. These interrogation centres would become a symbol of horror for ordinary Kashmiris, and come to be a blot on the reputation of the Indian security establishment.

Behind the soundproof walls of these buildings, a new narrative was created for Kashmir. Within their confines, the security forces tortured both militants and ordinary protestors.[7] The torture, in turn, fed the anger and fury of the local narratives against India. Regardless of the explanations supplied by security agencies, the secret compounds of the interrogation centres tarnished the credentials of Indian democracy, while feeding the ranks of militancy. And as violence rose, security deployment went up further, and so did the number of interrogation centres. Meanwhile, Pakistan had, over the years, established an efficient network of informants, couriers, gossipmongers and overground workers with extensive funding channels. As it pumped in more money and militants into Kashmir, India increased its own deployment of security forces and created even more interrogation centres. The business of militancy was flourishing.

The modern history of Kashmir can, in fact, be narrated through the interrogation centres. Hari Niwas, the grand palace of Maharaja Hari Singh, overlooking the Dal Lake, became one such centre.[8] Another building, with an equally captivating view of the valley, was notoriously named Papa II. Numerous people have died in its torture chambers.[9] After it was shut down, Papa II became the official residence of former chief minister Mehbooba Mufti.[10] Amidst the spectacular landscape of Kashmir, one person's home becomes another person's graveyard; someone's torture cell could be someone else's bedchamber. In the Valley, grief and happiness are intimate lovers.

The raiders of 1947 got delayed in Baramulla and did not reach Srinagar in time to capture its airbase by 24–25 October, as was originally planned. This gave New Delhi the time to rush in troops. The 1 Sikh, a regiment under Commanding Officer Lieutenant Colonel Ranjit Rai, was diverted from its internal security duties in Gurgaon, and rushed to the Delhi airport. At around 3 a.m. on 27 October, while the regiment was airborne, Rai was assigned his task and given a couple of maps to help him plan the operations. Over the next few hours, three Dakota aircrafts of the military and six civilian planes together carried out twenty-eight sorties. Among the pilots in that mission was Biju Patnaik, a legendary pilot-nationalist-politician whose son, Naveen Patnaik, is presently the chief minister of Odisha. That same evening, as Rai led a column towards Baramulla to prevent the advance of the raiders, he was shot dead in a paddy field.

Every year, the Indian Army commemorates 27 October as 'Infantry Day' in memory of the defence of Kashmir. Since that day, the Indian military presence in J&K has gone up seismically. Three army corps are based in the state—16 Corps in Jammu, 15 Corps in Srinagar and 14 Corps in Leh. At one point, 16 Corps was bigger than the entire British Army.

Over a thousand Indian soldiers died in the 1947–48 operations. A few months after Rai's death, another senior officer, Brigadier Mohammad Usman, died fighting the Pakistani forces, but managed to secure Naushera. He became an instant legend, a personification of India's inclusive, secular values. A brigadier at thirty-five, Usman had turned down the Pakistani leadership's offers to join the Muslim nation, choosing to remain in secular India. His sacrifice triggered a strong wave of national sentiment in favour of secular values. Every generation of the Indian Army has found its martyrs and medals in Kashmir—of the twenty-one Param Vir Chakra (PVC;

the highest military medal for valour in battle) awarded so far, twelve were for actions in Kashmir or along its borders. The first five PVCs were all awarded for operations in J&K. The record of the Ashoka Chakra, the peacetime equivalent of the PVC, is not very different either. The significance that Kashmir holds for the Indian Army is also evidenced from the fact that it has lost more soldiers fighting insurgency in the Valley than in wars with other nations, or indeed any other operation. By my calculations, it has more active troops deployed in J&K and along its border than anywhere else—the real numbers are not known but are estimated to be a few hundred thousand. It is no secret that the army has been forced to do counter-insurgency work, when its real duty is the guarding of India's borders. In my view, the army leadership has not done enough to persuade successive governments to follow up its military successes with peaceful negotiations.

In 1990, as Kashmir violence flared up and Punjab was still on the boil, the army came up with the idea of raising a paramilitary force trained to deal with the local population, with a strategy that combined both hard power and a soft approach. Three of the earliest Rashtriya Rifles (RR) battalions raised in 1990 were sent to Punjab and Kashmir. The battalions were fully manned by army personnel, but drew significantly from non-infantry arms, including army service corps and artillery. Infantry only provided 50 per cent of the strength. After a few months of training in dealing with insurgency, the RR is sent into action. Today, it has at least sixty-two battalions deployed in Kashmir, with an average of 800 soldiers in each.[11]

Around the time that RR was formed, the Parliament passed the J&K Disturbed Areas Act and the Armed Forces (Jammu and Kashmir) Special Powers Act. Once an area is declared as a 'disturbed area', the AFSPA comes into effect, to empower the troops operating there. This legislation draws its legacy from a similarly named British law passed during the Second World War, and was first enacted in parts of the Northeast to deal with the Naga insurgency. AFSPA slowly spread across that region, and finally made its appearance in J&K in 1990. The act grants the armed forces—including non-commissioned officers—wide-ranging powers to deal with a potential terror threat, from shooting to kill anyone to destroying a building. Under AFSPA, no security personnel can be prosecuted without sanction from the Union government.

While this is not a generalisation about the security forces at large, the draconian AFSPA has created people like Major Avtar Singh of 35 RR battalion. In a rare moment of justice in those chaotic times, the Kashmir High Court ordered an SIT to investigate the mysterious death of human rights activist Jaleel Andrabi, whose body was found in a jute sack in Jhelum river. All evidence pointed towards Major Singh. The SIT also stumbled upon something else—to cover up his tracks, Singh also killed four counter-insurgents who helped him in murdering Andrabi. Besides, the Kashmir police also learnt that Singh was possibly involved in five other killings back home.

Sometime in 2000, the Kashmir police traced him to a territorial army regiment in Karnal, Haryana. They landed up there with a high court order, but the army would not hand him over. Towards the end of the year, the police filed a charge sheet, but the murderer was still missing from their custody. Even though the court had imposed restrictions on his movements, Singh easily slipped out of India with his family while court proceedings were underway. One may well question whether he could have left India without active encouragement from the army and other arms of the state.

In 2011, an Indian woman in California reported a case of domestic abuse. When the police arrested and interrogated the husband, he turned out to be Avtar Singh. The local police realised that he was on the Interpol wanted list. Interpol was alerted, and India was told that Singh was in California. But New Delhi was not interested in him. A few months later, in the summer of 2012, the local police got a call from Singh, who said he had killed four people. By the time the police reached his home, Singh had shot himself and his family dead.[12]

The army is only one piece of the Indian security web in the Valley. Until the 1960s, the IB was India's prime and only federal intelligence agency dealing with J&K. By the late 1960s, R&AW was established to deal with external intelligence, and within a few years, started its operations in Kashmir. As India struggled with internal strife and external threats, new intelligence agencies and security arms were added. Almost two dozen intelligence agencies of various kinds exist in India today, some are part of larger forces like the paramilitary or state police, others, like the NTRO, are standalone agencies. Many of them have a significant presence in the region.

Militancy is a messy affair—a minefield where every right step helps crush a terrorist network, but every misstep is a human rights violation. In Kashmir, many Indian agencies have failed, and continue to fail, a key test of democracy—accountability—and must share the blame for their part in escalating the violence. For a very long time, the army officially encouraged the killings of terrorists. The number of 'kills' was used to assess its men on the ground, resulting in many fake encounters. Very often, officers have faced professional backlash for not pursuing the aggressive 'kill' strategy. For instance, my schoolmate, the late Brigadier Pramod Kumar, refused to be part of a staged encounter when he was a company commander with 1 Sector of the RR in 2000. He was subsequently punished with adverse remarks by his brigade commander, and ended up with three unfavourable reports from that posting. Until he succumbed to cancer a few years ago, Pramod repeatedly petitioned the army headquarters and the MoD against the negative remarks and the resultant slowdown in his promotions.[13] The remarks were ultimately set aside during the course of his career, but he became a brigadier after much delay, and the officer fell behind in the steep pyramid of army promotions. What happened to Pramod at the beginning of the new millennium is a story that needs to be examined in greater detail. We will return to it soon.

The day after that phone call in April 2001, I was up very early in the morning and quite restless. Would I be interviewing a famous militant or foolishly walking into a trap laid by a terrorist group? I could not rule out the possibility of kidnapping, given that it might prove to be a bargaining chip for the militants. Alternatively, Majid Dar, who was in the mood to pursue peace, might want to send out a fresh appeal through me. In conflict zones, there are no certainties, nor too many choices.

It was too early to call anyone, so I wrote an email to my brilliant and compassionate editor at Rediff.com, Nikhil Lakshman, telling him about the interview, giving him the numbers of my local contacts who had helped me get in touch with Dar, and promising to alert him after the interview. My driver and guide, Mohammed Shafi, who had worked with many visiting journalists, drove me to the spot. At the North Gate, I stood with a shoulder bag, while the city lay asleep around me. I felt like I had walked into a picture postcard: snow-capped peaks in the distance, tulips in full bloom, spring still in the air. A few minutes later, a bearded man on a rickety scooter stopped beside me and asked for proof of my identity. Once he had verified it, he asked me to sit pillion on his vehicle. He began riding slowly, looking around to check whether we were being tailed. A few metres ahead, the man asked: 'What is in your bag?' My notebook, camera and recorder, I said. He stopped, turned the scooter around, drove me back and asked me to hand over the camera to Shafi.

We rode down winding alleys, to ensure both that we were not being followed and that I was sufficiently confused about the route. We halted outside a house. Three people were tending a small garden here. The gardening activity was actually covert protection for Kashmir's most important militant commander. In the morning light, I could clearly see the cold Kalashnikov muzzles tucked inside their long pherans. A few minutes later, I was seated in a drawing room and a middle-aged lady was serving me tea in silence. Then, in walked Majid Dar, a tall, strapping man with a neatly trimmed beard. Greeting me with a warm hug, Dar said he had agreed to meet me because of my articles, which he often read when he was in Pakistan-occupied Kashmir (PoK), and considered mostly fair and balanced.

I began by asking him about his initiation into militancy. Dar recalled his primary-school days, when the movement for the right to self-determination was in full swing under the leadership of Sheikh Abdullah, and how it impacted him. 'At home, we used to hear stories about these processions, demonstrations etc. I was born in this atmosphere and grew up in these circumstances. So it was obvious that it had an impact on us,' he said. As a student, he began to take part in Abdullah's movement. By the early 1970s, Dar was making regular trips to jails and interrogation centres.

Around this time, there were new rumblings in the subcontinent. Pakistani troops had unleashed a reign of terror on East Pakistan. Hundreds of thousands were killed, thousands of women raped, millions forced to seek refuge in India, and an armed freedom movement was born. When the Indian security establishment was charged with training and organising the Mukti Bahini (the Bangladeshi freedom fighters), Brigadier Shabeg Singh was in charge of a large part of the operation. The Sikh officer cut off his hair to merge with the militia and fought alongside them.

On 30 January 1971, an Indian Airlines flight, Ganga, was hijacked by two Kashmiri youth carrying toy guns and fake grenades and taken to Lahore. Hijacking of civilian aircraft has been a regular tactic with Kashmiri and Pakistani militants ever since. A few hundred thousand Pakistanis came out into the streets of Lahore to give the hijackers a grand welcome. However, the Pakistani security establishment was suspicious of them, and suspected that most of the passengers were Indian government employees or their families. The hijack then became a reason for New Delhi to suspend all flights between East and West Pakistan via Indian airspace, which disrupted the airlift of Pakistani soldiers to the country's eastern wing. By the end of the year, Pakistan had been sundered in two, and Bangladesh born. In a swift military operation in December 1971, lasting barely fifteen days, the Indian forces, with the active support of the Mukti

Bahini, defeated Pakistani troops, and took almost 93,000 military personnel as prisoners of war. Among those to reach Dhaka was Shabeg Singh. He was decorated for his glorious service, celebrated as a hero, and soon promoted to the rank of major general. There is more to his story; more on that soon.

The creation of a new nation by breaking up one of the strongest American allies during the Cold War was a power move by Prime Minister Indira Gandhi. She was now unstoppable. In the Valley, Sheikh Abdullah began feeling the power of Gandhi's triumph when she emphatically declared that 'the hands of the clock cannot be turned back' on Kashmir. He was forced to rethink his resistance to New Delhi's domination. Abdullah had spent much of the previous two decades in jail, despite a brief rapprochement with Nehru in the months running up to the latter's death in 1964. The Indira–Sheikh Accord in 1975 brought Abdullah back as chief minister. His anti-India stance gave way to a more accommodative position. From an Indian perspective, the accord ushered in genuine democracy to J&K. He rehabilitated former militants with government jobs, and many of them retired as senior state government officials years later.

Jamat-e-Islami Kashmir, which has a conservative religious outlook and is often seen as pro-Pakistan, challenged the deal. Some of Abdullah's supporters too felt betrayed, and he was accused of selling off Kashmir to manoeuvre his return as chief minister after twenty-two years. Many, including Majid Dar, took to the streets to protest what they saw as a sell-out, and the state government violently cracked down on the demonstrations. 'Most of the time, the grounds for our detention were unconvincing and outrageous. To strengthen the case, we were charged under false reasons. We were cruelly treated in lock-ups. Our freedom was snatched away from us for even the slightest of reasons,' Dar told me.

Syed Ali Shah Geelani, the firebrand Jamaat-e-Islami member of the state assembly, became a vocal organiser of protests against the accord. Dar would often shutter his dry-cleaning shop in Sopore to join the local Jamaat protests. Under the Indira–Sheikh Accord, cases against militants like Qureshi were withdrawn, even though many of them rejected the accord itself. Those opposed to Abdullah formed a new front by merging several small splinter groups, including Qureshi's Al Fatah, and formed the People's League. In 1982, Abdullah passed away while he was chief minister, and his son, Farooq Abdullah, took over.

The relatively peaceful era of democracy in J&K was disrupted by the Congress within two years of Farooq becoming chief minister. Unhappy with his leadership style and the perceived marginalisation of the Congress in the administration, the national party prompted Farooq's brother-in-law, Ghulam Mohammed Shah, to break away, and provided him with support to form a government.[14] That regime did not last long.

The Congress party has long stirred up Kashmir for its narrow political gains. These manipulations and power games would peak in 1987 under Prime Minister Rajiv Gandhi, giving birth to the present Kashmir insurgency.[15] The Congress has had two broad attitudes towards the region. In the Nehruvian era, J&K was seen as at the heart of India's secular credentials, but under Indira and Rajiv Gandhi, all policies concerning the area have been governed by political expediency. Unlike the Congress, the BJP as well as the broader Hindutva ecosystem has had a consistent political stand on the Valley. In the early years after Independence, striking a discordant note with rest of the Indian political leadership, Dr Syama Prasad Mookerjee resigned from Nehru's cabinet because he was strongly opposed to Article 370, which granted the state a special status. Mookerjee condemned the fact that J&K was allowed its own flag, that other Indians were not allowed to settle down there and that there was the need for a special permit to enter the state. He died in Srinagar in 1953 while in custody.[16]

Mookerjee, who was aligned with the RSS and was a vocal advocate of the rights of Hindus, saw the state through the Hindu–Muslim binary. This perspective continues to guide the BJP, the successor to Mookerjee's Jana Sangh[17]—a fact that has considerably influenced the party's sense of security matters, terrorism and even its definition of the Indian state. In my assessment, it is due to this narrow view of Kashmir that the BJP, and the larger right-wing establishment led by the RSS, are often at the forefront of defending excesses by the security establishment. The party might give in to Chinese grandstanding or American persuasion, while flexing its muscles at Pakistan and swinging, in my opinion, the wrecking ball at Kashmir.

Majid Dar, accompanied by his four divisional commanders, dramatically announced a ceasefire on 24 July 2000. New Delhi was quick to reciprocate. But there were obstacles to peace every step of the way, not least from the ISI.

The ISI-controlled LeT and other militant groups went on a rampage. LeT stormed the RR brigade headquarters in Bandipura, killed thirty-one Amarnath pilgrims and eighteen sleeping labourers in Qazigund, wiped out seven members of a former militant's family, shot dead eleven Hindus in Doda, and butchered eight village defence committee members in Kishtwar. On 3 August, when Majid Dar and his commanders were to secretly meet with the Union home secretary and senior officials in Srinagar, some in the J&K police ensured the meeting would become a media spectacle, to the utter shock of everyone involved. Even as local media persons prepared to travel to Pahalgam, where Prime Minister Atal Bihari Vajpayee was visiting the massacre site of the pilgrims, they were alerted to the event in Srinagar. Though the militants requested camera crew not to shoot them, as their lives would be imperilled, the media did not relent, leading to a short fracas between the parties. After discussing the modalities, the militant commanders finally had to scale the walls to escape attention. On his way back, at Srinagar airport, Vajpayee gave his stamp of approval to the talks by saying: '*Talks insaniyat ke dayre mein hongi*.'[18] The talks will be held within the humanitarian framework—he was not insisting on the framework of the Constitution.

Within the political establishment in Pakistan, early reactions to the ceasefire were positive, with Foreign Minister Abdus Sattar saying that Islamabad would support the decision of the Kashmiris. But its security establishment was quick to realise that lasting peace could undo its own significance in the Valley. Reports emerged that the Hizbul supremo, Syed Salahuddin, had been put under house arrest in Pakistan before he emerged to demand that Pakistan be included in the talks. By 8 August, Salahuddin, who had been part of the secret parleys with New Delhi until then, withdrew the ceasefire from his Islamabad base.[19]

In my meeting with Dar, ISI was the elephant in the room. Just a few months earlier, everyone with a stake in Kashmir—Dar, New Delhi, Kashmiris, peaceniks, Pakistanis, militants—had been given a taste of the ISI's power in the Valley.

At some point in my interview, I asked Dar: According to the Indian intelligence, you are funded by the ISI?

Dar: Ask them how true that is. I don't know.

Me: Pakistan does not give you any money?

Dar: I am sitting here. For me, my people give money. I don't take money from Pakistan.

Me: But Pakistan openly says that they are supporting your movement.

Dar: The people of Pakistan do give money. They openly collect money. In recent times, there has been some controversy after the interior minister opposed the open collection of funds. They wanted to stop it, but people still give.

Throughout our conversation, it was clear that Pakistan and the ISI were integral parts of the Kashmir insurgency, though Dar was loath to admit it. For him, Pakistan had become an irritant because it was not sincere about finding peace in Kashmir. He was determined to break away from its clutches, but he no longer found support in New Delhi. Dar and his efforts would die a violent death a few months after our meeting.

After several cups of tea and a long interview, where we

discussed attacks launched by his cadres, his family and if Islam justified suicide attacks, I switched off my dictaphone. Outside, the gardeners continued to tend to the plants, while bright sunlight had suddenly lit up the city. Dar then made a request: could I please inform a particular senior IB official and anyone else in the security establishment I had access to that they needed to do more if he were to propose a second ceasefire offer? Most Hizbul cadres would openly support him, he said.

'I am not a messenger, but a mere reporter,' I replied, while acknowledging that I knew the official he was referring to.

'Aren't people's lives more important than your journalism?' he asked, as he hugged me goodbye.

We returned to my vehicle quickly enough, because the rider was no longer trying to shake off a possible tail. All the same, I was running late for my next appointment at the 15 Corps headquarters, the fortified military bastion at another end of the city. Though relieved and free, I did not have the time to go back to my rooms and call my editor in Mumbai to confirm my safety. I would learn about the few hours of panic in the newsroom only much later.

My appointment with the general officer commanding the 15 Corps, Lieutenant General John Ranjan Mukherjee, the most senior military officer in the Valley, had come through on a formal request. A pleasant and seasoned soldier, Mukherjee had the earnestness of a genuine leader. I mentioned in passing that Majid Dar had said that New Delhi will have to do more to give them confidence if they were to come overground with a new ceasefire offer. Though the lieutenant general was eager to discuss the matter, his juniors argued against any further leeway for the militants. I suspect that their arguments were led not so much by the possibility of peace in Kashmir as by other tactical concerns and an unpronounced fear of losing power. They appeared singularly unconcerned about the deaths and suffering of both ordinary people and the security personnel posted in the state.

The very next day, my interview[20] with Majid Dar was republished prominently in most Kashmiri newspapers. Soon enough, I got a call. Someone claiming to be a senior intelligence officer was on the other end, saying that a red car driven by a young Sikh was coming to my house to pick me up. He wanted to meet me urgently. Yet again, I had no choice but to obey the caller. This time I did not even have the time to organise myself or email my editor. The car was outside. At the imposing bungalow where the officer headed one of the Indian agencies, he handed me a drink and the transcript of an intercepted radio communication between two militant commanders. Pakistan-backed groups were expressing displeasure at the interview and at Majid Dar, and a potential threat to my life figured in it too. My almost two-month-long sojourn in Kashmir ended soon after.

Less than a year after my interview, Dar was shot dead in Sopore. Militants and groups close to the ISI were the most obvious suspects for the murder of Kashmir's most powerful hope for peace, but there was little clarity about what really happened in Dar's final days. In 2018, I asked Fazal Haq Qureshi about his friend's death. 'He had gone to meet his mother before he took the biggest decision of his life, to come overground with most of the Hizbul cadres. After meeting her, he was to travel across the border to meet with cadres on the other side. It would have been historic,' Qureshi said. If this was true, it would have been tectonic. Dar would have quit militancy with a vast majority of Kashmir's largest militant group, its cadres mostly drawn from the local population. It could have changed the future of Kashmir.

For most actors in the Kashmir issue, the benefits of strife far outweigh the dividends of peace. After years of being an underground guerrilla, Majid Dar may have realised the futility of violence. Some say he came upon that realisation while on pilgrimage to Mecca. However, there were other interests at play in the region.

When Majid Dar emerged after meeting his mother, two gunmen sprayed him with bullets, snuffing out the last key militant leader willing to trade his weapons for peace.

As much as the insurgency is a story of violence, it is also a story of how those who benefit from the business of militancy have subverted peaceful efforts. This would be seen over and over in Kashmir, but also elsewhere across the country.

When the Congress was wiped out in the general elections after Emergency, according to the late journalist Kuldip Nayar, its leaders got in touch with Jarnail Singh Bhindranwale, the fiery head of Damdami Taksaal, an important Sikh seminary. He was propped up as a counter to the Akali Dal that had defeated the Congress.[21] In the 1977 elections, the ruling Congress under Giani Zail Singh—he would later on become the president of India—had been reduced to third position in Punjab. Against this political reality, the Congress decided to fight the Akali Dal's politics of Sikhism by forwarding their own religious figure. Sanjay Gandhi and his associates zeroed in on two candidates. Nayar quoted a close aide of Gandhi and former Madhya Pradesh chief minister Kamal Nath as saying: 'The first one we interviewed did not look a courageous type. Bhindranwale, strong in tone and tenor, seemed to fit the bill. We would give him money off and on, but we never thought he would turn into a terrorist.'[22]

The Congress ended up creating a monster that would wreak havoc for years to come and shake New Delhi to its core.

The first sensational murder connected to Bhindranwale was that of Lala Jagat Narain, the founder of the *Punjab Kesari* newspaper, on 9 September 1981. Narain, a freedom fighter who had spent time in jail during the Emergency, was a fierce critic of Bhindranwale, and also a witness in the case about the attack on the Nirankaris.[23] Nayar writes that the Punjab police was thwarted in its attempt to arrest Bhindranwale for Narain's murder by two key Congress leaders: Zail Singh, who was the Union home minister after the Congress's triumphant return to power at the Centre in 1980, and the chief minister of Haryana, Bhajan Lal, who had recently defected with several legislators to the Congress.[24] At Chando Kalan village in Haryana, where Bhindranwale was when the police came for him, violence broke out between the police and his supporters, and two buses were torched, destroying, among other things, his written sermons, the dearly held written records of his teachings.

Meanwhile, across the border, Pakistan, smarting from the humiliation of 1971, was desperate for opportunities to exact revenge, and swiftly waded into the mess in Punjab. It provided arms and ammunition to the militants, and allowed them free entry and exit into Pakistan. Islamabad also helped mobilise support for Khalistan activists around the world. According to local reports and observers, General Zia-ul-Haq took a great deal of personal interest in the affairs of Sikh militancy.[25]

In 1982, Delhi was preparing to host the ninth Asian Games, not just a major sporting meet, but also a showcase event for Rajiv Gandhi, who was being groomed by his mother, Prime Minister Indira Gandhi, to succeed her.[26] Led by Harchand Singh Longowal, the Akali Dal—which was by this time aligned to Bhindranwale's agitations—announced protests in the national capital during the Asian Games. The state response was brutal, victimising ordinary Sikhs.[27] The havoc it created further fed Bhindranwale's militant posture.

Rajiv Gandhi, who was initiated into Indian politics with the Punjab militancy, drew the wrong lessons from it, and turned to similarly unimaginative political machinations in Kashmir a few years later.

With every violent crackdown by New Delhi, the Sikh militancy further hardened. Meanwhile, based on the accounts of arrested militants, Indian agencies claimed that Pakistan had hosted up to 3,000 Sikh militants at the peak of the insurgency. The leaders of most militant groups were stationed in Pakistan, and ISI provided them with arms, ammunition and training, and helped them cross the international border. The militancy also increasingly became anti-Hindu, with targeted killing of Hindus in buses, trains and open areas. As the situation worsened, Prime Minister Indira Gandhi was forced to dismiss her own party's government in Punjab on 6 June 1983.

In the summer of 1984, the Indian Army was deployed in the state. The police was brought under military command, and the 9th Division, commanded by Major General Kuldip Singh Brar, was moved from Meerut to Amritsar. Lieutenant General Ranjit Singh Dayal—the legendary soldier who led the improbable capture of Haji Pir Pass from Pakistan in 1965, and was now the chief of staff of the Western Command—was appointed as security advisor to the Punjab governor. Several Sikh soldiers were placed in visible positions in the Indian Army's operations.

Overnight, the Bihar regiment moved its soldiers to surround the Golden Temple, where extremist Sikhs under Bhindranwale were holed in. However, this was no ragtag group of Sikhs—its defences were led by Major General Shabeg Singh, one of the architects of the 1971 Bangladesh war strategy. Believed by many to have been ill-treated by the army, Singh, who was court-martialled a day before his retirement, became a vocal Sikh activist, ending up in Bhindranwale's camp.[28]

In a television interview with journalist Shekhar Gupta in 2012, General K.S. Brar, who led the operation on the Golden Temple, was candid about Shabeg Singh. 'He was my instructor in the academy. I was his cadet. Then, in the 1971 war, we both linked up when we were going into Dhaka.' Back then, Brar was commander of the 1 Maratha, one of the first battalions to enter Dhaka on 16 December 1971. Shabeg Singh and the Mukti Bahini he raised had reached Dhaka with them.

Operation Blue Star caused major damage to the Golden Temple complex, and severely strained the Sikh community's ties to India. A couple of days after it ended, almost the entire 9 Sikh Regiment, based on the outskirts of Sri Ganganagar in Rajasthan, mutinied. Around 600 armed soldiers drove around the town's streets shouting slogans in support of Bhindranwale. They shot dead a policeman and then split into two—one group went towards the national capital, the other towards Pakistan. As news of the mutiny emerged, the Sikh Regimental Centre in Ramgarh, Bihar, was in a churn too.

Close to 1,500 soldiers, both fresh recruits and liveried, attacked the armoury and carried away weapons. When news of the second mutiny reached the commandant, Brigadier S.C. Puri, he, along with two other officers, drove towards the soldiers. The soldiers fired at the car, injuring the brigadier.[29] The other officers rushed him to the military hospital, but Brigadier Puri died soon after.

The soldiers drove out of Ramgarh in a convoy of vehicles, including many civilian cars they had forcefully taken, towards Amritsar. The army mounted roadblocks, sent several units in search of them, and carried out recce by helicopters. It was something the army had not anticipated—a hunt for so many of its own. There were standoffs and exchanges of fire at various places, and media reports later claimed that over a hundred people may have died in the firing.[30]

On 24 August, an Indian Airlines flight from Chandigarh to Srinagar was hijacked by Sikh militants. They demanded that the Airbus A300 be taken to the US, but it went to Lahore, Karachi and then Dubai, where it finally landed without any bloodshed.

The overwhelmed Indian security establishment promptly blamed Pakistan for instigating the army mutinies.[31] However, the army's own court of enquiry unequivocally ruled out outside interference, and blamed Indian leadership and other factors. The unrest in the ranks did not end here. There were reports of small-scale mutinies from Jammu, Pune and from outside Bombay, and allegations that soldiers had been smoking and drinking inside the Golden Temple complex.[32] Two months after Operation Blue Star, when the army was finally asked to pull back, there was a huge pile of complaints of atrocities from across the state. The army leadership denied these allegations outright, even though its troops had arrested over 5,000 people and carried out numerous raids.[33] The government also passed the Terrorist Affected Areas (Special Courts) Act 1984, with stringent conditions for proving a person's innocence.

In Punjab, petty political interests combined with a less-than-robust security establishment brought the crisis to a head. This is what happened in J&K too. Despite the repeated failure of India's intelligence-gathering activities in Punjab, there was no noticeable effort to consciously avoid repeating those mistakes. India paid dearly for Operation Blue Star when Indira Gandhi was assassinated by her Sikh bodyguards in October 1984.

As the year was winding up, the cycle of violence grew vicious. The anti-Sikh riots in the aftermath of Gandhi's assassination pushed dozens of Sikh youngsters, including some from places like Delhi, to take up arms. Funding from the affluent Sikh diaspora picked up. Sikh militancy was no longer a localised affair, but a global movement with active support from Pakistan's ISI, branches in various countries and robust funding. On 23 June 1985, Canada-based Khalistani militants placed bombs in Air India flight 182, which blew up at 31,000 feet over the Atlantic Ocean, killing all 329 passengers and crew aboard. It was the most gruesome terror act in the skies until the 9/11 in the US. A Canadian enquiry commission into the attack said of their own security establishment: 'Excessive secrecy in information sharing prevented any one agency from obtaining all necessary information to assess the threat. Excessive secrecy also prevented those on the frontlines from obtaining information necessary to put in place security measures responsive to the threat.'[34] These words still ring true, most certainly for India; inter-agency cooperation remains weak.

In New Delhi, the new prime minister, Rajiv Gandhi, made efforts to bring normalcy to Punjab. He sent senior Congress leader Arjun Singh as governor, released several prisoners, including Akali Dal President Harchand Singh Longowal, and reached out to moderate factions. On 24 July 1985, the Rajiv–Longowal Accord was signed, in which the Union government accepted most Akali demands, including expanding the scope of the judicial commission of enquiry into the 1984 anti-Sikh riots, no reduction in army recruitments from Punjab and rehabilitation of army deserters. The accord, however, was not very popular, and Longowal was shot dead by Sikh militants within a month of it.

By 1986, a few hundred militants were back at the Golden Temple, Hindus continued to be targeted in sensational killings and considerable resources were flowing into the militancy, especially from Pakistan, where the ISI was actively stoking the embers. Besides, thanks to the Union's blunders and the Congress's miscalculations, the demand for Khalistan was only growing.

Even as Punjab was on fire, Prime Minister Rajiv Gandhi became distracted by an opportunity in J&K.

'Then came the election of 1987,' Majid Dar told me as we sipped warm cups of tea. My interview had run into well over an hour. I was on my second cup of tea and a bit more relaxed too. As we started discussing the 1987 elections, he turned visibly angry.

It was the year 1984 that, in fact, shaped the 1987 J&K elections too. The Congress had actively encouraged a split in the NC, causing a government formation that lasted only two years. In 1986, the Ghulam Mohammed Shah government was dismissed in the wake of communal riots in the state, and the resultant imposition of governor's rule. The Congress now reached out to Farooq Abdullah for an electoral alliance, promising to lift the governor's rule and facilitate his return to power.

The assembly elections were held on 23 March 1987. In the fray against the Congress–NC alliance was the Muslim United Front (MUF), comprising parties like Jamaat-e-Islami and Ittihad-ul-Muslimeen. The only prominent anti-NC force not in the MUF fold was the People's Conference, led by Abdul Ghani Lone, which fared badly.

The state, especially the Kashmir Valley, witnessed spirited campaigning in the lead-up to the elections. But instead of allowing free and fair elections, the establishment in both New Delhi and Srinagar is believed to have manipulated the polls.[35] Voters were openly intimidated, ballot boxes tampered with, candidates threatened and election officers were actively involved in overturning results.

Defeated candidates were also found to be declared winners. One candidate who had retreated in despair after losing was summoned back to be declared winner.[36]

Bizarre scenes were witnessed in constituency after constituency. An election observer saw an NC–Congress candidate huddled with the district magistrate and the counting officer. The counting officer insisted that he wanted to complete the counting, and would not accept the claim that the opposition candidate was anti-national. As they were deep in discussion, a senior officer rang up and instructed the counting officer to ensure the NC–Congress candidate was the winner. In Wachi constituency, Pulwama, the secretary to the Election Commission of India (ECI) himself oversaw the manipulation, and declared that the winning MUF candidate had been defeated, according to famed Kashmiri writer-poet and civil servant G.N. Gauhar, who was secretary of the J&K Delimitation Commission and was a central election observer during the polls.[37] Gauhar alleged a similar drama took place in Bandipora constituency. In Amira Kadal and Habba Kadal constituencies, two ministers entered the fray. 'In both these constituencies, the ministers lost, but not only they were declared elected additionally after the declaration of fraudulent results, they got the workers of the MUF tortured in police stations,' Gauhar claimed.

A generation that was attempting to join the Indian democracy would appear to have been rudely shooed away, with active assistance from the security establishment on the ground. Many would no longer recognise the landscape of the 1987 election. Supreme commander of the Hizbul Mujahideen and one of India's most wanted, Syed Salahuddin—born Mohammad Yusuf Shah—was a candidate from Srinagar's Lal Chowk constituency. He won a landslide victory against Ghulam Mohiuddin Shah, then a powerful minister in the Abdullah ministry.[38] However, the district magistrate stalled the announcement of the result, and announced the NC leader victorious.[39] Salahuddin and others objected, and policemen from the Maisuma police station dragged them in full public view down Lal Chowk, to the police station. They were then sent to a jail in Jammu. In another constituency, a winning NC candidate demanded that his victory margin of just a few hundred votes be multiplied ten times.

Syed Ali Shah Geelani, separatist leader and leading anti-India voice in the Valley today, contested from Sopore. As the chief of MUF, he would have become chief minister if the party had won a majority. Yasin Malik and Javed Mir, who pioneered militancy in the valley, were polling agents for the MUF. Separatist leader Shabir Shah's brother Mohammad Saeed Shah was the candidate from Anantnag.

That was the last time that the separatist leaders were part of an Indian electoral process, and the Kashmir Valley would never be the same again. In the face of outright manipulation, many of them took up arms, several died and most of them continue to boycott Indian elections. When Rajiv Gandhi and Farooq Abdullah apparently sabotaged a democratic election, as reports suggest, I think they thrust a knife deep into the idea of India. It would appear that the 1987 elections laid the grounds for a whole generation's final boycott of India, which is said to have further triggered the rise of an all-out and popular militancy. It is my view that the perceived myopic Gandhi–Abdullah alliance was one of the biggest political missteps in modern India.

By June that year, the last round of elections, in Leh, Kargil and Bhadrawah, were concluded. The ECI, the courts and every other democratic institution either remained silent or took active part in satiating the hunger of the powers that be. The tactical art of looking away at crucial junctures that India's institutions have perfected is at the heart of what challenges the country's democracy today. A big part of that mute-spectator status is achieved by the looming shadow of the police, intelligence and investigation agencies.

The Valley sank into a deceptive calm before the storm burst.

'Pindi, Pindi, Pindi!' A few months after the 1987 elections, bus attendants in Kashmir Valley shouted 'Pindi' from their vehicles at bus stops, offering to drop people to the border free of cost if they were headed to Rawalpindi. Hundreds of angry youngsters would board these buses, or use other means, to cross the border. After a few days of trekking, they would reach training camps in PoK.

This is how MUF candidate Yusuf Shah, aka Syed Salahuddin, turned into a guerrilla leader. Yasin Malik and Javed Mir joined hands to form the Jammu and Kashmir Liberation Front (JKLF), which would lead the resurgence of militancy in the region. JKLF traces its origins to the armed faction of the Plebiscite Front, founded in 1955 after Sheikh Abdullah was ousted as prime minister and jailed in 1953.

The Front would play a key role in ushering hundreds of Kashmiri youngsters into militant-training camps in Pakistan. One of its founders, buried in an unmarked grave in Delhi's Tihar Jail in 1984, was now resurrected as an icon for the restless region. Maqbool Butt, a resident of Kupwara district's Trehgam village, and other activists had established the National Liberation Front, the precursor to JKLF, in 1965 to lead an armed struggle to free Kashmir. Butt's fierce commitment to Kashmiri independence meant that he ran afoul of authorities on both sides of the border. He has the unique credit of being an enemy to both India and Pakistan—tortured and jailed in both countries before being hanged by India in February 1984.

Until 1987, Butt's story had been part of a marginal narrative. With three colleagues, he had secretly crossed over to Kashmir from Pakistan to initiate an armed rebellion in 1966, but Indian security forces had already been tipped off by a local informant. As the two sides exchanged fire, police officer Amar Chand and Butt's colleague Aurangzeb were killed. Butt and two others were arrested and tried for murder and illegal border crossing, among other charges, and given capital punishment. In Srinagar Jail, the young inmates would not give up. On the morning of 8 December 1968, the three of them escaped through an almost forty-foot-long tunnel. They reached

Pakistan, but were soon arrested there. Butt relentlessly campaigned for free Kashmir on both sides of the border, and in 1976, he was arrested once again on the Indian side of the LoC, where his death sentence was still valid. His supporters hijacked a plane and staged other terror acts to free him. Butt even petitioned the Indian president for clemency. However, the kidnapping of Indian diplomat Ravindra Mhatre in the UK, on 3 February 1984, and his subsequent murder three days later, to demand Butt's release, dramatically turned the narrative against him. He was hanged on 11 February inside Tihar. He had been a well-liked prisoner in Tihar Jail, who fought for the rights of other inmates. Within the jail, he is still known to be a good-natured ghost, and many inmates claim to have seen his spirit near the gallows.

Among the first acts of the newly resurgent JKLF was to assassinate High Court Justice Neelkanth Ganjoo, who, as a sessions judge, had awarded the death penalty to Butt in 1968. Ganjoo was on the busy Hari Singh Street in Srinagar on 4 November 1989 when JKLF militants shot him dead.

Kashmir was on the boil. Militants began to target informants and anyone aligned with the Indian state. IB officials were shot dead across the valley—R.N.P. Singh in Anantnag, Kishen Gopal in Badgam, M.L. Bhan in Nowgam and T.K. Razdan in Srinagar.

Before we discuss the bloody phase triggered by the rigged 1987 elections and Kashmir's descent into a prolonged chaos, we need to step back. For, in New Delhi, Prime Minister Rajiv Gandhi had begun dreaming of new adventures. Ebullient and seemingly in a great hurry, Gandhi and his security establishment did not have the patience to examine the bushfires in Kashmir. Their attention had turned towards the Indian Ocean, where a tiny island nation was in the throes of its own civil war.

7

Our Boys

On a summer evening in July 1987, a few men were hunting down tourist maps of Sri Lanka in the crowded streets of Hyderabad. They were soldiers preparing for a perilous mission: the 54 Infantry Division of the Indian Army would soon be leaving on a dramatic military operation; they were to be deployed beyond the national boundaries without a UN mandate.

Starting the morning of 30 July 1987, hundreds of soldiers of the division were airborne and headed to Sri Lanka. Their mission was to implement the recently signed Indo–Sri Lanka Accord, separate the Sri Lankan Armed Forces and the Liberation Tigers of Tamil Eelam (LTTE), accept the surrender of arms and ammunition from the LTTE, and facilitate the political process of finding a lasting solution to the violent ethnic crisis in the island nation. The Indian Peace Keeping Force (IPKF) was heading to a foreign land to keep peace.

What resulted, however, was ferocity of a sort that the Indian military was not prepared for. Already, the Indian security establishment had been sucked into Punjab and Kashmir, and was drifting aimlessly in the Northeast, where the army has had a continued presence since almost immediately after Independence.

'They [the Indian intelligence agencies] had no intelligence to give me about the terrain or the enemy. I had to buy tourist maps in Hyderabad before I went into operations. I had to borrow a Sri Lankan photocopying machine to make copies of the maps for my staff,'

Major General Harkirat Singh, who commanded the 54 Division then, recalled during an interview with me in early 2000.[1] Even a decade later, Singh's imperial moustache trembled as he recalled the mission that scarred his otherwise brilliant career. 'Everybody did [their] own and we landed in what looked like the refugee camps I had seen in Chabua, Assam, when we were fighting the Chinese. Everybody was just being inducted; nobody knew anything,' Singh admitted.

Apart from having to cope with induction into a foreign territory, there was also a complete lack of understanding about the landscape and the forces at work there. 'I should have got a proper intelligence summary saying this is the terrain and this is the enemy strength. I should have been given proper operational instruction . . . A proper overseas [chain of] command should have been formed. Nothing was done. The air force commanded its own troops, the army its own and the navy its own. Who was left to coordinate? Nobody,' the major general recalled.

The overall commander of the IPKF, Lieutenant General Depinder Singh, had similar observations. 'I wish I could write that, as I flew into Palaly, I had a clear vision of how the job in hand had to be tackled. Alas, quite the contrary; the operational instruction issued to me was delightfully vague, merely directing me to implement the accord,' Singh wrote in his book, *Indian Peace Keeping Force in Sri Lanka*.[2]

In Colombo, playing the commanding role in India's Sri Lanka policy was career diplomat Jyotindra Nath Dixit, who would go on to become the national security advisor in 2004, a year before his death. When I met him ten years after IPKF's humiliation, Dixit largely blamed Major General Harkirat Singh, but agreed with him about the lack of intelligence. '[Intelligence agencies] said these are boys who were trained by them from 1977 or whatever . . . All of them . . . all fifty different groups. LTTE, EPRLF [Eelam People's Revolutionary Liberation Front], all sorts. They said these are our boys, we know them very well, they owe so much to us, so once they say yes, they will not fight us. That was their judgement,' Dixit told me.

Under Rajiv Gandhi, the Indian security establishment reflected the prime minister's political dominance in India: it was repeatedly willing to take risks, even the occasional military adventurism. Kashmir, Punjab and the violence in the Northeast did not force a mature analysis within the system. As India began emerging as a regional security power, I believe, many decisions were made to align with the political interests of the young and powerful prime minister—whether it be the rigging of the J&K elections in 1987 or the machinations in Punjab (by first Indira and then Rajiv). The Indian establishment had also adopted the strategy of propping up armed groups to check majoritarian hegemony or uncomfortable political realities. They would prop up a virulent insurgent in Punjab, or rush troops in to help Sri Lankan Tamil militants, and if the situation got out of hand, use military power to handle it. These were not the balanced, professional decisions of a mature security establishment.

The situation as it unfolded after the IPKF landed showed how little the security and intelligence networks had studied Sri Lankan Tamils—especially the LTTE—or their history. This meant that the force was not ready for the wave of suicide bombings and other assaults that would lead to one of the Indian Army's worst military humiliations, and eventually to the assassination of Prime Minister Rajiv Gandhi.

The failure in Sri Lanka goes to the heart of my argument: that a security establishment without biases and dark corners, and with deep understanding of the situation on the ground is critical for a democracy. LTTE is an excellent case study for understanding modern terrorism, and for underlining the fact that violence by non-state actors is not the monopoly of any religion or region. To observers who had studied the culture, such as historian Rajan Gurukkal, a pre-eminent expert on south Indian history, the Sri Lankan militancy rekindled the romance of the Heroic Age among the Tamils. 'In every civilization, there is a phase called the heroic age. An archaic type of heroism is visible in advanced tribal societies [even today]. In some societies, these heroic values continue for a longer period, or the heroic age meets a natural death when advanced agricultural cultivation takes off,' Gurukkal told me when I met him in Thiruvananthapuram. India's most perfect form of heroism can be seen in early Dravidian culture, like in Greek culture, he said.

Modern literature on terrorism has not fully understood what led to the formation of the LTTE, which was dominated by Hindus but also included a fair number of Christians, and went on to become one of the deadliest terrorist groups in history, with a special unit for suicide attacks. Their men and women, cyanide capsules dangling from their necks, could easily have been warriors walking out of south Indian folk traditions.

The strife had stoked to life a long historical tradition of the Heroic Age in Tamil culture, wherein the ultimate responsibility of a young person was to sacrifice their body in the service of their society. This archaic heroism continues to be celebrated through Tamil literary texts, stone memorials for heroes and numerous other ways.

LTTE cadres, therefore, were not only committed to their freedom and their leader, but also went on to rewrite modern warfare through the abundant use of their own bodies as weapons.

Within days of the IPKF's deployment, the LTTE had turned on the Indian military. In three years, India lost close to 1,200 soldiers, with almost three times that number injured.[3] Over the years I have heard many in the intelligence, military and diplomatic corps, who had closely interacted with the LTTE earlier, complaining furiously that their 'own boys' turned on them. This was not supposed to be like the Afghan mujahideen or Islamic terrorists whose twisted religious beliefs celebrated martyrdom, they believed. The Tamils were supposed to be a benign militant group that checked the majoritarianism of the Sinhalese and protected their own interests. The LTTE's ferocity, especially its ability to recruit hundreds of suicide bombers, however, was proof that offering the body as a weapon was a pan-religious reality among the Tamils of Sri Lanka.

This tendency to misinterpret religious belief to justify violence and terrorism is not unique to any culture, community or religion, nor are suicide squads. In the Bible, Samson is assisted by divine intervention to bring down the supporting pillars of a temple on the Philistines, killing himself as well. In the Mahabharata, on the twelfth day of the great battle, Susharma—the king of Trigarta who had allied with the Kauravas—his brothers and a large number of their soldiers went through funeral ceremonies for themselves, declared themselves a suicide squad and went out to kill Arjuna. From the Jewish sect of Sicarii to the Hashishin among Ismaili Shia Muslims; from the Dutch who blew themselves up using gunpowder during the battle for Taiwan in 1661 to a farmer strapped with explosives in a New Zealand court at the beginning of the last century; from suicide attacks by Aceh's Muslims against the Dutch to the Japanese kamikaze pilots committed to giving up their lives during the Second World War—the history of suicide attacks is both secular and global.

As an unusual heat wave gripped Kerala just months after the devastating floods of 2018, Professor Rajan Gurukkal sat down with me in his office to give me a grand tour of history. He pointed out that among the reasons that forced a large migration of Tamils from India to Sri Lanka centuries ago were the repeated droughts in Ramanathapuram district, which separates the Palk Strait from the Gulf of Mannar, near Sri Lanka.

Among the many Tamil communities that live on the northern border between Tamil Nadu and Kerala, hero worship is a powerful reality even today, Gurukkal said. In the Heroic Age, each young man was considered a hero. In south India, this could be seen in early Dravidian culture among the Nair and Ezhava communities in northern Kerala, he said, explaining the hero culture thus: 'When the action happens, I have no idea about myself, except in terms of my use in the fight. There is no other interest, I have no relatives, no mother, no wife, no children; I don't think about anything else because I am a warrior. Till the last point of death, I am a fighter. I do not run away.' If a young man runs away from battle, his own mother would be ashamed of him, according to the region's oral literatures. To celebrate and maintain the hero cult, monuments and memorials are erected, and celebratory songs are penned.

The Indian establishment repeatedly ignores the fact that violence is secular. However, even most academic studies appear to have missed the fact that militancy, especially in its highest form of suicide attacks, has long been a tradition in the southern parts of India.

'I will make a statement to hand over arm[s] at the public meeting scheduled for the 4th August 1987 at 5 p.m. Thereafter, we will work out the modalities of handing over the arm[s].' LTTE supremo Velupillai Pirabakaran—his preferred spelling, but public literature uses Prabhakaran more often—signed the above note in English on 3 August 1987 and sent it to the IPKF commander. He signed off as the 'leader' of the Tigers. The two crucial missing 's' may have been due to the militant's weakness in English or an ominous sign of things to come. Pirabakaran symbolically led the surrender, and until 21 August, LTTE cadres laid down arms in batches before the IPKF.

The surrender was not a smooth exercise. India suspected the LTTE was only surrendering obsolete weapons, while Pirabakaran continued to be mercurial. The peace efforts in Sri Lanka always ran up against extremist positions—political opposition from Sinhalese groups, Buddhists monks who advocated a strong line against Tamil separatists, Indian Tamils who were not very impressed with New Delhi's line and, finally, the Tigers' supremo himself.

Within days, the LTTE stalled the surrender process by submitting alleged evidence that the R&AW, which had originally armed and trained them, was now equipping other Tamil groups. Intermittent violence between the LTTE and other Tamil militant groups also began.

On 11 September, the IPKF commander was called to Colombo for a meeting with Dixit and other diplomatic staff. Major General Singh claimed that he was told by Dixit that the Force's ultimate objective was to discredit the LTTE before the Tamil population, but not fully destroy them.[4] After this meeting, the fog of war descended on the Indian narrative. The narrative changes depending on who is telling the story. Did the high commissioner ask Harkirat Singh to kill Pirabakaran? Did he ask the army to discredit the Tigers? Or were Dixit and New Delhi, despite the Tamil group's strident stand, committed to peace in the island nation? These crucial questions have no definite answers even today.

The IPKF had also begun to get inputs that the LTTE and Sri Lankan security forces' collective anger against what they perceived as Indian hegemony brought them closer.[5] However, Colombo had a powerful group of politicians, led by Prime Minister Ranasinghe Premadasa and the minister for national security, Lalith Athulathmudali, who were publicly opposed to peace overtures with the Tamil group. Differences of opinion between India, the Sri Lankan government and the Tigers began to crop up on a number of issues.

All of this meant that peace was elusive.

On 15 September, Thileepan (born Rasaiah Parthipan), the leader of the LTTE's political wing, began a fast unto death to protest the Sri Lankan government's failure to fulfil its obligations under the Indo–Sri Lankan Accord. He accused India of not doing enough to implement it. After refusing food and water for almost twelve days, Thileepan died at the Kandaswamy temple in Nallur, Jaffna, on 26 September. As the twenty-three-year-old was breathing his last, Pirabakaran was on his way to meet Dixit. While the meeting between the two was underway in an IPKF post, a huge crowd of agitated Tamils assembled outside to protest Thileepan's death. After some persuasion, the crowd dispersed peacefully. Three cadres of the Tigers began a fast in Trincomalee, Batticaloa and Mulaitivu. With the efforts of the Indians and other intermediaries, the fast was called off on 29 September.

On 2 October—Mahatma Gandhi's birth anniversary and Dussehra fell on the same day that year—Major General Harkirat Singh and Pirabakaran were scheduled to meet in the evening to exchange festive-day greetings. That day would decisively alter the situation. A white van with red stripes halted near the town hall in Trincomalee, and the militants inside opened fire on an IPKF post, killing Sepoy Gorakh Ram of 26 Punjab and injuring another soldier. The Indian Army deduced that the killing was either by the Eelam People's Revolutionary Liberation Front or the Sri Lankan Home Guards, because the van used in the killing had earlier freely entered the secured Fort Frederick. The IPKF now filed a complaint with Sri Lankan Army officers about violation of the accord by their force.

A few hours after the meeting between Major General Singh and Pirabakaran came news that would transform the island's tenuous peace into bloody pandemonium. The Sri Lankan Navy detained seventeen LTTE cadres who were crossing over from Tamil Nadu to Sri Lanka in a boat. The government forces hurriedly shifted them to Colombo. They had recovered from the group a couple of weapons, and a revolver that had been gifted to Pirabakaran by his mother, and was therefore very special to him. Given IPKF's mandate under the bilateral agreement to separate the two warring factions, Harkirat Singh ordered the IPKF to surround the cadres at Palaly airport in Jaffna, so that the Sri Lankan troops would not be able to take them away. The seventeen cadres, including two of their area commanders, sat in a cabin at the airport, while the sixty Sri Lankan soldiers guarding them were surrounded by a much larger IPKF contingent, including a mechanised company and the 10th Battalion of the Parachute Regiment.

A day after the standoff, Dixit and Lt General Depinder Singh met the Sri Lankan president and other senior officials in Colombo to seek a diplomatic solution. But India was not banking on the negotiations alone. In the northeast, the IPKF was beefing up its deployment. The 10 Para took control of Trincomalee airport, while other units fanned out, intending to prevent Colombo from sending more forces into Trincomalee.

The Colombo meeting failed, and Sri Lankan authorities refused to release the apprehended cadres, and insisted on taking the Tigers to Colombo for investigations. The IPKF was ordered by headquarters to lift the blockade against local troops. On 5 October, as soon as it withdrew from the Palaly airport, government troops charged at the seventeen cadres. Each one of them consumed cyanide capsules in a last act of resistance.[6] The LTTE leaders who had visited the detained cadres may have handed over the capsules, according to Indian officials. Indian Army doctors stationed close by managed to revive five of them, but twelve died instantly. [7] Among the dead were two senior commanders—Kumarappa and Pulendran. Only a few days earlier, the IPKF had facilitated Kumarappa's wedding by flying in his fiancée from Batticaloa in a military helicopter.

Reacting to the mass suicide, the LTTE slaughtered over 200 Sinhalese residents, and over 10,000 were driven out of their homes in the northern and eastern parts. Three days later, it executed eight Sinhalese prisoners in its custody, and dropped their bodies outside Jaffna Fort, only a few feet away from an Indian military post.

Amidst the gathering storm, the Indian Army chief, General K. Sundarji, flew into Palaly. On 8 October, he handed over a bunch of pink papers to the senior generals, a summary of his recommendations to adopt hard action against the LTTE. The action plan had Rajiv Gandhi's approval, he said.[8] Both Major General Harkirat Singh and Lt General Depinder Singh told him it was not wise to enter into an all-out conflict with the LTTE immediately.[9] But the die was cast. It was time to go to war against their allies.

Two days later, it began to rain blood. Militants hijacked a jeep with five soldiers of 10 Para battalion in it and killed them. Four were killed and seven injured when a Central Reserve Police Force (CRPF) convoy was attacked. Militants fired mortars and automatic weapons at the headquarters of the 5th Battalion of the Madras Regiment, a military patrol returning to Jaffna Fort was fired upon, and the Dutch Fort in Jaffna came under mortar firing.

The IPKF drew up a plan for an offensive: capture LTTE television and radio stations; take control of their stronghold of Jaffna town; prevent more militants from reaching the stronghold; and clear out Jaffna suburbs and a few other key areas, including a couple of islands. The operations had to be carried out against the wisdom of all their training. The troops had no air cover, no artillery support and very limited operational freedom. They had come prepared to keep peace, not wage war.

Based on intelligence supplied by the Sri Lankan forces that Pirabakaran was at his headquarters in Kokkuvilon on the outskirts of Jaffna, the Indian military decided on a Special Forces-led operation. The football field of the Jaffna University campus was selected as the landing zone. Two units—10th Para Commando and 13th Sikh Light Infantry (LI)—would carry out the operations. They began around midnight on 11 October.

It was a flight into a death trap. The LTTE had been listening in on Indian communications and was ready for their arrival. As soon as the helicopters landed, they were subject to heavy firing. Only a total of 120 para commandos and just thirty of the intended 360 Sikh LI soldiers managed to land.

The remaining men could not be inducted because the helicopters had been severely damaged. Meanwhile, the thirty Sikh LI soldiers did not know that the others were not coming in. Their radio operator had been shot dead, and his radio set damaged. They had thus lost all contact with operational headquarters within minutes of landing.

The commandos spread out, took cover and carried on to their task: to raid LTTE headquarters. Major Birendra Singh, leading the 13th Sikh LI, did not join them because he had been instructed to wait for his battalion commander, who was advancing by land towards Jaffna at 3 a.m. The major and his twenty-nine soldiers ran out of ammunition by noon the next day. The three last survivors carried out a bayonet charge once their bullets were exhausted. Two of them died, one was injured and captured. Sepoy Gora Singh survived to tell the story of their horrors and bravery. The fight put up by the soldiers that day would rank as one of the finest battlefield moments in modern military history, but there was no one to celebrate their heroism, and no time to pause and ponder. The Indian military would soon be swamped.

The para commandos, meanwhile, moved towards their target. According to Lt General Depinder Singh, they captured a local Tamil along the way, and he offered to guide them. This youth then took the famed Special Forces on a wild goose chase before leading them into a trap. Over the next several hours, they were engaged in an intense firefight with the LTTE.

Indian Army formations—including three infantry brigades, mechanised infantry battalions and other support units—that moved towards Jaffna faced stiff resistance.[10] Every inch they cleared would be occupied by the Tigers in no time. Every now and then, groups of civilians would approach the troops on the pretext of submitting a memorandum, and once they were close enough, they would disperse as if on cue, and militants would appear from behind them to shoot at the soldiers. On a few occasions, soldiers who were leaving houses after searching them were shot down by women.

In Anai-Kottai, an Indian company ran into another ambush. Isolated, their ammunition almost exhausted, they were surrounded by a few hundred LTTE cadres, speaking in English over a megaphone, asking them to surrender. Captain Sunil Chandra, who led a small team that fought its way to bring ammunition to the besieged company, was killed sometime later. At Suthumalai, a platoon of soldiers had to wade through a marshy area in heavy rain, and hack rows of cacti to get to a bend in the road. As they emerged, the LTTE showered them with bullets.

On 21 October, around 11 a.m, helicopters and cannons of the Indian military fired at Jaffna Teaching Hospital, the premier healthcare institution in the peninsula. Over the next twenty-four hours, there was a bloodbath inside the hospital premises. Depinder Singh claims that his troops were attacked by LTTE cadres who had taken shelter in the hospital. Others called it a massacre by Indian troops. By the end of the firefight, almost seventy people, including doctors, nurses and patients, were dead. Indian troops were also accused of burning the bodies. This kind of publicity was the last thing that the soldiers, caught as they were in a bizarre battle, needed.

The Indian security establishment and political leadership lay, it would appear, thoroughly exposed. To me, the country's forces looked utterly unprofessional, and its intelligence questionable. A group of determined militants on a small island were teaching it to pay closer attention to history and not be blindsided by biases. It was not a lesson that the Indian establishment would absorb, however.

The IPKF finally captured Jaffna on 28 November, after six weeks of fighting. In that time, 319 Indians were killed, while 1,039 were injured. According to the Indian Army, the LTTE lost 1,100 cadres.[11]

But the fight was not over yet. The LTTE had merely withdrawn into the nearby jungles.

Tamil disquiet has a long history in Sri Lanka. The seeds of the community's nationalism were sown in the early nineteenth century, by the Tamil Hindu backlash against Protestant missionaries. It took on a more cohesive form after Sri Lanka's independence in 1948, when the country began to adopt a more aggressive majoritarianism, beginning with the declaration of Sinhala as the only official language. Discriminatory policies against Tamils in government jobs and higher education in the 1970s pushed Tamil nationalism towards a more virulent form.

As the situation worsened, Prime Minister Indira Gandhi's government decided to provide tacit support to Tamil militancy. Was the government arming Tamils to check the majoritarianism of the Sinhala-controlled government, or was it an effort to create a Tamil homeland in Sri Lanka? Its goals were not well calibrated, and there is still no reliable evidence on the strategy. From 1980–81 on, India began providing Tamil activists with logistical and military assistance through R&AW. In 1983, the intelligence wing established almost three dozen training camps across India, from Chakrata in Dehradun to Sirumalai in Tamil Nadu. Most reliable estimates suggest that almost 500 LTTE core members, including its entire leadership and about a hundred women militants, were trained in India.

Over the years, much credible evidence has emerged on India's policy of arming the LTTE. The Jain Commission, which enquired into the assassination of Rajiv Gandhi, recorded this, so have several Indian officials over the years.[12] Writers like Neena Gopal have drawn parallels between the situation in Bangladesh and Sri Lanka.[13] From both the countries, thousands of refugees were flowing into India, and in both countries, India propped up armed movements as a strategy. There were at least thirty-eight militant groups fighting for the establishment of Eelam, an independent Tamil nation, but by the mid-1980s, only two were active—LTTE and EROS (Eelam Revolutionary Organisation of Students). Their ranks began to swell as Colombo failed to fulfil the promises made to moderate democratic Tamil factions. According to Dixit, by the end of 1986, between 15,000 and 17,000 armed youth were operating in the Tamil-dominated areas of Sri Lanka.

A few months after he swept to power in 1985, Rajiv Gandhi decided to end all assistance to Tamil militants. He wanted to transform New Delhi's role from a partisan player to that of a mediator. This notwithstanding, by the end of 1986, the LTTE's publicity material spoke of a 'Greater Tamil Eelam', which included Tamil Nadu, the northeastern provinces of Sri Lanka and the Tamil population areas of Southeast Asia and Mauritius, echoing the glorious past of the Chola dynasty. The group began to send its cadres to train with the Hamas and other Palestinian groups in Libya, Lebanon and Syria. At one point of time, the LTTE even had its cadres training with the Israeli Mossad in the same facility where Sri Lankan soldiers were also training.

The turning point in the clashes between Sri Lankan forces and the LTTE came in 1983, when the latter killed thirteen soldiers. The incident sparked off the Black July riots in which about 400 Tamils were killed. The Sri Lankan military too joined in the frenzy. In a *Sunday Times* report dated 27 January 1985, veteran journalist Mary Anne Weaver wrote about a massacre in Tamil-dominated Mannar after an army jeep hit a landmine, killing a soldier and injuring three others: 'Thirty soldiers then went on a six-hour rampage around Mannar. They attacked the central hospital, stopped vehicles and shot the occupants dead on the spot. They lined up 15 employees of a post office and killed eight. They opened fire on peasants in fields, attacked a convent and stripped nuns of watches, gold crucifixes and chains. At the end, nearly 150 people lay dead; 20 are still missing, mostly young male Tamils taken to army camps.'[14]

The violence intensified with each passing day. On 14 May 1985, Marcelline Fiyuslas, aka Lt Col Victor, a Catholic from Mannar region, led an LTTE operation outside Tamil territories for the first time. His group hijacked a bus, entered the historic city of Anuradhapura and opened indiscriminate fire on people at the main bus station. They then drove to the Sri Maha Bodhi shrine, and killed monks, nuns and civilians worshipping there, before driving to the Wilpattu National Park and killing tourists.[15] By the end of the day, 146 people had been slaughtered.

As violence peaked, the Rajiv Gandhi government stepped up its mediatory efforts, despatching senior officials to Colombo, and appointing J.N. Dixit as the new high commissioner to Sri Lanka. Meanwhile, the Sri Lankan government was gathering support and logistics from Pakistan, Israel, South Africa and other countries. In early 1987, it launched Operation Liberation in the Jaffna Peninsula, and on the night of 25 May, a division strength of Sri Lankan forces moved into the town, with President Jayewardene's order to 'raze Jaffna to the ground, burn the town and then rebuild it'. Soon, Jaffna was under siege.

On 2 June, the Indian government decided to send essential supplies to Jaffna. Nineteen Indian fishing boats carrying forty-odd tons of pulses, rice, kerosene, bread, salt, vegetables and other essentials were nearing Jaffna when the Sri Lankan Navy blocked them. The Indian boats quietly withdrew. Two days later, India launched Operation Poomalai from three air force bases in south India. An AN-32 transport aircraft accompanied by four Mirage fighters took off for Sri Lanka to drop twenty-five tons of essential supplies to the Tamils. The airdrop put an end to the Sri Lankan military operations, and it agreed to allow relief supplies via sea. But the period also saw a complete freeze in contact between Indian and Lankan authorities.

By the end of June, the LTTE began sending informal messages to the Indians that they would be willing to accept a compromise if the agreement was drawn up with a guarantee from the Government of India. As New Delhi reached out to Colombo with this missive, the LTTE also sent out one of its own—both a message and a foretelling.

On 5 July, Vallipuram Vasanthan, aka Captain Miller, drove a truck filled with explosives into Nelliady Madhya Maha Vidyalayam, a school that the Sri Lankan Army had turned into a military base only a few weeks earlier. By many accounts, Miller was actually tied to the vehicle to ensure that the truck bomb went off without any glitch and LTTE cadres following the truck could quickly capture the school. Captain Miller had revived a long-forgotten cultural tradition—of young men volunteering to die for a cause. He was the first in a wave of suicide warriors that the LTTE sent out across the subcontinent to assassinate political leaders such as Rajiv Gandhi and carry out massive attacks in crowded places, creating a new template for terrorism in modern history. Vasanthan's face was put on the insignia of the Black Tigers, the suicide squad of LTTE. Since then, 5 July has been commemorated across the Tamil diaspora as the Black Tigers Day (Karumpuli Naal), and a shrine was erected in the school with his statue.

Over the years, the Tigers created a broad spectrum of commemorative features to celebrate their martyrs: from organising

Maaveerar Naal (Great Heroes' Day) to Black Tigers Day, from creating well-maintained cemeteries (thuyilumillam)—at least twenty-seven by dependable counts—to erecting headstones. In doing so, the LTTE and the larger Tamil diaspora were borrowing from a long tradition of celebrating fallen heroes. With a number of Christians in its ranks, the LTTE was a secular organisation. The establishment of cemeteries was likely to have been a combination of both Christian traditions and old south Indian traditions of 'hero stones' in memory of fallen heroes.

Academic writings and other reports from Sri Lanka estimate that a considerable section of the Christian leadership among the Tamils were LTTE supporters. In 1995, when the Sri Lankan military captured Jaffna, Father S.J. Emmanuel, vicar general of the Jaffna Catholic Diocese, was reported as saying: 'They [LTTE] are the children of the Tamil people, the sons and daughters of Tamil soil. They cannot be isolated and separated from the Tamil masses.'[16] According to J.N. Dixit, too, Tamil Christian priests were overwhelmingly in favour of the LTTE.

As the Sri Lankan military smashed into Tamil areas towards the end of the insurgency, one of the first actions it took was to destroy these cemeteries and headstones. In many instances, military camps were set up on top of the cemeteries. By 2016–17, however, reports showed that the locals were restoring these spots to their venerated status. In a set of poignant photographs from Kanagapuram in Kilinochchi, locals assembled the broken headstones into a moving symbol of their memories. In 2017, hundreds assembled to commemorate Great Heroes' Day at the cemetery.

Across Karnataka and the border regions of Kerala and Tamil Nadu, hero stones have been erected for centuries. Over 2,650 such stones have been discovered in Karnataka.[17] There are several hundred stones in Tamil Nadu, and while the stones themselves are rare in Kerala, in Malayali history and culture, there are many narratives about suicide squads. On the banks of the Bharathapuzha river in northern Kerala, for instance, a festival called Mamankam, held every twelve years, turned into an annual stage show for suicide squads ('chavers' in Malayalam). Fascinating though it is, Mamankam is also a chilling narrative about the willingness to die as part of a cult of heroism.

The festival, dated to around 1000 CE, began as a trade fair in Tirunavaya, on the dry riverbed of Bharathapuzha, which flows from Tamil Nadu into northern Kerala. The festival took a chilling turn after the Samutiris, then the Hindu chiefs of Kozhikode, captured Tirunavaya, in present-day Malappuram district, from its original chieftains of Valluvanatu around 1480 CE. The Samutiris turned the festival into a show of their power and personally presided over the celebrations. In turn, the Valluvanatu chiefs began sending select teams of suicide warriors to assassinate the Samutiri. Members of a few select landed Nair families were chosen as the chavers, suicide warriors, who, Rajan Gurukkal said, would run through the security ring of the royal guards to reach the Samutiri. The chavers did not succeed in their assassination attempts, and their bodies were usually pushed into a pit by elephants. On one such attempt, the Samutiri suffered an injury to his temple, according to the local folklore. Despite the overwhelming odds, Mamankam after Mamankam, privileged youngsters went to the festival as chavers, never to return.

There are several other references in Tamil folklore to selfless warriors who gave up their lives for the greater good, and of fury and rage against inequity. One of the most celebrated Tamil epics, *Silappadikaram,* is about Kannagi's anger and revenge at the injustice meted out to her husband by the king. She tears off one of her breasts, and her fury sets the city of Madurai on fire.[18] That unbridled fury against injustice is deeply ingrained in the Tamil sentiment.

Another deployment of suicide attacks in recent Tamil history can be found in the story of Velu Nachiyar, the queen of Sivaganga, who fled her kingdom with her daughter after it was annexed by the Nawab of Arcot and the East India Company in 1772.[19] Building strategic alliances, including with Hyder Ali of Mysore, the queen launched a military operation to regain her kingdom. One of her key associates was Kuyili, a Dalit woman known for her unflinching loyalty. Kuyili and a small band of women fighters sneaked into the Sivaganga Fort on the tenth day of Navaratri, pretending to be devotees. As they approached the armoury, Kuyili doused herself in ghee and set herself on fire. Almost the entire armoury stock was destroyed, and the British had no chance against Velu Nachiyar, who reclaimed her kingdom.

'Martyrdom is not just an individual's courage, but also the celebration of the larger kinship's participation, their collective will. If the individual has a rethink, it cannot happen. It would be extremely shameful, and it won't then be limited to him. His own mother will tear out her own breasts out of shame,' said Gurukkal.

The LTTE was drawing from this old culture of celebrating suicide deaths. Starting in 1989, the group and its broad set of sympathisers around the world began to organise the Maaveerar Naal on 27 November, Lt Shankar's death anniversary. Every educational institution in Tamil areas, every village and even the Tamil diaspora participated in this celebration of their fallen heroes. At the culmination of a week-long event, Pirabakaran would deliver a speech, which began precisely at 6.05 p.m., the time when Lt Shankar died.

Tamil Christians also participated in the LTTE's celebration of martyrs, according to many analysts of the period. Starting in the early 1980s, Christian Tamil youth joined the LTTE in large numbers. US-based academic S. Ratnajeevan H. Hoole, who has been at the receiving end of the Tigers' ire, pointed out in a research paper in 1996 that Catholic priests in Tamil areas would urge the congregation from the pulpit to give a son to the LTTE, like God gave his only son Jesus to the world.[20] As the Tigers' influence began to rise in the northeast, so did the influence of pro-LTTE priests within the church. A fair number of Catholic Church and Church of south India priests in the northeast of the country were active propagandists for the LTTE, Hoole and others have pointed out.

Besides commemorative events and memorials, the Tigers regularly published glossy books with photographs of their martyrs. According to pro-LTTE writer Sachi Sri Kantha, in 2003, a memorial souvenir titled *Sooriya Puthalvargal* was published, its ninety-six pages detailing in Tamil the bravery of 240 Black Tigers, including some who were yet to carry out suicide attacks. 'These were the contemporary practitioners of altruistic suicidal act in the battleground of Ceylon, perfected by Guru Drona in the Battle of Kurushetra nearly 5,000 years ago,' Kantha wrote in June 2004.[21] 'All were superheroes of a higher order for Tamils like me. They belong to my extended family, and they are the real things, unlike the glib Hollywood generated entertainment icons like Rambo and Terminator.'

'The most difficult part of my entire command was managing the withdrawal of the IPKF. At one stage, we had 70,000 troops. We slowly brought them down to 50, 40, and then to 30,000. When you are on a narrow bridge head, with the LTTE all around, and you are getting no military assistance from the Sri Lankan army, and the LTTE free at that stage, the prime concern for me was the lives of my soldiers,' Lt Gen. A.S. Kalkat, who took over command of the IPKF from Lt Gen. Depinder Singh, told me.[22]

Ever since they landed in Sri Lanka, the Indian soldiers had found themselves in a difficult situation—neither of the two parties in the conflict seemed to be happy to have Big Brother around. The Indo–Sri Lanka Accord was the result of India's tough posturing, its willingness to stand guarantee for the LTTE and bring them to the table, and the commitment of the then Sri Lankan president J.R. Jayewardene. On the Sri Lankan side too there were dissensions, and many leaders did not approve of the agreement.[23] Portending things to come, on 30 July 1987, a day after the accord was signed and a few minutes after Indian Prime Minister Rajiv Gandhi ignored the advice of officials, including Dixit, to avoid physical proximity with Sri Lankan forces, and inspected a guard of honour, a naval rating reversed his rifle, held it by the barrel and swung it at Gandhi, injuring him.[24]

By the end of 1989, the LTTE and the Sri Lankan establishment had struck an informal understanding that they would both target the IPKF. The Lankan forces even equipped the LTTE in their common fight. Anti-Indian sentiments had been on the rise after the IPKF deployment, while for Pirabakaran, the force was now a sworn enemy.

Rajiv Gandhi lost the general elections in 1989 in the aftermath of the Bofors scandal and other factors. His one-time trusted finance minister, V.P. Singh, was at the head of an Opposition coalition. Within weeks of becoming the prime minister, Singh ordered the withdrawal of the IPKF, bringing the thirty-two-month-long deployment to an end in March 1990.

On 24 March, the Sri Lankan Army organised a formal send-off for it. Mutual suspicion hung in the air even as the country's foreign minister, chiefs and senior officers of the armed forces, and the media gathered. 'While we were pulling back, we had our party standing by on all sides to make sure that someone did not double-cross or conspire against our soldiers. We had even helicopters standing by to extricate,' General Kalkat said.

Back home, there was to be no succour. 'The humiliation was not in Sri Lanka, because there was no humiliation [there]. The humiliation came when we came back to India. The question people asked was, why did we go there, what were you doing there? And the main thing was the so-called boycott of IPKF soldiers when they arrived at Madras port. I think that was a needless act. It was no good. I think the DMK [then in power in Tamil Nadu] was the one,' Kalkat said.

In my assessment, the Indian security establishment had also failed to anticipate how the Tigers were perceived among Tamil society at large. For many, it was no rogue militant group, but a group of freedom fighters, nurtured, funded and politically supported by them. Among the diaspora, the LTTE resurrected a certain 'continuation of old anthropologic values, of which kinship of a wide network is key', Rajan Gurukkal pointed out.

The last shots of the civil war were fired around 9.30 a.m. on 19 May 2009. Sergeant Muthu Banda radioed his commanding officer, Colonel G.V. Ravipriya, that he had spotted among the mangroves of Nandikadal a body that looked like that of the LTTE chief. There were five other bodies around him, which the Sri Lankan military believed were of his bodyguards. Many dispute the official claims, as the end of the Tigers came at a time of intense human rights violations by the state, with the silent blessings of a large section of the international community, including India.

In over three decades of its armed struggle, the LTTE staged, by many yardsticks, an unparalleled level of violence by a non-state actor. It is the only terrorist group to assassinate heads of two different nations—Rajiv Gandhi of India and Ranasinghe Premadasa, then president of Sri Lanka. The Tigers also assassinated one presidential candidate, seven cabinet ministers, thirty-seven members of Parliament, and several dozen other politicians. It produced almost 400 suicide bombers, with hundreds more waiting in the wings. Cyanide capsules hung as medals of honour around the necks of many cadres.

However, the biggest differentiator of the Tigers was their ability to generate so many suicide bombers. Since suicide terrorism reappeared in Lebanon in the 1980s and through recent history, including Al Qaeda's 9/11 attack, the LTTE has been the most prolific producer of suicide terrorists. There may not be another group in human history that inspired so many men and women to give up their lives, certainly not from a country as small as Sri Lanka. The Indian establishment had not anticipated this.

Unprofessional and secretive security establishments can be a threat to evolving democracies like ours. It might seem that India is safe from military coups and the subversion of governance, but there is enough evidence in these pages and elsewhere to show that the dark forces within our agencies need to be reined in. There is no other security establishment in the world that has tackled such a variety of non-state actors—Northeastern insurgents, many of them devout Christians; Islamist terrorists with a warped sense of justice; Hindu terrorists inspired by communal hatred; caste groups that butcher others; and secular groups such as Maoists that fight for other reasons. No other security establishment in the world has sacrificed so many of its men and women to terrorism. India has lost over 34,000 police personnel, mostly sacrificed in fighting insurgencies of various kinds;[25] it has the world's highest number of war widows at over 25,000, most of them victims of internal strife.[26]

The sheer diversity of the country's experience in dealing with unrest and militancy ought to have challenged the biases that have crept into the system. Yet, its presumption that terrorism is exclusive to Islam persists. Far too much of India's resources have been spent in tracking Islamic terrorism, while some of its deadliest enemies have been secular Maoists, Hindus or Christians.

The result of this bias is visible in administrative structures and practices. R&AW, for instance, does not employ Muslims in its ranks. The Special Protection Group (SPG) excludes Sikhs. The IB, it appears to me, is continuing to rely heavily on interrogation reports that have been repeatedly proven to have been manipulated by its own officers. The NIA, created after the Mumbai attacks of 2008, also appears to have sacrificed its professionalism at the altar of political masters.

8

The Militancy Enterprise

In the cold January of 1990, which changed everything, these two men were just thirteen years old.

On 19 January, Rahul Pandita returned home from a game of cricket to an early dinner, and soon fell asleep. 'I am in deep slumber. I can hear strange voices,' he recalled years later. His father woke him up saying, 'Something is happening.' Rahul could hear people talking loudly on the streets outside in Srinagar. 'Then a whistling sound could be heard. It was the sound of the mosque's loudspeaker. We heard it every day in the wee hours of the morning just before the muezzin broke into the azaan. But normally the whistle was short-lived; that night, it refused to stop. That night, the muezzin didn't call.' They heard a long drawl, and then the loudspeaker began to hiss 'Naara-e-taqbeer, Allah hu Akbar', Rahul has written in *Our Moon Has Blood Clots*, a powerful retelling of his life as a refugee in his own country.[1]

It was the cry for riots, Rahul says. 'Within a few minutes, battle cries flew at us from every direction. They rushed towards us like poison darts.' From mosques, songs eulogising the mujahideen of Afghanistan started playing, and then, according to Rahul, the crowd chanted slogans like, 'We want to be with Pakistan, without Pandit men but with their women.' Rahul's mother rushed to the kitchen, grabbed a long knife and returned. 'If they come, I will kill her,' she said, looking at his elder sister. 'And then I will kill myself.

And you see what you need to do,' the mother told the men in their family.

Over an hour's drive from Rahul's house, Basharat Peer was back home in Anantnag from his boarding school for the winter vacation. 'Today I fail to remember the beginnings. I fail to remember who told me about azadi, who told me about militants, who told me it had begun. I fail to remember the date, the place, the image that announced the war of my adolescence,' Basharat wrote in his award-winning book, *Curfewed Night*.[2] In the book, he remembers the long, sad night of 20 January—he may have got it wrong, it could be the next day—after BBC World Service announced that the CRPF had opened fire on a protesting crowd at Gawkadal Bridge in Srinagar, killing fifty people.[3]

'As the news sank in, we all wept,' Basharat says. Next morning, his village was still wrapped in mourning when a young man shouted: 'Hum kya chahte?' (What do we want?) People responded 'Azadi!' (Freedom!) It was the beginning of Kashmir's long, and continuing, struggle for freedom from India.

Rahul and his family spent a few more traumatic days in Srinagar before boarding a taxi for Jammu, abandoning their twenty-four-room house, and Basharat witnessed the brewing discontent as his friends, cousins and other acquaintances took up arms to stage a full-fledged militancy.

For the young, these memories could be defining. When I was about six years old, a small communal fight broke out in my village. My chaachan, father, tried to mediate, and was attacked. I have blurred, indistinct memories of the incident and what happened after—a distant noise, standing with our ammachi, mother, outside our house because it had been taken over by a group of people, sleeping on the cold cement floor of a relative's house. I also remember my grown-up cousins wandering around with knives a few days later. I wonder what the children on the other side were feeling. What were their nightmares like? Did they too fear a police crackdown or a violent retribution? Were they, like us, awake and tormented at night? The immense anger and bitterness that the incident left behind took years to overcome, and our village still struggles with the scars of that day. This is what riots and civil wars do. All it takes is a moment to spark off violence. It could be someone pursuing political gain, or there might be genuine grievances that burst out spontaneously. The scars and trauma of such communal conflagrations endure for generations.

Rahul and his family struggled to find normalcy in Jammu, shifting from a cheap hotel to a dharamsala, and then to a single-room accommodation, the enormity of what had happened to the Hindus in Kashmir Valley slowly sinking in. The growing anger against New Delhi among the Muslims of the Valley had blinded a section of them, turning them into communal killers, rapists and arsonists. Militants showed off the killings they carried out; young boys claimed to have emptied Hindu houses; and neighbours helped the militants hunt Hindu households. The rage of the disenfranchised lashed their neighbours. In my assessment, what appears to be the repeated political blunders, the alleged manipulation of elections and the Union's narrow interpretation of grievances probably contributed to creating a fertile ground for militancy in J&K.

Hundreds of Kashmiri boys and men crossed over to PoK for arms training. What was a trickle after the 1987 elections soon became a deluge. Automatic rifles and other sophisticated weapons poured into the Valley. Over several weeks that winter of 1990, thousands of families, mostly Hindus, fled Kashmir—the official count put the number at around 62,000 families, numbering anywhere between 300,000 to 600,000 people.[4] The scenic valley was now a battlefield. Both Basharat and Rahul would find their lives disrupted forever. However, they were luckier than most. Many of their childhood companions, like Rahul's cousin Ravi or friend Latif, or Basharat's cousin Tariq, died as the insurgency burst out in the early 1990s.

Across the border, the Pakistani establishment was waiting, both to exact revenge for past humiliations and to reclaim Kashmir, ready with the experience of a decade of running the world's most ferocious and most expensive insurgency. What the ISI had just accomplished in the Afghan war had no parallels in modern history: coordinating an operation involving several global powers, who provided the resources to train men to fight the Soviet Union troops in Afghanistan. The ISI ran the operations of the war, from collecting money and arms from the US, the UK, Saudi Arabia and others to training militants and even coordinating their operations. It was touted as a Holy War, and brought together thousands of Islamic fighters—mujahideen, soldiers of God—from around the world, among them Osama bin Laden. These fighters rushed to Pakistan, and from its training camps crossed the Durand Line into the Afghan battlefield. Praising Allah, believing in post-death felicitations and privileges, these mujahideen fought a ferocious battle against one of the world's most powerful militaries. In the process, the Pakistani state learnt an important lesson: that insurgency was profitable business. Foreign donors were pouring billions of dollars into the country, with limited audit or accountability. Terrorism was good business if one could stomach a bit of anarchy, which Pakistan had enough experience with.

Brigadier Mohammad Yousaf was commanding an infantry brigade when he was summoned to the ISI to take over its Afghan Bureau in 1983. By then, the ISI had already been involved for four years with the mujahideen resistance, which began to take organised shape in 1979, after the USSR sent in over 100,000 soldiers in a brutal crackdown in favour of Kabul's pro-Soviet regime. From 1983 to 1987, Brigadier Yousaf ran a team of ISI operatives—sixty officers and 300 senior soldiers. 'During my four years, some 80,000 Mujahideen were trained; hundreds of thousands of tons of arms and ammunition were distributed, several billion dollars were spent on this immense logistic exercise and ISI teams regularly entered Afghanistan alongside the Mujahideen,' Yousaf admitted in his book, *The Bear Trap*,[5] co-authored with retired military officer and writer Mark Adkin. It remains the most authentic account of the Afghan operations to emerge from within the ISI.

In April 1988, when Rawalpindi was rocked by a massive explosion at the Ojhri Camp, which held the entire military stock for the Afghan operations, Brigadier Yousaf says an estimated 10,000 tonnes went up in flames, including 30,000 rockets and numerous Stinger missiles.

The Soviet Union, with its state-controlled economy in a shambles, continued to lose face and men in Afghanistan, and decided to withdraw its troops in 1988. When the Soviet troops marched in, Afghanistan's population was some fifteen million; by the time they left, it had shrunk to eight million,[6] and over five million had been driven out as refugees.[7] A CIA assessment said the ISI-led operation resulted in over 10,000 Soviet military deaths and a total casualty of about 35,000 among the Soviet troops.[8] Over a million civilians had died in the conflict, besides 90,000 mujahideen.[9] The communist empire collapsed soon after the Soviet withdrawal—the Berlin Wall came down, East European despots were thrown out and the Soviet Union itself disintegrated. On the other side were the mujahideen, and they had tasted blood. They needed a new battlefield.

The ISI too was now ready to turn its full attention to Kashmir. Its Directorate S—in charge of external operations in both Afghanistan and Kashmir—inducted thousands of new officers. Most of the Directorate S staff were former members of the army's SSG,[10] which had been created and trained with American assistance. 'Black Label sipping Pakistani generals with London flats and daughters in Ivy League campuses had been managing jihadi guerrilla campaigns against India and in Afghanistan for two decades,' noted Steve Coll,[11] veteran US journalist who has written some of the most authoritative books on terrorism in South Asia, especially on the Al Qaeda and ISI. According to Coll's estimates, the ISI had 25,000 staff.[12] In comparison, despite being more than four times the size of Pakistan, India's largest agency, the IB, according to my contacts, has about

20,000 personnel. The ISI is led by senior officers drawn from the three military arms—and they serve at the intelligence agency for two to four years on an average—as well as a large number of military officers who may have missed their promotions and an equally large number of civilian staff. Besides, there are hundreds of freelance agents.

While India has a massive security presence in the Valley, if they trust you, many Kashmiris will tell you that the ISI is the most powerful, if invisible, organisation there. This, in spite of the fact that the ISI does not have a physical office or formal set-up in the area. It is easy to assign it the blame, and call it an evil empire with immense financial clout. The ISI's influence does, after all, show up repeatedly, and often violently. However, what also needs close scrutiny is how the Indian establishment has repeatedly, and mostly violently, pushed the average Kashmiri away from the idea of India. And also how certain sections of it have operated below the democratic radar.

Among the many challenges to India's democracy, the rise of its security establishment is the least examined. While Indian readers are familiar with the way the security structures in neighbouring countries, such as Pakistan, Bangladesh, Myanmar and Sri Lanka, went about demolishing their own democracies, the monster taking shape within has largely gone unnoticed. Nurtured in the turmoil of Kashmir, Punjab, the Northeast and Maoist-affected regions, it would soon spread to the rest of the country.

January 1990, which transformed the lives of both Basharat and Rahul, had been in the making since the 1987 elections. However, neither the political leadership nor the security establishment was looking at the many auguries that it needed to course-correct urgently—the eerie silence that enveloped the Valley immediately after the elections, the people who travelled across the border to take up arms, the lessons from Pakistan's securitised state, the collapse of the Soviet Union, the recent humiliation in Sri Lanka, and scores of other signs.

The V.P. Singh-led coalition government was sworn in at the Centre on 2 December 1989. The new prime minister appointed Mufti Mohammad Sayeed as the home minister, the first Kashmiri Muslim to hold the post. Six days later, on Friday, 8 December, Rubaiya Sayeed, a medical intern at the Lal Ded Memorial Hospital in Srinagar, boarded a minibus on her way home, which was in Nowgam, less than ten kilometres away. This was her routine, and everything appeared normal, from the freezing winter chill to the uncanny stillness of the Valley. When two men boarded the bus in Ram Bagh, nobody noticed. As the bus reached Bagat Kanipora, less than a kilometre from her home, three men sprang up. They pointed guns at Rubaiya Sayeed, forced her out of the bus, pushed her into a blue Maruti car and drove off. Her father was in Delhi, settling into his new job.

The abduction was conducted by JKLF militants, of which the former polling agent Yasin Malik was now a leader, and it demanded the release of several militants from jails in exchange for her release. Over the next 120 hours, Mufti Mohammad Sayeed reacted as an anxious father rather than the home minister, something he would regret later.[13] The Union government pushed for his daughter's safety above all else, even as Chief Minister Farooq Abdullah argued against capitulation. Finally, five militants were released on 13 December.

Rubaiya was home safe, and the Valley revelled in the victory of the militants. If the Indian government could be brought to its knees so easily, then full freedom for Kashmir was achievable, they argued. On the streets, hundreds of thousands carried placards with slogans like 'Jo kare khuda ka khauf, uthale Kalashnikov' (All god-fearing men, pick up the gun). Masked militants now roamed the streets, hundreds crossed over into Pakistan and killings became routine in the Valley.

Jagmohan Malhotra was rushed in from Delhi as governor. As a career bureaucrat who was part of the Gandhi family coterie, he had played a key role in the national capital during the Emergency, and had been J&K governor between 1984 and 1989. Jagmohan was perceived in the Valley as a pro-Hindu administrator. Protesting his appointment, Farooq Abdullah resigned and took a flight out to London. On the morning of 19 January 1990, Jagmohan flew in to Jammu in a small BSF aircraft for his second stint as governor. Meanwhile, security forces began a violent crackdown in Srinagar, going from house to house, dragging out men, humiliating women.

Late on the evening of 20 January, when Rahul and his family were frozen in fear and Muslim residents were agitated by the excesses of security forces, the state-run Doordarshan telecasted a special programme on the revolt in Azerbaijan and the Romanian Liberation, adding fuel to the fire in the Kashmir Valley. The next morning, crowds took to the streets, burning down public buildings, among them the State Industrial Development Complex office compound, Women's Polytechnic and Mehjoor Bridge. The security forces responded with ruthlessness. The death toll due to CRPF firing at Gawkadal Bridge was officially twenty-one, and then went up to fifty. But some reliable estimates have put it at around 160.[14] This was the massacre that Basharat and his family were hearing about on the radio in the evening.

A vicious cycle had begun. India had handed over the responsibility of dealing with its gravest challenge thus far to Jagmohan, a civil servant whose impartiality a majority of the locals did not trust. Jagmohan's own career captures the essence of my argument: that members of the security and permanent executives who are willing to do the bidding of their political masters thrive, despite the gravest allegations. Jagmohan played a critical role in the notorious clean-up of Delhi during the Emergency, and he was indicted by the Shah Commission for excesses. However, none of it affected his career. In 1990, when he arrived in J&K for a second stint, it was in the thick fog of war in the Valley. Many suspected that Jagmohan may have played a role in the exodus of Hindus, but there has been no proof of it. However, as soon as he arrived, the number of violent crackdowns, firings on protestors and search operations intensified.[15]

Though primarily targeting Hindus and the Indian security forces, the militants also hunted down intellectuals sympathetic to the Indian state. As for the security forces, in their hunt for militants, they were brutal to ordinary Kashmiris.

It would appear that neither the tottering coalition government nor the security establishment had realised the true ramifications of acceding to the militants' demands after they kidnapped Rubaiya Sayeed. They wanted to forget the incident like it were only a nightmare, but would not be able to. Without realising it, they had created a new template for insurgency in India: kidnap someone important and the government will bend. Kidnappings became routine in Kashmir.

A militant group kidnapped Tassaduq Ahmed Dev, brother-in-law of senior Congress leader Ghulam Nabi Azad, in September 1991, and the government released three militants to secure his freedom. Another militant was released to secure the freedom of Nahida Soz, daughter of former Union minister Saifuddin Soz, after she was kidnapped by the JKLF. When Indian Oil Corporation official K. Doraiswamy was abducted, the government released six militants to secure his freedom. Among those released was the militant who had been involved a few months earlier in the kidnapping and murder of the Kashmir University vice chancellor, Mushir-ul-Haq, and the general manager of HMT, H.L. Khera. When the son of former J&K minister G.M. Mir Lasjan was kidnapped, the government released seven more militants. The militants had figured out that India was a weak state with inefficient administrative mechanisms in Kashmir. If there had been one kidnapping in 1989, at least 169 abductions were reported in 1990, and by 1993, the number was up to 349.

In the second week of February 1994, the security forces intercepted an autorickshaw in Khanabal, discovering two unlikely passengers—Maulana Masood Azhar, the Pakistani general secretary of the Harkat-ul-Ansar, a militant group primarily comprising

Afghan war veterans, and Sajjad Afghani, one of the group's senior-most commanders, with experience in the Afghan battlefield and now leading the Kashmir operations. Azhar was in the Valley to smoothen out a factional feud within the terrorist group.

But unlike other militants, he had not scaled the Pir Panjal ranges to arrive there. He flew in via Dhaka to the Indira Gandhi International Airport in New Delhi on a Portuguese passport that had been issued to a Gujarat-born man named Wali Adam Issa. Azhar checked in at the capital's premier Ashoka Hotel, and then travelled to Srinagar. Violent jihad, now a multi-layered global operation, was flush with funds and ambitious targets. Azhar had been globetrotting for some time, spreading the message of violence to the rest of the world, especially since the Afghan operations were winding up. Like many other mujahideen from the Afghan battlefield, he believed that the world was just years away from turning into a single Ummah, a homeland of Islam. One week, he was fundraising in Abu Dhabi and Saudi Arabia; the next, he was in the UK, giving speeches to youngsters and raising money; and the week after, he was in Somalia, advising local terrorists.[16]

After February 1994, ensuring Masood Azhar's freedom became a key Harkat-ul-Ansar agenda, one they would not give up on for the next six years. A few months after he was arrested, kidnappings by militants moved out of Kashmir and into the Indian mainland. In New Delhi, a suave young man, calling himself Rohit Sharma, befriended four foreigners and tricked them into visiting a village that he claimed had been bequeathed to him by a recently deceased uncle. Three of them, all British citizens, were taken to a village near Saharanpur, less than 200 kilometres from the national capital, and kept chained there. The fourth, an American, was held captive in a hideout near Ghaziabad. Then 'Rohit Sharma' sent a note to both BBC and Voice of America offices in New Delhi, demanding the release of ten militants, including Masood Azhar. This was October 1994. The kidnapping was detected accidentally, and for some time, the police had no clue who the kidnapper was. It is not clear how his identity was finally revealed, but the Uttar Pradesh police soon learnt that he was Ahmed Omar Saeed Sheikh, a London School of Economics dropout, son of a wealthy Pakistani family in the UK, and a fanatical member of the Harkat-ul-Ansar. Sheikh was desperate to free his mentor Masood Azhar and spirit him out of India. The young man spent three years in Meerut District Jail, before he was shifted to Tihar Jail in the national capital.

A few months after Sheikh's kidnapping drama, a previously unknown terror group called Al-Faran kidnapped six Western trekkers—two Americans, two Britons, a German and a Norwegian. One American escaped, the Norwegian's body was found with head severed, and there has been no trace of the other four.[17] The terror group's demand was the release of a group of militants, with Azhar atop the list. For once, the government refused to give in to their demand. In hindsight, one wonders if the government's tough position was because those kidnapped were foreigners, and whether there was a presumption that global pressure would get the hostages freed. The Al-Faran kidnapping was not the end of Masood Azhar's tryst with India—just as the world was on the brink of a new millennium, the scale of terror would get much larger.

The way I see it, a confusion had crept into the Indian security establishment in the 1990s. Its repeated humiliation as well as the hostility of locals in the Kashmir Valley appears to have dragged it down a rabbit hole, where repeated human rights violations, abductions, rapes and other criminal acts were perceived to be becoming ever more ordinary. Indian security forces were repeatedly failing the test of the Constitution. While it is true that the forces were operating in difficult circumstances, it is also a fact that they were not a ragtag army of militants, but the security arm of a democratic republic. The failures taught Indian agencies several important lessons, but they also took away some truly wrong ones.

After the Gawkadal Bridge massacre, the police filed FIR No. 3/90 at the Kralkhud station against the riotous mob. There was no mention of the massacre by the CRPF. Even today, the case has not found judicial closure.[18] It was the beginning of a pattern in Kashmir. The situation is difficult: if you miss a militant, he could take you down; if you do not stop a violent crowd, it could lynch you. However, there can be no justification for ignoring the rule of law, and certainly not for the perpetration of criminal acts or for the lack of accountability. It is in the most extreme circumstances that a democracy and its institutions are tested, and Kashmir was one such. Delhi failed the test repeatedly, in my opinion, with disastrous consequences for democracy itself. When a democratic nation fails, its dark corners are strengthened.

In February 1991, Indian Army troops stormed into the twin villages of Kunan and Poshpora outside the town of Kupwara, forced the men out of all the homes and confined them in two houses, and then allegedly went about raping and assaulting women and children.[19] There have been several enquiries, claims and counterclaims, but the survivors of the atrocity are yet to find justice.

The intense conflict of the 1990s in Kashmir, with heavy casualties on both sides, as well as gross human rights violations, left a lasting impact on Indian security forces. I believe that besides the hollowing out of their democratic credentials, communal biases too began to visibly creep into the system. There is no date that can be put to when it started, or how it progressed, but a decade into the fight in Kashmir, certain arms of the Indian security establishment were almost entirely free of accountability and operating in a sinister manner. This frightening development did not receive public scrutiny nor was it subject to legislative debates. Over time, it is my assessment that, these sections of the establishment began to play a powerful role in shaping public debates and political positions, threatening the very edifice of democracy.

As Kashmir was erupting, the world was entering a new order. On 9 November 1989, in the most visible thawing of the Cold War, the

Berlin Wall came down. It was history's greatest street party. More than two million East Germans flooded into West Germany during the weekend that followed. The modern-day empire that was the Union of Soviet Socialist Republics (USSR), seven times larger than India, with eleven time zones, was in ruins. And in Kabul, a mother and her two daughters took a secret flight out to New Delhi, while her husband stayed back.

Afghanistan president, Najibullah, the Butcher of Kabul to many, was the Soviet-backed president of Afghanistan from 1986 until the turmoil reached his palace in 1992. On 17 April, at around 3 a.m., Najibullah boarded an armed convoy from his presidential palace to the Kabul airport. He was to take a chartered aircraft headed for India, which had offered him asylum, and join his wife and two daughters. The airport was under the control of Abdul Rashid Dostum, an Afghan Uzbek, who had raised a militia with active support from the president to take on the mujahideen fighters. But Najibullah was in for a nasty surprise. Dostum's people would not let him enter the airport where, in the chartered aircraft meant for Najibullah, sat Behon Sevan, a senior UN official in Kabul who would accompany the Afghan president. Trapped in the city that he once ruled, Najibullah was forced to seek asylum in Kabul's UN compound, from where the Taliban fighters dragged him and his brother out in 1996, and strung them from a traffic tower outside the presidential palace. His wife and two daughters would spend years in silence in a stately mansion not very far from the Indian Parliament.

With Najibullah seeking asylum in the UN compound, the mujahideen had finally won after fourteen years of fighting. A transition government, supported by various mujahideen groups, took over the state. Burhanuddin Rabbani became the president of Afghanistan, but the peace was short-lived. Rabbani would soon go back on his power-sharing commitment, and Gulbuddin Hekmatyar's powerful mujahideen group, called the Islamic Party (Hizb-e-Islami), surrounded Kabul, leading to fresh unrest. For the mujahideen and the ISI, their big victory had made an impact on the world stage: they had forced out the Soviet troops and overthrown the pro-communist regime in Kabul. They needed a new destination, a new Islamic war. It was Kashmir that they set their sights on. Kashmiri separatists too eagerly welcomed the seasoned fighters from Afghanistan. They called them the 'mehmaan mujahideen', or guest fighters. Not only were Kashmir's amateur fighters getting the power and support of the battle-hardened foreigners, but their cause was finally global.

In September 1992, the Kashmiri newspaper *Afaq* interviewed a group of Afghani veterans. One of them, Akbar Qureshi, said that the jihad in Kashmir would be harder than that in Afghanistan, but they would win. Among those featured was Ibne Masood, a Sudanese civil engineer specialising in improvised explosive devices, or IEDs, who was now with the Hizbul Mujahideen. Masood said that over 6,000 foreign militants were ready to come to Kashmir. The third militant featured was Abdul Rehman, member of a rich Bahrain family.

According to Indian estimates, the forces killed 536 local militants in 1990, and fourteen foreigners. By 2000, the number of foreigners killed, 870, was more than the local militants killed, 742. By the next year, the number of foreigners killed was 1,032 against 710 local militants. During 1991–94, the security forces arrested forty-nine Pakistani militants, and killed eighty in Kashmir. During this period, six Afghans were killed and eighty arrested. Also among the dead were an Egyptian, three Sudanese, one Lebanese, three Bahraini and two Saudi Arabians.

When I met Majid Dar in 2001, I asked him about the Afghan angle. Dar told me that he had been to Afghanistan two or three times, and had met Gulbuddin Hekmatyar, Rabbani and others. Some of the earliest Kashmiri militants too talk about having been to Afghanistan in 1989 and later, and a few of them were at the Jalalabad front with the mujahideen.[20]

I asked Majid Dar: 'Do you have any foreign-trained boys for making IEDs? I mean from Western universities etc.?'

'No. But we had a Sudanese boy—an engineer. His name was

Ibne Masood. He achieved martyrdom in Sopore, four or five years back. He was a chemical engineer, and he trained a lot of people,' Dar said.

Apart from fighters, a massive amount of money too flowed into Kashmir—from Pakistan, the expat Kashmiri community and the larger Muslim communities across the world. The ISI led these efforts, devising complex informal transaction routes, activating traditional hawala networks and even exploiting formal banking channels. The Indian investigation agencies did find a fair number of bank transactions into suspect accounts in Kashmir in the early 1990s, but it was the hawala route transactions that accounted for the bulk of the funds. South Asia's simple, reliable and below-the-radar banking system had its origins in necessity rather than criminal intent. For traders and businessmen involved in large-scale transactions, the hawala route made it easier to move money across countries; for migrants, it was the easiest way to send money home. Hawala flourished also because of the absence of modern yet affordable banking in large parts of the region.

For the Kashmiri militants and their backers across the border, it became an easy system to route money through.

On 25 March 1991, a senior Hizbul Mujahideen operative, Ashfak Hussain Lone, was arrested in the Chitli Kabar mohalla of Old Delhi. He was found carrying several bank drafts for significant amounts of money. Investigation into his arrest led to the unravelling of a sensational hawala network, which exposed the fact that the militancy enterprise was not that different from the business of Indian politics. Further investigations took the police to two hawala dealers in Bombay, which led them to the Jain family in Delhi. The CBI filed an FIR on 4 March 1995 against S.K. Jain, his employee J.K. Jain and others under the Prevention of Corruption Act and the Foreign Exchange Regulation Act, which was later replaced by the Foreign Exchange Management Act.

The diaries recovered from S.K. Jain documented not only Kashmiri militants who received money through their hawala network, but also senior political leaders across the spectrum, such as BJP leaders L.K. Advani and Madan Lal Khurana, and Congress leaders such as Arjun Singh, N.D. Tiwari and Madhavrao Scindia, among several dozen others. The hawala scandal investigations were bungled, the CBI failed to find corroborative evidence and the charges collapsed in courts. The public outrage against the CBI's sham performance and a PIL resulted in a landmark Supreme Court ruling in 1997, providing the CBI with considerable autonomy, a process that could have ushered in transparency within the security establishment.

The fight for Kashmir grew nastier. Locals continued to pour into militant camps, hundreds of foreigners were coming from across the border, the average Kashmiri was hostile to the Indian security forces and no good intelligence was available. To deal with the challenges, India needed something more rooted in the local realities. And there was help available—Pakistan was, by now, aggressively promoting the Hizbul, which wanted Kashmir to be part of Pakistan, and discouraging groups such as the JKLF, which wanted independence.

Many militants were upset with Pakistan's new position, and sometime in 1994, arising from this disgruntlement and Indian desperation, the idea of state-sponsored militias, comprising surrendered militants, took birth. It was not a novel idea. Throughout history, nation states have had armed militia to add to state-sponsored violence, better control crowds or coup-proof rulers in unstable countries. Militia, ultimately, is unaccounted-for state violence. Kashmir would be no different.

As I see it, once the strategy kicked in, the army, paramilitary forces and the J&K police virtually competed to create their militias. These renegades served two primary purposes: target militants and help security forces with information. Folk singer-turned-militant Mohammad Yusuf Parray, better known as Kuka Parray, started the Ikhwan-ul-Muslimeen that primarily targeted Hizbul militants and members of Jamaat-e-Islami; former militant Javed Ahmed Shah formed a group that worked closely with the Special Operations Group (SOG) of the state police. By the end of 1994, all the groups came together. Together and separately, it appears to me, they became the lawless arm of the state—professional blackmailers, mercenaries, rapists and criminals-on-hire. Some of them also became politicians. In 1996, when the first legislative assembly elections were held after the manipulated 1987 polls, Kuka Parray was a candidate. Leading a party called the Jammu and Kashmir Awami League, he contested from Sonawari constituency in Bandipora, and was pitted against Mohammad Akbar Lone of the NC. In Saderkoot Bala village, a group of elders campaigned aggressively for Lone. Parray won the election with 15,601 votes against Lone's 14,875. It was time for his militia to celebrate.

About twenty Ikhwanis descended on the village of Saderkoot Bala, even as the results were being declared across the state, and surrounded the house of Ghulam Qadir Dar, who had actively campaigned for the NC candidate. By 7.30 p.m., they had surrounded his house and were shouting for him. His family hid Dar in the attic of the house. When his wife stepped out to tell the Ikhwanis that he was not home, they mowed her down. His son, daughter and nephew were next in line. After emptying over 150 cartridges at Ghulam Qadir Dar's home, the Ikhwanis moved to the house of two other NC supporters.

At Saifuddin Dar's house, the family had just finished dinner, and the patriarch had sat down for a smoke when the Ikhwanis arrived. By the time the twenty-strong team left, seven people in the village lay dead.[21] Ghulam Qadir Dar and Saifuddin Dar's families had no trouble identifying some of the killers. The local police filed a case and booked nine Ikhwanis. The situation then became bizarre. Dar says he would often be summoned to the local army camp and interrogated, and forced to withdraw the case.[22] One of the killers, Mohammad Ayoub Dar, was recruited as a member of the Jammu and Kashmir Territorial Army.[23] Another accused, Wali Mir, became an NC activist.[24] Rashid Billa, the Ikhwan who led the massacre, was shot dead in his house by militants in April 2017.[25] Kuka Parray, the folk singer who became a militant and then pioneered the Ikhwan concept, became an MLA, and was murdered in September 2003 by suspected militants as he left a school compound after witnessing a cricket match.[26]

What happened in Saderkoot Bala village, and in several other instances, was yet another side of India's war on terror. In September 2002, in the run-up to the state assembly elections, I went to meet Liaqat Ali Khan, former chief of Ikhwans in Anantnag, and now a candidate in the elections. While declaring their commitment to free and fair elections, his present and former militia colleagues told me that they did whatever the local police chief told them to do. Khan lived in a well-guarded government bungalow, and his Ikhwan colleagues occupied houses vacated by Pandit families, some still bearing the imprint of the decade-old violence. The lifestyle of Ali Khan and his team betrayed the strong state patronage enjoyed by the Ikhwans.

The Ikhwan plan was simple. The security forces hired ex-militants, empowered them to kill and terrorise people, and then let them join politics. These militia men, in turn, wanted undemocratic elections. From the circumstances, as far as I can see, the Indian forces were either silently complicit or they were actively engaged. The Kashmiris appear to have been allowed to commit heinous offences upon each other.

Despite the huge toll it took on the society, and on the discipline of the security forces, the strategy of arming a section of the society against another would be deployed years later in the Naxal belt, yet again to disastrous consequences. In 2005, as Maoist violence flared up, the Chhattisgarh government formed the Salwa Judum, armed it and let it loose on the local population and the Maoists. Until the Supreme Court declared it illegal in July 2011, the Salwa Judum was a terror group for most locals.

It was not always the militia that did the dirty work. There were repeated indications during my reporting that, at least in some instances, there was silent political endorsement of extrajudicial actions, which might also include the possibility of permitting security forces into carrying out killing operations without fear of paying the consequences.

The violence in Kashmir was relentless. By 1999, there were almost 3,000 incidents of violence per year, and that year saw 821 civilians, 1,082 suspected militants, 355 special forces and 305 foreign militants killed.[27] The security establishment was up against the wall. Meanwhile, Masood Azhar, the Harkat-ul-Ansar idealogue who had been in Indian jails since 1994, was not forgotten. As the old millennium came to an end, and the world slipped into a festive mood, five men in Kathmandu readied for a new operation to secure Azhar's release. They would not only disrupt the holiday spirit, but dramatically alter the Indian security establishment forever. Their impact is yet to be fully understood, but the after-effects of that hijack can still be felt to this day.

9

The Hijack and its Aftermath

Christmas festivities were underway, even as the world prepared for the year 2000 with some worry. Amidst this, on 24 December 1999, at 4.20 p.m., an Indian Airlines aircraft, IC-814, took off from Kathmandu's Tribhuvan International Airport.

As the flight purser, Anil Sharma, emerged from the cockpit after serving tea to the pilots, Captain Devi Sharan and First Officer Rajinder Kumar, a big-bodied man in a grey suit and ski mask pointed a pistol at him, a grenade in the other hand. The man stormed into the cockpit, announced the hijack and commanded Captain Sharan to divert the aircraft in a westerly direction. Four other hijackers got up from amongst the passengers to take charge of the passenger cabin.

It was almost 5.30 p.m. Prime Minister Atal Bihari Vajpayee was on a flight too, and not very far from the hijacked aircraft. His flight did not have an onboard phone, but the pilot, of course, was in touch with the ground. Yet, no one bothered to inform the prime minister. In the national capital, government business was slowly winding up. In South Block, Cabinet Secretary Prabhat Kumar and National Security Advisor Brajesh Mishra were wrapping up a meeting when the alert came in. Across the road, in North Block, IB Chief Shyamal Dutt dialled Home Minister L.K. Advani to inform him of the hijack.

In Vasant Vihar's Priya complex, at the Rediff.com office, we were finishing up early when the phone rang. Journalist Suhasini

Haidar, who worked with CNN International and occasionally wrote for Rediff.com, was at the other end. She was at the Delhi airport for another story, and had accidentally run into the most sensational piece of news: the IC-814 hijack. After a few cross-checks and a newsflash on our website, I got on my rickety scooter and headed to the airport, with only a thin sweater for protection. At the airport, panic was spreading; the display system showed that IC-814 was delayed, and the crowd was abuzz with speculation that something had gone wrong. Sometime later, an official confirmed to the gathered relatives that the flight had indeed been hijacked.

This was not how the Indian security establishment had hoped to wrap up the twentieth century. The decade, and especially the year 1999, had been really tough. A few months earlier, hundreds of Pakistan-sponsored intruders occupied Indian territories along the LoC in Kargil sector, forcing India into an armed conflict in which it lost over 500 soldiers. The Kashmir militancy recorded one of the highest casualties thus far.

While intelligence failure has been blamed for the Kargil intrusions, level-headed academic research[1] lays the blame elsewhere. On 2 June 1998, almost a year before the Kargil conflict, the IB chief had personally written to the prime minister, marking a copy to others, including the director general of military operations, about preparations for a large-scale infiltration from the Pakistan side. The Kargil-based 121 Infantry Brigade's commander, Brigadier Surinder Singh—who would be dismissed after the war and would go on to sue the army for it—had warned his superiors in August 1998 of the heightened threat.[2] He informed them of increasing cross-border firings and the possibility that the situation at Kargil would escalate. The R&AW, in its half-yearly assessment of September 1998, had warned of a 'limited swift offensive'.

As far as I can see, blaming intelligence failure was an effective strategy, and everyone in the command-and-control structure who inadvertently facilitated the Kargil war received medals and accolades. Kargil ought to have been a wake-up call, one that forced a re-examination of the fault lines in the security establishment. It is my view that a large part of the intelligence generated by Indian agencies had no takers, either due to lack of credibility or because the various arms of the security system were operating in silos.

Another aspect needs examining here. Over the past decade of fighting in Kashmir, I have come to believe, the forces were repeatedly found to be faking narratives, staging fake encounters[3] and making absurd claims. It is this background that leads me to believe that the security establishment had probably internalised a distrust of intelligence inputs. Many sources have repeatedly told me that inputs piled up—some genuine, others fake—but no one paid enough attention to processing them. In my opinion, there appears to be a slow degeneration which was visible only to discerning eyes and those with deep access into the security establishment.

To return to flight IC-814, the Crisis Management Group—the CMG, India's apex body for dealing with national crises, and headed by the cabinet secretary—finally assembled at 6 p.m., almost an hour and a half after the hijack. Until then, no one had bothered to ask the anti-hijack squad of the NSG to be ready at the airport, nor to trail the aircraft, nor were there any other cohesive orders. As the senior officials walked into Rajiv Gandhi Bhawan, next to Safdarjung Airport, confusion prevailed. And the aircraft that landed in Amritsar was able to leave Indian airspace.

No reliable specifics have emerged from that crucial CMG meeting. Years later, then R&AW chief, A.S. Dulat, in his book, *Kashmir: The Vajpayee Years,* said the CMG 'degenerated into a blame game, with various senior officials trying to lay the blame for allowing the aircraft to leave Indian soil on one another; the cabinet secretary, being the head of the CMG, was one target, and the NSG chief, Nikhil Kumar, became another. It was a fraught time and nerves were unfortunately constantly on edge.'[4]

The Cabinet Committee on Security, comprising senior ministers, met at Vajpayee's official residence. Confusion seems to have been the prevailing mood there too. I was at the international airport, with the relatives of passengers onboard the IC-814, as were other journalists. The panic among the relatives is all mixed up in my mind with the incoherent response of the Indian establishment.

By 29 December, Indian negotiators had pared down the demands of the hijackers to the release of three terrorists—Masood Azhar, of course; Omar Sheikh, the UK citizen who kidnapped foreigners in Delhi in 1994 to get Azhar released; and Mushtaq Ahmed Zargar, a Srinagar resident who led a group notorious for targeted killing of Hindus in the late 1980s. The Cabinet Committee decided to give in to the final demands of the hijackers and release the three terrorists. Azhar was jailed in Kot Balwal in Jammu; Zargar was in Central Jail in Srinagar and Omar Sheikh was in Delhi's Tihar Jail. There is still no clarity if the government paid any ransom, though early during the hijack, the terrorists had demanded US$ 200 million as well as the release of thirty-six terrorists from Indian jails.[5]

Dulat was tasked by the Cabinet Committee to rush to the winter capital of J&K, Jammu, to convince Chief Minister Farooq Abdullah to release both Azhar and Zargar and bring them to Delhi. He landed there on the evening of 30 December. For both Abdullah and Dulat, there was a sense of déjà vu. Almost a decade earlier, when Rubaiya Sayeed was kidnapped, Dulat was the chief of the IB station in Srinagar and Abdullah was the chief minister. 'In both the episodes I had asked him to release jailed terrorists, and in both episodes he had initially refused, saying presciently that doing so would have dire consequences for militancy in his state. In both episodes I persuaded him to ultimately give in, on orders from the top in Delhi,' Dulat recalled in his book.[6] In both instances, and at various points in between, there seem to have been clear warnings about what appears to be the lack of cohesive policies, accountability and growing unprofessionalism in the security establishment, I believe.

On the morning of 31 December, Masood Azhar and Mushtaq Ahmed Zargar were brought to the Gulfstream jet belonging to the Aviation Research Centre, the aviation arm of the R&AW, in which Dulat had landed in Jammu. The two terrorists, blindfolded, sat in the rear of the aircraft, in the middle hung a curtain, and in the front sat the R&AW chief. The flight was quiet. As soon as they landed in Delhi, the two terrorists were taken to another aircraft, where Foreign Minister Jaswant Singh was waiting to head for Kandahar. They had already placed Omar Sheikh, the LSE student who would later murder journalist Daniel Pearl, in the aircraft. In an absurd display of the Indian state's incoherent strategy on terrorism, India's foreign minister and three of its most dreaded terrorists took the same flight to Kandahar. Years later, Jaswant Singh called it a 'painful chapter of my life, something that I don't want to revisit'.[7]

While the agencies were able to quickly figure out who the hijackers were, and who was backing them, one thing became clear: Pakistan had a substantial network in Kathmandu, and there were local elements supporting the Kashmiri cause. With the help of the Nepali security forces, Indian agencies stepped up the process of identifying and rounding up people who were suspected of aiding terrorists—a key suspicion lingered that the city was also a major centre for hawala transactions linked to the Kashmir militancy. Many of the arrested, all of them Kashmiris based in Kathmandu, were brought across the border and handed over to the IB for interrogation.

In New Delhi, a comprehensive review of aviation security was initiated, and the government began identifying those with suspect credentials, with a view to denying them the right to operate in aviation. Two new directors on the board of Mesco Airlines were denied permission by the home ministry because they were facing CBI investigations. Congress leader Satish Sharma was denied permission to be on the board of the Delhi Flying Club because of a criminal case against him. Security at airports was strengthened. In Nepal, India bargained for better security check for passengers boarding India-bound flights, and the Indian Airlines hired sky marshals on some sensitive sectors. There were indications that the government and security agencies were finally on the right track.

However, the government's firmness and the resolve of the security establishment began to unravel quickly. The home ministry played a questionable role in providing security clearance to Jet Airways promoter Naresh Goyal, who was accused of links to underworld criminals by intelligence agencies—a fact that I have documented in detail in my earlier book, *A Feast of Vultures*—while refusing security clearance to others who were merely accused of some financial misdeeds.[8]

A macabre drama would play out around the Kashmiris rounded up from Nepal. The understanding with Nepali agencies was that the arrested would be released after detailed interrogation. But many of those picked up from Nepal and handed over to the IB mysteriously disappeared.

In 2007, a journalist friend sent an old, fragile Kashmiri man to my office in the INS Building. At the time, I worked for the Mumbai-based newspaper *DNA*. The old man alleged that both his sons, traders in Kathmandu, had been missing since early 2000. His efforts had produced some leads: the Nepal police officials told him that they had detained the brothers and handed them over to India's IB at the border. He wandered from office to office, from journalist to politician, desperate for any news of his children. The old man told me that he knew where his sons were brought to, and took me on a drive to an IB office in Delhi's RK Puram area.

Over the next several weeks, as I worked on the story, I pieced together that at least seventeen people who had been picked up from Nepal around the time of the hijacking and handed over to the IB, had gone missing.[9] I ran the names of these people against records of inmates of Indian jails. They were not in any of the jails. However, I did learn that Kashmiris were being kept in detention in twenty-four jails across the country. I met with a senior intelligence officer who had held a key post during the hijacking period. He said that when the Indian government mounted pressure on Nepal after the hijack, the smaller nation had agreed to step up an already existing informal understanding to arrest those suspected of involvement with Kashmiri militants. It was an accepted practice, but very rare. Those detained by the Nepal police were brought to the border and handed over to IB officials, who were often accompanied by Delhi police personnel. After interrogation, these people were handed over to the police forces, who, in turn, documented them in arrest records as terror suspects. Earlier, when such suspects had been occasionally extradited from Nepal, they were shown as having been arrested from railway stations or crowded bus stands. However, after the hijack, the pattern changed. The national capital witnessed several encounters, some staged suspiciously in crowded places, and there were some in Uttar Pradesh as well.

In the months after the hijack, there was pressure on the Nepal authorities from the relatives of those arrested from the country. 'We had queries from Nepal authorities, and that is when we started looking around,' a senior intelligence official told me. He said there was even written correspondence between agencies. 'Nothing came of it. It wasn't a coincidence that a series of encounters followed the hijack,' he said. The most controversial of those encounters was on 3 November 2002, when the policemen from the Special Cell of the Delhi police claimed to have eliminated two suspected LeT terrorists in the basement of Ansal Plaza. No independent judicial process was followed in these encounters.

What would have been the right response? The Kargil conflict a few months earlier had already exposed a deep crisis within India's security establishment. The hijack rang yet another rude alarm bell. The government should have got down to the business of fixing the problems visible—from reliable and timely intelligence to swift operational responses.

There were almost two dozen agencies in the country dealing with intelligence gathering, analysis and distribution. How efficient were they? How much of their information was fake, and how much reliable? How did the system eliminate the vast network of informants and sources that provide bad material?

The second part of the analysis should have been focused on the movement of information across agencies, across states and between various stakeholders—was the turf battle among agencies an impediment to India's war on terror? Finally, it should have investigated India's operational responses, of deploying the action arms—the NSG, police or the army—quickly and effectively.

None of this happened. And so, things only got worse. In my assessment, instead of finding the real enemies of the nation, Indian agencies hunted down those who were accessible; instead of searching for terrorists, it appears that they rounded up innocents. Instead of improving intelligence-gathering and analysis, it seems they faked more intelligence. After Kandahar, I believe that sections of the security establishment and the government drifted even further into undemocratic postures.

Remember my schoolmate, the late Brigadier Pramod Kumar, who refused to be part of a staged encounter in 2000 when he was a company commander with 1 Sector of the RR? Kumar's genial appearance belied his nerves of steel. Around the time he refused to fake an encounter, another group of young officers in the same sector were ordered to carry out an operation, and they readily agreed.

In March 2000, just three months after the IC-814 hijack, India was readying for the visit of US President Bill Clinton, the first by a US president in twenty-two years, and there were hopes that the sanctions America had imposed on India after the 1998 nuclear tests might be lifted. On 20 March 2000, while Clinton was still airborne, almost two dozen men in military fatigues arrived in Chittisinghpora village, a quaint, Sikh-dominated village in Anantnag district. The terrorists in army fatigues arrived in military vehicles, and asked men, including young children, to line up outside the two gurudwaras in two different parts of the village. A man, whom the group addressed as 'CO sahib', fired in the air and, on cue, terrorists in both locations started shooting down the people lined up, all the while shouting 'Jai Hind, Bharat Mata Ki Jai and Jai Mata Di'. The terrorists also took occasional sips of liquor while firing. Nanak Singh, the only person to survive the massacre, would forever recall the names with which the killers addressed each other: Pawan, Bhansi and Bahadur.[10]

A few hours later in New Delhi, National Security Advisor Brajesh Mishra blamed the terrorist groups LeT and Hizbul Mujahideen for the massacre. The *Frontline*, a liberal Left magazine of the *Hindu* group, claimed that just before the terrorists pressed the trigger, one of the Sikhs recognised a killer and asked: '*Chattiya, tu idhar kya kar raha hai?*' (Chattiya, what are you doing here?)[11] The magazine added that investigators had figured out that Chatt Guri was the nickname of Mohammed Yakub Magray (who is referred to as Wagay in some records). In a report in its next edition, the magazine gloated, in a style that is typical of Indian reporting on terrorism: 'It took some of the best interrogators from the ruthlessly efficient Jammu and Kashmir Police SOG almost 48 hours to break Magray. He was, it turned out, a Hizbul Mujahideen operative active on the organisation's wireless network with the code-name Zamrood.'[12] From Zamrood, the magazine claimed, the investigators quickly deduced that the LeT had carried out the attack—the deadliest communally targeted killing of a minority group in J&K ever.

With this information, 1 Sector RR under Brigadier Deepak Bajaj carried out a swift operation. A colonel and two majors led the operation, along with police personnel from the SOG of the state police. Five days after the Chittisinghpora massacre, on the last day of President Clinton's visit, in the presence of Union Home Minister L.K. Advani, who was visiting the grieving village, the senior superintendent of police (SSP), Farooq Khan, claimed that five foreign terrorists responsible for the massacre had been eliminated in a joint operation by the RR and the SOG in the forests of Pathribal. Advani, the most influential minister in Vajpayee's government, was quick to congratulate the forces for eliminating the 'the butchers responsible for Chittisinghpora massacre'. The army gave Advani a detailed briefing on the brisk operation, and a situation report of the 1 Sector RR recommended officers who led the operation for commendations. The *Frontline* called it a 'dawn raid' led by Farooq Khan and Colonel Ajay Saxena, during which they also recovered assault rifles, grenades and two wireless sets.[13] 'We expect further success soon,' Khan told the magazine.

Other Indian publications made similar sensational claims, oozing nationalistic jingoism in their coverage. On the floor of the J&K state assembly, Chief Minister Farooq Abdullah claimed a day later that all the five killed were militants in combat uniform involved in the Chittisinghpora massacre. Brigadier Bajaj sanctimoniously said to the *Frontline*: 'The fact of the matter is that we can't protect everyone, everywhere, all the time. People have to learn to protect themselves too.'

Even as the media was spinning the official narrative, Movli Qasim Ali in Pathribal recognised one of the so-called killed terrorists as Jumma Khan, a fifty-year-old acquaintance. The government claims collapsed. It turned out that the army and the SOG had abducted five innocent villagers as night progressed on 23 March, and on 25 March, they were shot dead atop a hillock called Zoontengri, and the bodies were then burnt and dressed in military fatigues.[14] With the help of some locals, they buried the bodies in different graveyards.

After several years of investigation, the CBI counsel told the Supreme Court in March 2012 that 'it was a fake encounter and cold-blooded murders'. The apex court allowed the army to decide if a general court martial or a criminal court must be assembled to try the criminals in its ranks. The army ignored both suggestions, and using the cover of the Army Act, the case was closed.

Within hours of the identity of the murdered villagers emerging, the people of Chittisinghpora burst out in anger. On the afternoon of 3 April, about 2,000 civilians, including the family members of those killed in the encounter, marched down from their villages in the hills to the office of the deputy commissioner of Anantnag, demanding justice as well as the return of the dead bodies for burial. As the noisy procession reached Brakpora Chowk, the security agencies opened fire on them, killing eight people and injuring over thirty-five. The villagers returned home with more dead bodies.

The state government announced an SIT into the Pathribal fake encounter case. But whom did they appoint to head it? Farooq Khan, the SSP who played a leading role in the encounter.[15] In the case of the Brakpora killings, retired Supreme Court judge S.R. Pandian was appointed to a single-person enquiry commission. On 27 October 2000, Justice Pandian submitted his report, which indicted the police and CRPF for the murder of peaceful protestors. He also said the 'faked encounter killings in Pathribal' was a critical reason for the firing on the protestors.[16]

The bodies of those killed in the fake encounter were dug up on 6 April 2000 by a team of forensic experts, amidst heart-wrenching scenes. A year later, the Hyderabad laboratory that was carrying out DNA testing to confirm the identity of the victims, by matching with samples collected from their relatives, wrote to the J&K police saying that there was a deliberate effort to derail the testing. In place of a female relative's sample, blood from an unknown male had been sent. Instead of another female relative's blood, what the police sent was a sample containing the blood of two men. The search for the Chittisinghpora killers continued. The J&K police in September 2000 arrested two Pakistanis and claimed they were responsible for mowing down the Sikhs. Their trial was shifted to Delhi by a Supreme Court order. In 2012, the Delhi High Court acquitted the two, saying there was no legal evidence at all to show their involvement. Both were quietly repatriated to Pakistan.

A new twist in the Chittisinghpora murders was provided by David Coleman Headley. He told Indian investigators that an LeT terrorist named Muzzammil had told him that he was one of the terrorists who carried out the killings. According to Headley, Muzzammil was also behind the attack on the Akshardham temple in Gujarat in 2001, for which six innocents were tortured and jailed by the Gujarat police for over a decade, only to be acquitted in 2014 by the Supreme Court. While the security establishment was eager to play up the Chittisinghpora claims, his claim regarding the Akshardham attack was quietly ignored.

Investigations into the attack on the temple complex in Gujarat had taken on a menacing tenor. Two terrorists stormed the stunning Akshardham complex and killed thirty-three people and injured several more. When the NSG neutralised the terrorists the next morning, many of us reporters were already gathered outside.

The Gujarat police's claims about the terrorists were countered by the J&K police who said they knew the real Akshardham attackers. Finally, the Supreme Court pronounced its judgement on the attack on 16 May 2014. It acquitted all six persons accused by the Gujarat police, including three on death row. 'Here, we intend to take note of the perversity in conducting this case at various stages, right from the investigation level to the granting of sanction by the state government to prosecute the accused persons under POTA, the conviction and awarding of sentence to the accused persons by the Special Court (POTA) and confirmation of the same by the High Court. We, being the apex court cannot afford to sit with folded hands when such gross violation of fundamental rights and basic human rights of the citizens of this country were presented before us,' the apex court ruled.[17]

The judgement pointed to the reckless, communal and political nature of the security establishment that was taking shape in Gujarat, in line with the divisive politics of the Gujarat government under the then chief minister, Narendra Modi, who was also home minister for the most part. It was hardly an unheard-of political strategy. During the Emergency, Indira Gandhi had shown how it could be done. Many chief ministers, across several states, followed suit. However, there was one vital difference in the way Modi approached the game.

His actions appear to be openly communal, and seem to be targeting members of a clearly identified enemy: Muslims. I believe there appear to be circumstances suggesting that fake encounters were staged to create a certain narrative. And there was no punishment for those who faked these events. When such police officers were caught, the state government actively organised to support them.

In the Akshardham case, the Supreme Court pointed out that the Gujarat ATS, led by D.G. Vanzara, had been shooting in the dark for about a year. 'Then on the morning of 28.03.2003, the case is transferred to Crime Branch, Ahmedabad. This was followed by D.G. Vanzara giving instructions to the then-ACP G.S. Singhal (PW-126) about one Ashfaq Bhavnagri (PW-50). PW-126 was thereafter made in charge of the case on the same evening at 6:30 p.m. and the statement of PW-50 was recorded at 8 p.m., i.e within one and a half hours.'[18] So, if Vanzara was the source of such a critical piece of information that led to the breakthrough, then, the apex court wondered: 'This shrouds our minds with suspicion as to why such a vital witness, D.G. Vanzara, who discovered the link to the accused persons, was not examined by the Special Court (POTA). The courts below accepted the facts and evidence produced by the police without being suspicious about the extreme coincidences with which the chain of events unfolded itself immediately that is, within 24 hours of the case being transferred to the Crime Branch, Ahmedabad.'[19]

On the day the Supreme Court acquitted all accused in the Akshardham temple attack, Indian democracy witnessed one of its most dramatic moments: election results in the 2014 general elections showed a sweeping victory for the BJP under Narendra Modi.

Apart from lambasting the process followed, the reckless nature of police investigations and the failures of the lower courts, the Supreme Court said about the state's chief minister, Narendra Modi, who sanctioned the prosecution of the innocents: 'The present case does not show that the sanctioning authority had applied its mind to the satisfaction as to whether the present case required granting of sanction.'[20] The prosecution could not prove that the sanction was granted either on the basis of an informed decision or on the basis of an independent analysis. The apex court tersely said of India's incoming prime minister: 'This would go to show clear non-application of mind by the Home Minister in granting sanction. Therefore, the sanction is void on the ground of non-application of mind and is not a legal and valid sanction under Section 50 of POTA.'[21]

For the euphoric new prime minister, or the larger society, the apex court's order held little meaning. India was ushering in a government with a clear mandate, and after ten years of an often corrupt and mostly lacklustre governance under Dr Manmohan Singh, India wanted decisive leadership, the wiping out of corruption and to emerge on the global stage.

But to return to the beginnings of the new millennium, it wasn't just the IC-814 hijack that shook up the system. The 9/11 attacks too were a key turning point for the Indian security establishment. The government moved quickly to support the US position on terrorism, and began to put in place domestic initiatives that were not sufficiently rigorous. Wahid, whom we met in Part One of this book, was one of its many victims.

The new millennium saw the rise of the Indian security establishment and its capability to wreak havoc on India's democracy, the criminal justice system and constitutional accountability. A new, ferocious chapter in counterterrorism strategy was unfolding. The police, intelligence and investigation agencies' invasion of the lives of ordinary citizens was no more something that happened in a distant corner of the country, in Kashmir or the Northeast. It would soon become the everyday reality of Indians across the nation, without exception.

10

Our Brutal Existence

Desperate phone calls and odd requests are part of a reporter's life. Even by those standards, the call I received in early 2010 was bizarre. A reputed doctor from Kochi told me what his family and several others spread across India had been facing in the recent past—events that, at the peril of using a cliché, I can only call Kafkaesque. My friend Manoj Das, then editor of the *Times of India* in Kerala, had asked him to speak to me.

In Kochi, this doctor, his wife, also a doctor, and his mother-in-law were facing imminent arrest by the Punjab police, a contingent of which had flown down to the seaside city. Accompanying them was a PR blitzkrieg, accusing the family of being part of a large criminal conspiracy. The pliant local media in Kerala reported that the well-respected family, including the doctor's mother-in-law, a retired college professor, were all part of a grand scheme to cheat Jay Polychem, a south Delhi-based firm.

In Mumbai, another Punjab police team took away a migrant from Nepal, who had kept his HIV positive status low-key and was trying to build a normal life. On the outskirts of Delhi, in Faridabad, they arrested a pregnant woman, her husband and brother-in-law.

According to the police, all these people were conspiring to implement a plot devised by an engineer, who was now a petrochemical trader, from the Kochi family, who once worked for Jay Polychem. The doctor who called me was the trader's brother-in-law.

The nightmarish experiences of these seemingly unrelated people had their origins in Mumbai several years earlier. Samdeep Mohan Varghese joined Reliance Industries in 1994 as a management trainee and rose through the ranks. In about a decade, he had become the head of a section in the petrochemicals division. Sam regularly met with the buyers of their products. Among these clients were two brothers from Delhi—Sandeep and Satinder Madhok—whom he met for the first time in 1997. 'They were pleasant, charming actually,' Sam recalled. He would meet them occasionally at industrial get-togethers in India and abroad. In 2000, the brothers told Sam that they planned to aggressively expand the petrochemical business via Delhi, Singapore and Houston. They offered him a position in their company as head of a division. Sam was not interested. However, his situation in Reliance soon changed. In a reshuffle, he was moved to the office of the executive director, where there was much more power but the work was too bureaucratic for Sam's liking. Meanwhile, the Madhoks were relentlessly wooing him. In 2002, Sam accepted their offer. The move came with a salary hike of almost 300 per cent, and the option to work out of Houston or Singapore.

Sam moved to Delhi, and began operating out of the Defence Colony headquarters of Jay Polychem. The Madhoks were keen to impress and win him over. They told him about their political connections—the younger scion of a Punjab political family was a regular at their office, they were particularly close to a powerful woman politician of Uttar Pradesh, they were also in the charmed circles of the members of other parties. As Sam settled into his new job, he began to realise how the Madhok business worked: there was not enough trading, and a lot of bags filled with cash moved in and out of the office. There were secure locations in the office for storing, counting and sorting cash. Sam was focused on starting the Houston office, and kept pestering the Madhoks about it. By August 2008, he had landed in Houston on a business visa. The work visa, the Madhoks told him, would come later. It was an immensely frustrating time—he did not have the proper documents, nor did money come in on time. However, Sam carried on, and began interviewing potential candidates to join the Houston office. But then the global recession of 2008 struck. The Madhoks told him to stall the expansion plans and shift to the Singapore office. There, Sam felt more confident, because a well-respected industry name from Shell joined too, as did his former boss from Reliance. However, the Singapore facade collapsed before long.

'Where it actually started going wrong was when they were looking for trade finance lines [to facilitate international trade] from different banks. I had a lot of friends in the banking sector in Singapore, so they wanted me to make fake presentations. They wanted me to exaggerate their trade volume by ten times, from a few hundred million dollar turnover to a few billions. I refused,' Sam said. Things went downhill pretty quickly from there. Without a work visa, no proper salary and increasing friction with the management, Sam had enough. He hired a lawyer, who said he should resign from the company, so that they could sue for damages. Within days of the legal notice, Sam had his first nasty surprise. A police notice from Jalandhar arrived, asking him to appear for questioning in Punjab, because he had allegedly cheated the company.

The battle lines were drawn. Sam could not go back. Neither could the Madhoks. For both parties, the stakes could not have been higher.

Sam wrote a detailed complaint in November 2009 to the ED and the DRI. He also filed a complaint with the Singapore authorities.

Within days of his complaint, the company stepped up its response. On 30 November 2009, it filed a complaint with the Rajpura police station in Punjab against Sam and several others for publishing defamatory information about the company on a website they had created. The website had been registered only nine days earlier. By February 2010, an FIR had been filed.

A team of Punjab police personnel flew down to Kochi on tickets bought by Jay Polychem,[1] as if they were goons on hire. Sam's mother went to the Kerala High Court against the arrest, and it said the allegations were very vague in nature. A few days later, the policemen picked up the Nepali man from Mumbai. He had worked as a household help with Sam when he was with the Reliance group. The man was taken to Punjab, and tortured at the Rajpura police station for information on where Sam was hiding. Overseeing the interrogation was Sandeep Madhok, one of the Jay Polychem brothers.[2]

In Faridabad, a former neighbour of the Madhoks, who now worked for them, began facing an ordeal of his own. Amardeep had protested when he realised that some papers he had signed without reading were actually complaints against Sam. When Sam was in the Delhi office, he had been a kind boss who had even sponsored Amardeep's honeymoon to Kerala. The man resigned from the company in protest, but the ordeal was just beginning. One day, he was summoned to the company, and Sandeep Madhok and his brother beat him up with a belt, asking him to stand by their complaint against Sam. He refused. A few days later, a posse of Punjab police landed up at Amardeep's house, and told him that there was a case against not just him, but also his wife, sister and brother-in-law. He was taken to Punjab, and tortured at the Rajpura police station. Overseeing the torture session, once again, was Sandeep Madhok.[3]

Supervising the police operation was the then DIG of Patiala range, S.K. Asthana. As I began to piece together the police excesses for the *Times of India*, I called Asthana. 'I don't care about what you write in your paper,' he told me nonchalantly. In fact, he had a suggestion for me: ask Sam to come to Punjab and cooperate with the police. Asthana has in the past been accused of custodial death, was pulled up by the Punjab and Haryana High Court, and accused by the Election Commission of bias and transferred out.

It was surprising that the Madhoks, who were based in Delhi, should go to Punjab to file cases against Sam and the others. When I asked him about it, Sandeep Madhok, accompanied by a very aggressive and unruly lawyer, told me that one of the directors noticed the website while he was in Punjab. So an instant complaint was filed there. You are close to a powerful political family in Punjab, is that why you filed the complaint there, I asked. I got no response.

I was meeting with Madhok in his Defence Colony office, where hung large oil canvases that looked like cheap Chinese fakes. The brothers had reached out to me through a high-profile Delhi lawyer, who met me in a posh hotel and offered a bribe for not pursuing the story. 'I have a budget, we can share it. No one needs to know,' the lawyer said straightforwardly. After that effort failed, Madhok finally agreed to meet me.

Thanks to their proximity to the powerful political family, the Madhoks had powerful access to the might of the state police force. The aggressive fight against the Sikh militancy had left a deep impression on the Punjab police. The militancy had been put down, but the unruly side of the police was still very active and was not held to account. Jay Polychem just hired that side of the Punjab police.

Punjab, like J&K, Manipur and other states ravaged by insurgency, exemplifies my overall argument: that the non-military parts of the security establishment are tearing into the constitutional rights of citizens and have emerged as the biggest threat to Indian democracy. That the average Indian is afraid of dealing with the police is a telling fact.

When violence by Pakistan-backed terrorists spiralled out of control in Punjab in the 1980s, the state police was not prepared for it. After the Indira Gandhi assassination and the resultant anti-Sikh pogrom, the situation only worsened. And that is when the Rajiv Gandhi government decided to bring in Julio Francis Ribeiro, an IPS officer from Maharashtra police with an illustrious and storied career, to head the Punjab police force. He had been police commissioner of Bombay, chief of Gujarat police, director general of CRPF, and was known as the cop who smashed the smuggling rackets of Bombay. In March 1986, he took over as the DGP, and came in declaring a 'bullet for a bullet'. Meanwhile, the government had passed laws such as the Punjab Disturbed Areas Act and the Armed Forces (Special Powers) Act to provide better protection to security agencies operating in tough conditions.

By April 1988, when Ribeiro handed over the force to K.P.S. Gill, another tough-talking IPS officer, the police had allegedly killed over 800 suspected terrorists.[4] However, for all the tough action and posturing, the law-and-order situation had not improved: the number of hardened terrorists went up from just 101 to over 178 by the time Gill took over.[5] Ribeiro introduced financial rewards for policemen who killed terrorists. This practice became the template in large parts of Kashmir, Manipur and several states that were fighting Naxalites. In this model, the war on terror is equally a national service and a flourishing business. There are financial rewards available, you can settle private scores and impunity is assured.[6]

In Punjab, while the state apparatus efficiently documented human rights violations by militants, the misdemeanours of the police's killer squads, which began to pick up in the second half of the 1980s, went mostly unrecorded. Human rights organisations and activists were all facing either outright bans or police action.[7]

Then, along came Jaswant Singh Khalra, general secretary of the Akali Dal's human rights wing, who began an intrepid documentation of the secret cremations in Amritsar district. According to the law, the police are required to carry out the last rites of a body when there is no one to claim it. In Punjab, this was used to cover up criminal activities. Khalra began the laborious, but highly innovative, activity of collecting details of firewood-purchase registers maintained in the district's three crematoria. Even these numbers may not have fully captured the extent of the police killings—an estimated 300 kilograms of wood are required to burn a single body, but the police often burnt several bodies on a single pyre. Khalra methodically went about his harrowing documentation process.

Those who knew the Khalra family were not surprised by Jaswant Singh's courage even in a state that had gone from being terrorised by militants to being terrorised by the security agencies. His grandfather, Harnam Singh, was one of the founders of the Ghadar movement, and one of the organisers of the Komagata Maru passenger ship, which reached Vancouver with 376 Sikh immigrants but was turned away. The ship was forced to sail to Calcutta. When it arrived there in September 1914, British officials tried to identify Harnam Singh and Gurdit Singh, the organisers, and all hell broke loose. Passengers opened fire, wounding several officials. As British troops quelled the revolt, and began forcing the passengers onto a train, Harnam, Gurdit and twenty-eight others escaped. In November 1914, members of the Ghadar movement made their first attempt to provoke a mutiny in the army, but failed. The movement had been penetrated deeply by the British intelligence, and based on inside information, the police raided the Ghadar headquarters in Lahore on 19 February 1915, and arrested over a dozen leaders, including Harnam Singh, and confiscated weapons, bombs and rebel flags. Harnam Singh was acquitted in the Lahore conspiracy case, but was ordered to be kept under surveillance in his village, Khalra. He was allowed to marry, and Jaswant Singh's father was born of this marriage. When Harnam Singh's internment was revoked in 1922, he returned to Shanghai to continue his revolutionary activities, never to return.

As the Punjab strife deepened in the late 1980s and early 1990s, the mandatory post-mortem had been replaced, in government hospitals, by the filing of whatever information the police supplied. The doctors were merely required to sign the official document.

On 30 October 1993, when a body was brought in for post-mortem, the doctor noticed that the man was still breathing, in spite of a bullet injury to his head. When he drew the police officers' attention to it, they took the man away and soon returned with his corpse.[8]

The son of Baldev Singh, an ex-soldier of 9 Punjab Regiment, who fought in the 1965 war with Pakistan, and whose daughter Manjit Kaur was a star national weightlifter, was killed in an encounter by the police. The father was not allowed to collect the body, which was instead rushed to a pyre at the Durgiyana Mandir cremation ground. By the time Singh reached the venue, his son's head was burning, and the rest of his body was intact.[9] He was allowed to collect the ashes.

Khalra went to the Punjab and Haryana High Court with his findings. However, the court dismissed the petition saying that he had no locus standi in the matter. It was a bizarre argument for a constitutional court to have made, especially because, a few years earlier, the Supreme Court had expanded the scope of PILs to make justice more accessible to the disempowered.

On 16 January 1995, the Akali Dal's human rights wing held a press conference in Chandigarh to make public Khalra's sensational findings. The press release said that, based on firewood-purchase registers, they had identified 400 illegal cremations in Patti, 700 at Tarn Taran and about 2,000 at Durgiana Mandir cremation ground between June 1984 to end-1994.

Two days after this, then police chief K.P.S. Gill held his own press conference in Amritsar, where he claimed that thousands of Sikh youth had left for foreign countries using fake documents and names, and that Khalra was claiming those people as missing and killed by the security forces.[10] Gill also made the usual noises about ISI trying to revive militancy in the state. The public duel was just beginning.

A day later, on 19 January, Khalra called another press conference in Amritsar. He challenged the legendary police chief to an open debate, and repeated his claims that the police had murdered and illegally cremated hundreds of people. He signed off promising to release the details of the missing people soon in a systematic manner.

The Punjab police shifted gears, no longer bothered about the court of public opinion. It transferred the controversial police officer Ajit Singh Sandhu as SSP from Ropar district to Tarn Taran. He was already facing court cases related to disappearances of people, and activists held him responsible for hundreds of such cases. The phone line at Khalra's home started ringing at odd hours. When answered, anonymous callers threatened Khalra and told him to stop his activism for the disappeared if he did not want to disappear. When his wife picked up the phone, the other side would either go silent or shower her with abuses. Most calls came in the dead of night. Policemen began physical surveillance of him,[11] and some of them would even sheepishly ask Khalra for his day's travel plans so that they could report back accurately to their bosses. The police and state also deployed local political leaders to terrorise Khalra, according to those who have researched his death. 'Jaswant appeared upset when in February 1995, a Congress member of the legislative assembly (MLA) from Patti constituency invited him to his house and asked him not to pursue the matter of police cremations,' the book records.[12] The people's representative, like many before and after him, was acting as a police agent. There are several reasons why an MLA would betray his public responsibility: he may have received some favours, perhaps dark secrets that could ruin his life were available with the security establishment, or maybe he was actively cultivating them for his own ends.

Sometime in March 1995, Khalra visited the US and Canada, and met with political leaders and human rights activists. When he returned in July, he continued his activism. He declared that, at the Jain Sabha cremation ground, the police had cremated 1,135 bodies, and the total number of illegal cremations across the state was around 25,000.[13]

The local police responded to the new allegations in a written statement, in which they accused him of being in league with a militant group called Khalistan Command Force.

A few days later, IB officials dropped in to question Khalra about his foreign visits. 'In the second week of August, some officers of the Intelligence Bureau (IB) visited Jaswant Singh and questioned him about his foreign visits. They wanted to know the names of persons who had hosted him and had interacted with him. They visited him a number of times in the last two weeks of August to follow up on these inquiries.'[14] It seems to me that the IB was not greatly interested in the illegal cremations that Khalra had documented.

The IB has to its credit several incredible achievements in protecting India and subverting threats, but it has also shown a tendency to serve the political ambitions of those in power. Several observers and political leaders have for long advocated that the IB, and other intelligence agencies, must be ultimately accountable to the Parliament, where a committee of parliamentarians across party lines should scrutinise the agencies, the way that the Comptroller and Auditor General is ultimately accountable to the Public Accounts Committee of the Parliament. Some argue against the point, saying that politicians cannot be trusted with sensitive intelligence operations and information. That argument is significant because it is evidence of the security establishment's doctrine that it should have the final say on what is best for the country and its citizens. The implication here is that individuals can be sacrificed for the larger good of the society. It is an argument that smacks of authoritarianism and denial of individual liberty. Politicians may be corrupt or lazy, but they are ultimately elected by the people.

The Committee for Information and Initiative on Punjab (CIIP), yet another citizen's initiative for accountability in the state, moved the Supreme Court based on Khalra's findings. Five months after the apex court admitted the petition and asked for more details, the Punjab police practically challenged the court. On 6 September 1995, Khalra was washing his car outside his Kabir Park residence in Amritsar when police commandos showed up in two vehicles, and took him away. The local deputy superintendent of police, the chief of the local police station and others were present during the abduction.[15]

Khalra's wife and friends began a desperate search for him, and a couple of days after his detention, the president of the Shiromani Gurudwara Prabandhak Committee, the powerful organisation that manages gurudwaras in several states, sent a telegram to Justice Kuldip Singh of the Supreme Court. Five days after the kidnapping,

Justice Singh converted the telegram into a habeas corpus petition. In affidavit after affidavit, Punjab police officers and the state government lied, saying that Khalra was not in their custody. On 15 November, with the Punjab police stonewalling all efforts to track him down, the Supreme Court ordered the CBI to search for Khalra as well as to investigate his claims about the illegal cremations. In July 1996, the CBI submitted its interim report, saying that it had detected 984 illegal cremations at Tarn Taran from 1984 to 1994.[16] A few days later, the CBI told the court that nine police officers, including people who filed false affidavits before the court, were responsible for the abduction and disappearance of the activist. Appalling details of police brutality emerged later. Special police officer Kuldip Singh told the CBI that Khalra had been tortured and shot dead as night descended on 24 October 1995. The activist's body was cut up into pieces and dumped in Sutlej river, Kuldip Singh claimed.[17]

The CBI said in court on 30 July 1996 that the nine state police officers, acting on the orders of SSP Ajit Singh Sandhu, were responsible for Khalra's abduction and disappearance. Sandhu had already filed an affidavit saying he never threatened Khalra. The court asked the CBI to prosecute them for kidnapping, presuming that Khalra was still alive.

By December 1996, the CBI told the court that 2,097 illegal cremations had been carried out by the security agencies in the three crematoria of Amritsar district, and that it was able to fully identify 582 bodies and 278 partially, but that it could not identify the remaining 1,238 bodies.[18] Though the activists were not impressed, it was a huge step forward in India's efforts to hold the security establishment accountable. Despite all the work that has gone into forcing the official machinery into action, the process of accountability has not been taken to its logical conclusion even today.

For police officer Sandhu, the past was slowly catching up. He was arrested and jailed for the abduction and custodial death of Kuljit Singh Dhat, who, ironically, was a relative of the revolutionary freedom fighter Bhagat Singh. Before Sandhu could be charge sheeted in Khalra's disappearance and held accountable for the hundreds of crimes under his watch, on 24 May 1997, Sandhu threw himself in front of a train. A suicide note was recovered: 'It is better to die than live in humiliation.'

After attending Sandhu's funeral, his former boss, K.P.S. Gill, wrote to the prime minister, appealing for a fair approach towards policemen, and putting up a strong defence of the Punjab police: 'For over a decade, to wear a police uniform in the Punjab was to proclaim yourself a wilful target for preferential terrorist attack. Yet, thousands of men in uniform stood as a bulwark of democracy against the unconstrained depredations of the extremists. Thousands sacrificed their lives. Thousands of others witnessed the murder of their parents, their brothers and sisters, their wives and their children.' Gill was not wrong. But what he discounted was the fact that, in the low-intensity war that Punjab witnessed, the security establishment was still duty-bound to abide by the laws of the land. They were not expected to behave like the terrorists they were hunting. Even in the thickest fog of war, the law-abider and law-breaker must be distinguished.

Khalra was not the only activist targeted by the police. Activists are the amplifiers of a society and its staunchest defenders; silencing them ensures the silence of society at large. In Sangrur, Ram Singh Biling, a local journalist and the Sangrur district secretary of the Punjab Human Rights Organisation (PHRO), disappeared forever in police custody.[19] In April 1992, chairman of PHRO and retired high court judge, Ajit Singh Bains, was tortured and produced in public with handcuffs and detained under the draconian TADA.[20] He was accused of attending a secret meeting with militants, which turned out to be a deliberately false claim. The chief minister of the state himself defended the police action against Bains in the assembly, and accused PHRO of supporting terrorists.[21] A few weeks later, Param Satinderjit Singh, a student leader of Guru Nanak Dev University, was arrested from the campus, triggering student protests and a hunger strike by his father.[22] None of it had any effect; the student never returned. In August 1992, Malwinder Singh Malli, the general secretary of PHRO and editor of a local leftist magazine, was detained.[23] Some days later, human rights lawyer Jagwinder Singh was picked up in Kapurthala, never to be seen again.[24]

It appears to me that police actions like these, carried out with what would appear to be the active blessings of the political executive, paralysed Punjab's most potent human rights networks. Simultaneously, encounters and disappearances escalated. A newspaper report said that the police dumped the bodies of those killed in irrigation canals, and many of them washed up in Rajasthan, triggering official complaints from that state's chief secretary.

The story is the same in Punjab, J&K, the northeastern states, the tribal belts of central India and elsewhere. I conclude that when the professionalism of the security establishment is tested by militancy and when uncomfortable questions are asked of the police and the government, a certain part of the security establishment rises up to protect those institutions. Has it not always been the practice in illiberal democracies to silence those who speak up? In the silence of a society, the authorities can bury their crimes.

In 2021, there is an eerie resemblance between the Punjab of the 1990s and the India of today. Across states, those same tactics are being used against critics of governments. Gandhian activists have been turned into militants; revered teachers are accused of assassination conspiracies.

As for Punjab, it continues to fall short in its efforts to find a peaceful closure to the militancy days. As I wrap up this book in early 2021, over two and a half decades after the guns fell silent in Punjab, there has been no major progress in the efforts of the distraught families striving to hold the police accountable for over 8,000 disappearances. An estimated 1,600 villages in fourteen districts have at least one person who was forced to disappear by the police.[25]

In the 1980s, Punjab was in the grip of militancy and Kashmir was waiting to explode. In the Northeast, however, primarily Nagaland and Manipur, armed insurgencies had been ongoing for decades. Much of the militancy here had degenerated into extortion and criminal rackets. Ordinary people were terrorised by both the security forces and the militants.

To better understand the rise of a dark side within the security establishment, we must look closely at Manipur, especially in the early 2000s. The state had a new chief minister, Congress leader Okram Ibobi, and Yumnam Joykumar—a senior IPS officer who had learnt his lessons on tackling insurgency in Kashmir and Northern Ireland, where he went to learn counterterrorism strategy—was back in the state. Manipur massively expanded its police force, increasing the strength by almost 50 per cent, and ordered it to retaliate without hesitation.[26] The gruelling task of patient policing and depressingly slow judicial process was not for the new Manipur leadership. The Assam Rifles and other Central security forces provided further muscle power.

Thus began the killings, and by the early 2000s, state-sponsored encounter deaths had become a daily affair. The matter came to national attention in July 2004 after an early-morning raid by Assam Rifles, led by army officers on deputation, to arrest Thangjam Manorama, who they alleged was part of the People's Liberation Army of Manipur. Within hours, she was shot dead—according to the paramilitary force, the incident occurred when she tried to escape. Forensic examination found eight bullets wounds on her, including one on her genitals. They also found semen stains on her skirt. Manorama was abducted, raped and shot dead.[27] Five days later, a group of elderly Manipuri women demonstrated outside Kangla Fort, the historic seat of Meitei sovereignty that was now the headquarters of the Assam Rifles. They stripped and held up a white banner with crimson letters on it: Indian Army Rape Us. It put the spotlight on the situation in Manipur, but it would not stop the violence.

By this time, the state had a well-trained police commando force that had tasted blood. Among the commandos trained and equipped to kill was Thounaojam Herojit. On 23 July 2009, he rushed into a busy street in Imphal to take on an alleged militant. Herojit shot the man dead inside a pharmacy. However, the entire operation was caught on camera by a photographer. The shots proved beyond doubt that the alleged militant had actually been brought there by the police, taken inside and shot dead. In the chaos, a pregnant woman was also killed and five others injured. Babloo Loitongbam, a human rights lawyer who has played a pioneering role in initiating the process of peace-building, received these photographs. He handed them over to a reporter with the Delhi-based publication *Tehelka*, which carried the story on its cover.[28] Manipur instantly erupted in protests.

By 2013, the Manipur killings came to the attention of the Supreme Court, thanks to a petition moved by the Extra Judicial Execution Victim Families Association (EEVFAM). Leading the association's fight for justice in Manipur was Babloo, who with a small team, had identified 1,528 people killed by the security forces in staged encounters. The Supreme Court, on 4 January 2013, appointed a commission headed by a retired Supreme Court judge, Justice Santosh Hegde, to inquire into the first six cases listed by the petitioners. The court found it a simple matter to satisfy itself about the claims—it was proof of what an independent judicial enquiry can do to start the healing process.

The first of the six cases was of Azad Khan, from the village of Phoubakchao Maha Leikai, who was killed on 4 March 2009. After examining all involved, including several members of the security team led by Major Vijay Singh Balhara of the army, the commission said that the killing of Azad Khan was not an encounter but a cold-blooded murder.[29] The security forces had made no effort to capture or disable him. According to his family members, Azad and a friend were sitting on the veranda of his house, reading newspapers. His parents, aunt and a female cousin were also present when about thirty security personnel landed up at around 11.50 a.m.

They dragged him about seventy metres to the field on the northern edge of the veranda, and began beating him mercilessly. When his relatives protested, all of them and Azad's friend were pushed into a room in the house and locked inside. The room had a window that opened to the field where Azad was being thrashed. As his family and friend looked on, Azad collapsed to the ground. Then the security force pumped bullets into him, and threw a pistol next to the body. Azad was just twelve years old.

According to details submitted to the commission, Major Balhara, then with 21 Assam Rifles, had called up a havildar of the local police commando team, saying he had received information that militants were moving around in Azad's village. Where did Major Balhara receive his input? 'At about 10.00 hours, he received an input from an Grade A-1 source that there were two or three armed terrorists in the general area of Phoubakchao.'[30] Who was this Grade A-1 source? The army officer does not reveal this. It is an oft-seen pattern: the operation always begins with inputs from an unnamed source, and ends up in the death of either innocents or real terrorists, or occasionally, security force members. According to one of the sharpest intelligence analysts I know, a man who has studied the pattern of security killings, in many instances of senior officers being killed in Kashmir, there had been that tip-off from a source. We return again to the problems inherent in a system running on an industry of unaudited sources.

The Justice Hegde commission found that each of the six cases referred to it was a murder by the security forces. 'The continuous use of the AFSPA for decades in Manipur has evidently had little or no effect on the situation. On the other hand, the 6 cases, which have been shown to be not real encounters, are egregious examples of the AFSPA's gross abuse,' it said.[31] The commission's investigation led to another startling find, which has particular resonance in India today: 'Out of the 2713 cases registered in Manipur in the last five years attracting the provision of the UAPA, only 13 have been charge sheeted.'[32]

Manipur was attempting to come to terms with its violent past and present. Relatives and friends were pitted against each other in a small state, with a population of less than thirty lakh. On Christmas day in 2014, in a shocking moment of truth, a mass grave was discovered on the grounds of the Tombisana High School in Imphal town. It had seven skulls, several skeletal parts and some jewellery. The school had earlier been occupied by the security forces.

The year 2016 brought another dramatic turn of events. At a secret location, Herojit met with a group of journalists, and admitted that he had executed the unarmed young man at the pharmacy in 2009. Over the next several months, he helped the media and activists like Babloo understand the rot in the police system, because he had kept a meticulous diary of every killing he carried out. Herojit admitted to over a hundred killings. All the killings, he said, were done at the behest of his superiors.

Meanwhile, on 14 July 2017, the Supreme Court asked the CBI to probe EEVFAM's allegations that the security forces had carried out 1,528 extra-judicial killings in Manipur. The CBI shortlisted ninety-five cases for focused investigation. It began filing FIRs, but rarely named anyone. In many cases, it just copy-pasted the state police FIRs that contained unverified allegations against those killed. The Supreme Court had to step in and rebuke the CBI on the shoddy job it was doing. The results were instant.

Almost a year after it began investigating Azad Khan's killing, the agency filed an FIR into the killing of the twelve-year-old boy, and named among others Major Vijay Singh Balhara. By this time, Balhara had become a colonel commanding the 26 Mechanised Infantry Battalion. The FIR triggered a few hundred military personnel to file a petition in the Supreme Court demanding that enquiries against the armed forces be dropped because it demoralises the military. At last count, at least 739 personnel had filed petitions against naming Balhara. Notably, 107 of these were soldiers serving under him. The army headquarters claimed that it had no role in this flurry of petitions, and that every soldier had the right to legal recourse.

However, this display of trade unionism was a rare thing in the military. Almost around the same time, another group of serving army soldiers also filed a petition in the Supreme Court against action in the killing of a cattle trader in J&K.

The Manipur situation could have been even worse than the horror it already was. There were rumours at one point that a state-sponsored militia would be raised from among the civilians there, much like the Salwa Judum of Chhattisgarh.

Around 2005, Chhattisgarh was witnessing the entry of major new mining operations, and a Congress leader named Mahendra Karma started the Salwa Judum ('Peace March' in Gondi) as a voluntary group. It soon began receiving state patronage, and was given arms, training and financial support. The movement spread like wildfire, growing to over 4,000-strong. Tribals caught in the fight had to either join the Naxals or listen to the Salwa Judum. The militia recruited youngsters as 'Koya Commandos', and with the blessings of the state authorities, went into tribal villages to move them forcefully to camps. They also raped and murdered and burnt down villages. The Salwa Judum had no constitutional accountability, pitted people against each other and was worse than the Naxals that it was supposed to fight. At least the Naxals were explicit in their declaration that they did not accept the laws of the land. Here was a militia, with state backing, that was outright criminal. By the time the Supreme Court banned the Salwa Judum in 2011, there were far too many orphans, rape victims and other scarred people that the state had helped create.

The villages of Kondasawali, Karrepara and Kamaraguda in Sukma district tell the story of how the militia operated. In 2020, the NHRC ruled that state government officials abetted the crimes committed by the Salwa Judum in these villages. In 2007, seven people of the area were killed and ninety-five huts burnt down by the militia in its bid to establish its hold over the region. Other villagers fled, only to return by 2013, when they began their legal fight. The NHRC report said that the incidents had come to the 'notice of police, revenue and other officials of District Sukma soon after they had taken place, but police and district officials had deliberately turned a blind eye'.[33] Their refusal to 'to take cognizance of these incidents for seven years is also a very strong circumstance to show that these crimes had been abetted by the district officials of Sukma/ or state government officials of the State of Chhattisgarh'.

In such a long fight for justice, the Adivasi villagers—who are cut off from access to the structures of knowledge, not to mention other resources that are needed for justice—need the assistance of intermediaries, people who can help them access justice, provide support and boost their morale. This is the role that civil society, NGOs and activists play in a society, acting for the interests of the weakest sections, and as a bulwark against corrupt and cruel government machineries.

In the case against the Salwa Judum, the villagers worked alongside Sudha Bharadwaj, a US citizen who had returned to the country to work among the poorest Indians. When the NHRC order came in 2020, Bharadwaj was in Pune jail on accusations of sedition and of being part of a Maoist conspiracy, along with other civil society members who are now called the 'Bhima Koregaon 16'. In fact, Bharadwaj's own arrest and detention is proof of the central theme of this book, and of the severe threat to India's democracy today.

The story of how Sudha Bharadwaj ended up in Chhattisgarh, working with mine workers in tribal villages, is now well known. In 1984, a charismatic communist leader, Shankar Guha Niyogi, who had been arrested under the National Security Act two years earlier, visited Jawaharlal Nehru University to thank the students who had vigorously carried out a public protest and signature campaign to ensure his freedom. Bharadwaj, who grew up in the campus, was impressed by Niyogi's work and commitment. Sometime later, she went to visit Dalli-Rajhara in Chhattisgarh, where Niyogi's union ran schools and hospitals for the families of mine workers, and a couple of years down the line, permanently shifted there. She was soon confronted by the reality of India's lawlessness when Niyogi was assassinated in 1991. Fourteen years later, the Supreme Court convicted a hired killer, Paltan Mallah, in the Niyogi murder, but acquitted the local industrialists whom the trial court had convicted for the conspiracy to murder Niyogi.[34]

Bharadwaj now awaits her own turn for justice—justice that has constantly eluded the workers to whom she has dedicated her life, justice that her mentor Niyogi could not get even in his death.

Our investigation into Jay Polychem and the Punjab police appeared on the front page of the *Times of India* on 9 July 2010.[35] It had an immediate impact, with the Punjab and Haryana High Court taking *suo motu* cognisance of the report and listing it as a PIL. The court also put an end to the police harassment.

Sam was a fearless fighter. Once he decided to take on the Madhoks, he began cataloguing the company's illegal activities. He wrote detailed complaints to the Federal Bank, which had lent large sums to Jay Polychem. Sam cautioned the bank that it would end up losing all its money. This was sometime in 2010, much before loan defaults by big corporates would grab national attention. 'I knew the Madhoks were very friendly with the bankers, but I thought the Federal Bank, which is headquartered in Kerala, would have a better response. I was wrong,' Sam recalled years later. The bankers ignored his warnings.

Sam had also mounted an aggressive legal response to Jay Polychem's attacks. In July 2012, the Punjab and Haryana High Court ordered that the FIR against Sam and others be quashed, calling it frivolous.

In large part, Sam was able to fight back because of extremely efficient lawyers and some outstanding judges. However, some of his lawyers were not quite on the level. One of them, a high-profile man, repeatedly tried to mislead the court, saying he had no brief from his client, even though Sam and he were in constant touch. Sitting in Singapore and Jakarta, Sam could not have known what was happening inside a courtroom in India. When he finally realised that his own lawyer was scuttling one of the cases, Sam asked another of his lawyers in Delhi to take up the matter. But the Delhi lawyer refused. This too is part of the Indian legal system, where lawyers are sometimes available to conspire against their own clients, where corporates pay high-profile lawyers for not appearing against them, where the influential hunt benches and influence judgements in numerous ways.[36] All of this, combined with a feeble or corrupt media, only tightens the hold of the security establishment on India's democracy.

A month later, Sam travelled to India. He had to deal with some work, review the legal issues in Delhi, and most importantly, meet his ageing mother and relatives in Kerala. He had not returned since the police case was filed. Sam took off on 9 August 2012 in a Singapore Airlines flight from Jakarta, where he had found a job, and landed in Delhi around 3 a.m. the next morning. Tired and jet-lagged, Sam was hoping to rest before starting his day. But at the immigration counter, a nasty surprise awaited him. There was a lookout circular against him, the official said. Sam said the case had been quashed a month ago, and produced a copy of the judgement. It does not matter, we have explicit instructions to detain you, the official replied. Sam kept asking for the copy of the circular, but they would not show it to him. He was taken to an ante-room, while one of the officials dialled the Punjab police, who said they would immediately start for Delhi to take custody of Sam. Since he was by now well tutored in the ways of the Indian establishment, Sam had taken a small precautionary step: he had asked his Delhi lawyer to meet him at the airport. This ensured that he was not ill-treated and also got basic legal access. But that was not good enough.

By the end of the day, the duty magistrate remanded Sam to judicial custody. And Sam-the-whistle-blower landed up in Tihar

Jail, one of the most crowded and violent jails in the world. It was in Tihar that Sam had his first proper meal of the day—a vegetarian meal for an undertrial.

The Punjab police did not turn up the next day, so he ended up staying in jail over the weekend, during which, he says, he also got some unique insights into an average Indian prison. 'I saw warders distributing drugs to the inmates,' he said. On Monday morning, Sam boarded the jail vehicle with other inmates, and reached the Patiala court complex next to India Gate. A battery of lawyers appeared on behalf of Jay Polychem, and demanded that he be sent to Punjab. From the very beginning, the judge appeared sceptical. But a lawyer for the Delhi police convinced the court to extend the hearing to the next day, because they were awaiting some communication from the Punjab police. Incidentally, the Punjab police, which had told the immigration authorities on Thursday that they were starting from Patiala right then, had not covered the 250-kilometre distance to Delhi in five days.

Sam was finally released on Tuesday. The judge was dismissive of the state's claims, and found that Sam was telling the truth. Freedom from jail would not be the end of his ordeals, though.

After checking into a hotel, Sam got down to his official work. A day or so later, he and his lawyer decided to have lunch at the Andhra Bhavan canteen, a popular eatery near India Gate. As their car moved towards the Bhavan, they noticed four people on two bikes trailing them. When they parked the car, the bikes stopped. Sam got out of the car and ran towards the bikers. In panic, they abandoned one bike, and all four squeezed onto the other and got away. Sam called the Delhi police, and filed a complaint. The police seized the motorbike, but would not file an FIR. Sam's lawyers moved a magistrate's court, and forced the police to file the case. However, a couple of years later, the Delhi police closed the case saying that the bike belonged to someone who had come to a bank branch operating out of the Andhra Bhavan premises. There was no effort to track mobile numbers operational in the area at the time or conduct any other investigations.[37]

Over the years, Sam and I became warm acquaintances, and I kept track of his fight. Meanwhile, the Jay Polychem management tried all it could to stop me from pursuing the story. One day, a PR manager came to meet me and said that some of them—PR people, lawyers, even some journalists—made good money from the Madhoks, thanks to my story.

In recent times, as I got down to writing this book and setting up Confluence Media, Sam and I lost touch for a while. Then early morning on 5 December 2020, he sent me a WhatsApp message: 'When I highlighted this 10 years ago . . . no one bothered. Now, I heard these guys are in London. They left India a while back.' With the message he had attached a report in the *Hindustan Times* saying: 'CBI books Delhi company in Rs 1800-crore bank fraud case'.[38]

The story began: 'The Central Bureau of Investigation on Friday raided three locations, three days after booking a petrochemical trading company—Jay Polychem India Ltd—for allegedly cheating a consortium of 13 banks led by State Bank of India of Rs 1800 crore.' The report went on to say that the agency has issued a lookout circular against the owners of the company—Satinder Pal Madhok, Sandeep Madhok, Harmeet Kaur and Sumohita Kaur—so that they do not flee the country. A forensic audit by Ernst and Young showed large-scale syphoning off of bank funds, fictitious transactions, forgery and more, the CBI claimed. The agency also found that the Madhoks had created a fictitious web of vendors and customers, letters of credit to foreign companies that did not exist, fictitious receivables and much else. Sam estimates that the total money defrauded by the Madhoks would be about a billion dollars, over Rs 7,000 crores. 'Much of it,' he said, 'would be black money belonging to politicians and others, who would never complain.'

11

Gujarat Model

There was something magical in Delhi's air as 2010 was winding up. For journalists, it was the beginning of a short-lived golden period, because the mainstream media suddenly found the spine to investigate those in power and also to publish such stories. That period lasted for just about four years, until Narendra Modi, who rode to power on the back of the anti-corruption and anti-government sentiments kicked up by those media reports, entered Delhi with a brutal majority and an authoritarian manner of functioning.[1] Looking back from 2021, that period, only a decade ago, seems surreal.

I joined the *Times of India* as Editor, Special Projects in the summer of 2010, and was given a free hand to pursue any story. Within months, we published a detailed investigation into the Adarsh Housing scam. A housing complex in Mumbai, which was built for Kargil war veterans and war widows, had ended up in the hands of retired military chiefs, senior bureaucrats, and powerful politicians and their relatives. What sent shockwaves through military circles and society at large was that senior military officers, including a few former chiefs, who ought to have been protecting their personnel and their families, were cheating them.[2] Within days, the Maharashtra chief minister, Ashok Chavan, had to resign because two of his relatives had acquired apartments in the complex. There was the growing realisation at the time that mainstream media could hold powers accountable, and that Indian democracy was truly flourishing. A growing chorus by anti-corruption crusaders began to ripple across the country.

The blatantly illegal activities that went into the allocation of 2G spectrum to several companies were exposed in the media. The massive splurge on organising the Commonwealth Games was audited minutely. The powerful and the mighty, even senior cabinet ministers and chief ministers, were subject to enquiries by the media. By February 2011, Telecom Minister A. Raja, who oversaw the 2G manipulations, was arrested and sent to Tihar Jail. The India Against Corruption movement was picking up momentum across the country. By April 2011, activist Anna Hazare and his supporters began a high-profile protest in Delhi that brought thousands across India on to the streets. Candlelight marches, heated debates and screaming headlines all called for a corruption-free India. The most assuring aspect of it all was the sudden professionalism visible across the investigation agencies. Providing them with support and cover was a very determined Supreme Court.

But it was all a chimera. Underneath the bubbling enthusiasm of a maturing democracy, a dangerous politics was gathering strength. While there were scattered glimpses of Modi's style of governance from occasional reports and activist claims, the Gujarat administration under Modi was a closed system, with limited media audits and no whistle-blowers. Whatever was known came through critics and the occasional media leak. They were rare, and drowned out by the advertisement blitzkrieg around the Gujarat model of development.

But then, on 3 September 2013, D.G. Vanzara, an IPS officer who played a crucial role in Modi's counterterrorism strategy in the state, gave us a tiny glimpse of the administration's secrets. It can only be assumed that Vanzara was mighty pissed off after spending a long time in jail. There were thirty-two Gujarat and Rajasthan police officers, including six IPS officers, in various jails for their alleged role in the fake encounters that the Gujarat police had carried out over the years. What Vanzara did not know when he turned whistleblower was that, just ten days later, Modi would be anointed the BJP's prime ministerial candidate.

'With the passage of time, I realized that this government [Modi-led Gujarat government] was not only not interested in protecting us but it also has been clandestinely making all efforts to keep me and my officers in the jail so as to save its own skin from CBI on one hand and gain political benefits on the other,' Vanzara wrote in a resignation letter[3] that reveals more than the sum of its words does. It is proof of how the unaccounted part of the security establishment is deployed by politicians to construct political narratives, terrorise ordinary citizens, muzzle critics and bury the rule of law. In his letter lies the blueprint of what has taken over India under Modi.

Vanzara's letter said: 'It is everybody's knowledge that this government has been reaping very rich political dividends, since the last twelve years, by keeping the glow of encounter cases alive in the sky of Gujarat.' He should know, because he played a lead role in bringing that glow to Gujarat.

According to investigations by Gujarat government officials[4] and by a Supreme Court-appointed committee,[5] the encounter culture of Gujarat had an explicit political aim: creating the narrative of a terror threat, especially targeted at Modi, and whipping up Islamophobia.

In January 2019, a Supreme Court bench headed by Justice Ranjan Gogoi agreed, after much delay, to place in the public domain the final report by retired Justice H.S. Bedi into the seventeen police shootings between 2002 and 2006 in Gujarat when Modi was chief minister. The first of those encounters happened in October 2002. The police claimed to have arrested Sameer Khan Pathan from a city bus terminus on 27 September. They said that he had escaped to Pakistan from Gujarat with a forged passport after killing a constable in 1996, and there became a terrorist with Jaish-e-Mohammed. He came back to India via Nepal, with ISI assistance, and established terror hideouts in Mumbai, Rajkot and Bhopal. And then, the police claimed, he was tasked with killing Narendra Modi. On 22 October, the joint commissioner of the Crime Branch, P.P. Pande, claimed that Pathan was shot dead after he tried to snatch the official revolver of one of the officers. It was first of the many attempts by terrorists to kill Modi, according to Gujarat police claims of that period. It was also the first anti-terror operation under Vanzara. Justice Bedi said the killing of Sameer Khan was 'indeed the result of a fake encounter', and it was a 'custodial death'.[6] Justice Bedi also recorded the plight of Sameer's father, Sarfaraz Khan, who was dismissed from his job as a driver with the Ahmedabad Municipal Corporation after his son was declared an absconder. He ordered a compensation of Rs 10 lakh to the grieving father.

The Gujarat state government was opposed to the release of the report, though it is not clear on what grounds it was protesting. Was the state government not keen on upholding law and order? Was it hoping to protect criminals? Why was it keen that a commission report ordered by the Supreme Court, and written by a retired judge, be kept secret?

Vanzara's resignation letter says that the Modi government 'suddenly became vibrant and displayed a spur of sincere activities only when Shri Amitbhai Shah, former MOS, Home, was arrested by CBI. It so happened that Shri Ram Jethmalani, the most learned, senior most and highest paid advocate of India was engaged for Shri Amitbhai Shah who appeared on behalf of him at all levels of courts, right from the lowest CBI court, to Special Court, to High Court, to the Apex court of India and got him released on regular bail within record time of 3 months of his imprisonment'.

Vanzara was referring to the arrest of the current Union home minister, Amit Shah, on 25 July 2010 for his alleged involvement in the Sohrabuddin Sheikh murder case. Sheikh was killed in a fake encounter on 26 November 2005, admitted the Gujarat government before the Supreme Court, after a probe by the state police established that Sohrabuddin was not a terrorist, and that the Gujarat and Rajasthan state police came together to eliminate him, his wife, Kausar Bi, and, later, his associate Tulsiram Prajapati. Vanzara and team had then claimed that Sheikh was an LeT operative who was on a mission to Gujarat. The mission, yet again, was to assassinate Chief Minister Narendra Modi.

By the time of Sheikh's killing, the Gujarat police had staged half a dozen encounters, and in all of them, the alleged terrorists were on a mission to assassinate Modi. The police, with active assistance from other agencies, were working to please the chief minister, boosting his image as someone who is on top of terror threats, and carrying out cold-blooded murders in the process. According to evidence that later emerged, in the form of phone call logs, Amit Shah, then the state home minister, was suddenly in touch with the field officers of the Crime Branch during the encounter. His calls to DSP N.K. Amin began on 22 November around the time Sohrabuddin, his wife, Kausar Bi, and associate Prajapati were kidnapped by the police. Over the next few days, Shah called the relatively junior police officer several times. The calls dry up around 29 November, when Kausar Bi is raped and killed.

While the Gujarat police submitted two separate charge sheets in 2007 and 2008 in the case, the Supreme Court was not convinced by the probe.[7] In 2010, based on petitions and letters from the relatives of those murdered, the Supreme Court ordered the CBI to further investigate the crimes, and transferred the case to Mumbai.[8] The apex court also stipulated that a dedicated judge should hear the entire case and deliver the judgement.

Two Gujarat-based builders, Dashrath Patel and Raman Patel, told the CBI that police officers close to Shah had extorted money from them, and that the officers used Sohrabuddin's gang to threaten them. The builders also claimed that they got instructions from Shah to be discreet with the CBI. The builders had video-recorded a conversation they had with police officers, and gave three statements to the CBI, including one under Section 164, recorded before a judge. One of the witnesses said in the recorded statement that, based on a conversation he had with Sohrabuddin while in jail, Vanzara had contracted Sohrabuddin and two others to kill Haren Pandya.[9] The CBI came into the case several years later, and while it was able to prove a few things, the federal agency failed to build a watertight case.

Amit Shah was arrested in July 2010. Three months later, he was granted bail, but was barred from entering Gujarat so that he would not subvert the course of justice. He was allowed to return to Gujarat only in September 2012. The evidence against him, the proven murders by the police under his command and the courts' concerns about his conduct, none of it mattered to Chief Minister Narendra Modi. Since returning to Gujarat in 2012, Shah has had a glorious political career. As the country's home minister today, Shah is in charge of most of the non-military parts of the security establishment, which had once investigated him.

Vanzara says in his resignation letter that Amit Shah completely mismanaged the police department as the minister of state for home in Gujarat since 2002. 'I am sorry to state that instead of providing an innovative and benevolent leadership for keeping the police force of the state intact, efficient and fighting machine, Shri Amitbhai Shah introduced a much despised British policy of divide and rule coupled with equally dirty policy of use the officers and throw them by deliberately spreading disinformations about them, whereby he succeeded in creating the "crisis of confidence" among senior officers on one hand and the government on the other. That, in turn, destroyed the command-and-control mechanism of Gujarat Police which is considered to be a "soul" of any uniformed organization anywhere in the world.'

Vanzara says that, between 2002 and 2007, the officers and men of the state police's Crime Branch, ATS and Border Range 'simply acted and performed their duties in compliance of the conscious policy of this government'. He writes that when he was dealing with jihadi terrorism threats, 'I used to get daily dozens of phone calls from the Biggies of Gandhinagar who probably saw a savior in me/my officers, but by the time I/my officers outlived my/their utility and were arrested by the CID/CBI under the very nose of this government, nobody bothered even to formally ask us as to how we were!'

Vanzara goes on to make an important argument about the chain of command, and the flaw in the Gujarat encounter investigations: 'Gujarat CID/Union CBI had arrested me and my officers in different encounter cases holding us to be responsible for carrying out alleged fake encounters, if that is true, then the CBI Investigating officers of all the four encounter cases of Shohrabuddin, Tulasiram, Sadique Jamal and Isharat Jahan have to arrest the policy formulators also as we, being field officers, have simply implemented the conscious policy of this government which was inspiring, guiding and monitoring our actions from the very close quarters. By this reasoning, I am of the firm opinion that the place of this government, instead of being in Gandhinagar, should either be in Taloja Central Prison at Navi Mumbai or in Sabarmati Central Prison at Ahmedabad.'

Vanzara has a word of advice for Modi in his letter: 'It would not be out of context to remind him that he, in the hurry of marching towards Delhi, may kindly not forget to repay the debt which he owes to jailed police officers who endowed him with the halo of Brave Chief Minister among the galaxy of other Chief Ministers who do not bear the same adjective before their names. This, as per my humble opinion, is also a part of the repayment of debt to Mother India.'

Only a few days after Vanzara's letter, Modi was declared a prime ministerial candidate, and since then, the Sohrabuddin murder trial has taken some strange turns.

The investigation got underway after Sohrabuddin's brother, Rubabuddin Sheikh, wrote to the chief justice of India in December 2005 about his brother's killing and the disappearance of his wife. The apex court acted on the farmer's letter and asked the Gujarat police chief to enquire into the matter—it was in the spirit of a long tradition of the court coming to the aid of the weakest. Even as the court order got underway, Tulsiram Prajapati, the most important witness in the Sohrabuddin–Kausar Bi case, was killed in an encounter.[10] With this, the Gujarat police had shown itself capable of challenging the Supreme Court to a show of strength.

The Modi government in Gujarat filed eight action taken reports

(ATRs) before the court, and the state police arrested several police officers for the fake encounter. However, by 2010, the apex court took objection to factual discrepancies in the ATRs, and called in the CBI. A month down the line, with evidence, including Amit Shah's call details, the agency submitted a charge sheet saying Amit Shah was a co-conspirator in the murders.[11]

Judge J.T. Utpat, appointed by the high court to preside over the CBI special court on the Sohrabuddin–Kausar Bi–Prajapati murder cases, began the hearing in May 2013. Shah never appeared before Utpat. On 6 June 2014, two weeks after Modi was sworn in as the prime minister, Utpat let Shah's counsel know his displeasure at the accused not being present in court. He ordered Shah to appear on 20 June. Shah would not. The judge now fixed the next hearing for 26 June, while reprimanding Shah. A day before Shah was to appear, Utpat was transferred out by the Bombay High Court.[12] A few days later, on 9 July 2014, the BJP, now the ruling party, appointed Amit Shah, still an accused in the murder cases, its national president.

Justice B.H. Loya was appointed as Utpat's successor. Loya did not insist on Shah appearing before him, accepting his counsel's pleas about Shah being busy and in Delhi. However, on 31 October, Loya asked Shah's counsel why the accused did not appear in court even though he was in Mumbai, and fixed the next date of hearing for 15 December.[13]

A month later, Loya was dead. On 30 November 2014 the judge had travelled to Nagpur to attend a marriage ceremony, along with two fellow judges. He returned late in the night to the government guesthouse, Ravi Bhavan, where he was staying. From then on, the facts vary, depending on who the narrator is.

As of 1 December 2014, Loya was dead. Almost two weeks later, the two judges who accompanied Loya to Nagpur told the family that he died a few minutes after 12.30 a.m. The post-mortem report quoted the police as saying that Loya died around 6.15 a.m. However, Loya's family had started receiving phone calls from about 5 a.m., informing them of his death. Among the first callers was a local RSS worker.[14] No one knows how he came to be informed so early about Loya's death, or where he got the family's numbers from. The same worker would appear again at a hospital in Latur, where Loya's sister had dropped in on her way to her ancestral home.[15] The RSS has rejected the claims that any of its members were involved in Loya's death.

In November 2017, *Caravan* magazine carried a detailed report in which, for the first time, Loya's family members, including his father and two sisters, raised serious doubts about his death.[16] They hinted that it was murder. The family claimed that the body was not accompanied by any of Loya's colleagues, including the two judges who were travelling with him from Mumbai. Loya's wife, daughter and son travelled from Mumbai to Gategaon, their ancestral village where Loya's body was, accompanied by a few judges. Throughout the journey, one of the judges kept telling the family not to speak to anyone, the family claimed.

They noticed bloodstains on the shirt Loya was wearing; his spectacles were stuck under his body, the belt was twisted and the pant clip broken. When one of the sisters, a doctor herself, demanded a second post-mortem, Loya's judicial colleagues discouraged her, the family said. In the very first instance, the fact that the police had insisted on a post-mortem suggested that the death was being treated as unnatural. However, the police did not follow up with the preparation of a witness testimony (panchnama) that should have been handed over to the family. Loya's mobile phone was returned to the family only three or four days after the death—it had been wiped clean. And who handed the phone over? The same mysterious RSS worker. Loya's family had more startling claims. His sister said that Loya had been under tremendous pressure over the Sohrabuddin case. They said he had received an SMS a few days before his death, warning him, but that the mobile had since been wiped clean. The chief justice of the Bombay High Court, Mohit Shah, offered Judge Loya Rs 100 crore to acquit the accused, they claimed.[17] Shah has never responded to the allegations.

An unprofessional police force only served to deepen the mystery around Judge Loya's death. The case did not have the advantage of a professionally done panchnama, video recorded post-mortem and proper police assistance.[18]

The Loya murder case raised several questions. The opposition party, Congress, held a press conference to claim that two associates of the judge, who knew about the pressure he was under, had also died mysterious deaths. Activist-lawyer Shrikant Khandalkar was thrown off a building in November 2015, while a retired judge close to Loya died mysteriously while travelling in a train, Kapil Sibal of the Congress said.[19]

The government vigorously defended the narrative that Judge Loya had died a natural death. However, among lawyers who had known him for a long time, the honest judge needed a better closure at least. They petitioned the courts, demanding an enquiry. The petition found its way to the Supreme Court in early 2018. It would trigger a rebellion in the apex court.

12 January 2018 was an unprecedented day for the Indian judiciary. For the first time in its history, four of its senior-most judges, after the chief justice, called a press conference to complain about the administration of the Supreme Court. 'The administration of the Supreme Court is not in order. There are many things less than desirable that have happened in the last few months . . . As senior-most justices of the court, we have a responsibility to the nation and institution. We tried to persuade the CJI that some things are not in order and he needs to take remedial measures. Unfortunately, our efforts failed. We all believe that the SC must maintain its equanimity. Democracy will not survive without a free judiciary,' Justice Jasti Chelameswar told journalists.[20]

They were protesting the way cases were allotted to various benches. Justice Ranjan Gogoi, who went on to become the chief justice later that year, told reporters that the press conference was prompted by the controversy surrounding the death of Special CBI Judge B.H. Loya, and the way Chief Justice Dipak Mishra allotted the PIL on the death to Justice Arun Mishra.[21] Politically sensitive cases are usually heard by benches headed by senior judges in the Supreme Court, even though allotment of cases is the chief justice's prerogative. Justice Arun Mishra later recused himself from the case. A bench headed by Chief Justice Dipak Mishra dismissed the demand for a probe into the death of Judge Loya on 19 April 2018.

Within days of Loya's death, the high court appointed M.B. Gosavi to preside over the Sohrabuddin case. Judge Gosavi took up the discharge petition filed by Shah first, and heard the arguments for a couple of days. Two weeks later, on 30 December, he dropped all charges against Amit Shah.[22] It was exactly a month since Loya had died.

The dropping of charges certainly stretched the logic of an investigation and trial. A case is filed based on suspicion and preliminary indications, a trial is held to establish facts and find proof. Without this process, it was an unusual step for a trial court to dismiss charges against Shah. As the Supreme Court-appointed agency probing the murders, the CBI was duty-bound to appeal the discharge in the high court. However, it chose not to appeal. Rubabuddin challenged Shah's discharge at the Mumbai High Court, only to withdraw his application days later,[23] in yet another disturbing twist to the case.

Ever since Shah was discharged, the case only moved in one way. By the time the trial started, all senior police officers accused in the three murders had also been acquitted.[24] After that, only policemen lower down in the hierarchy were on trial. In June 2017, a fourth judge took over the trial: S.J. Sharma.

In December 2018, Rajnish Rai, the IPS officer who arrested the three senior officers involved in the encounter killings—Vanzara, Rajkumar Pandian and Dinesh M.N.—was suspended from service, even though he had submitted a request for voluntary retirement from service in August. A day after Rai's suspension, the trial court in Mumbai acquitted the remaining twenty-two accused in the case. Judge Sharma expressed sympathy for the families of those killed, but said that the court can only go by the evidence.[25]

It is hard to deny that the CBI's conduct in the trial scuttled the course of justice. While 700 witnesses were listed, it called only 210. There was a visible change in the CBI's attitude after the new government came to power in 2014.[26] Of the witnesses it called, ninety-two turned hostile. As for important witnesses like Rajnish Rai, they were never examined.[27]

While the judge was scathing in his attack of the CBI, he also criticised the agency for trying to frame Shah for political reasons, even though the Union home minister had been discharged much earlier. 'Having so examined the entire investigation and having conducted the trial, I have no hesitation in recording that during the investigation of these offences, the CBI was doing something other than reaching the truth of these offences. It clearly appears that the CBI was more concerned in establishing a particular preconceived and premeditated theory rather than finding out the truth,' the judge said.[28] However, the court did not censure or act against any CBI officials, nor did the agency take any further action.

The security architecture that Modi was shaping for Gujarat could not have come at a worse time. Reeling from the embarrassment of the Kargil conflict of 1999, the National Democratic Alliance (NDA) government had carried out sizeable reforms in the security establishment, which included setting up a new technical intelligence agency, the NTRO, appointing a full time National Security Advisor, setting up the Defence Intelligence Agency, and so on. One of the positive fallouts of the reforms was that they began to usher in a certain amount of transparency into the secretive world of intelligence agencies as well as the broader security establishment. There were debates about whether the Indian intelligence agencies ought to be brought under parliamentary supervision, like in most other democracies. Even conservatives agreed that some kind of audit of intelligence operations and expenses was a good starting point. The Multi-Agency Centre (MAC), a coordination centre set up under IB to work on counterterrorism, where twenty-two intelligence agencies shared inputs daily, turned out to be, in a limited way, a system of accountability. As MAC became active, a parallel trend began to emerge, which was brought to my attention by a senior intelligence officer: of different agencies scaling down their claims about the number of militants operating in Kashmir. The agencies were now asking questions of each other, he pointed out.

However, the spate of encounter killings in Gujarat, and the involvement of IB officials, had a sharply negative impact on the transparency wave. It was patently clear to many of us that the IB and other agencies began to clamp up, and mount an aggressive defence of their men, instead of examining facts. The way I see it, the activities of the IB's Gujarat division were questionable on many counts, but the IB leadership defended it. The developments in Gujarat sharply divided the security establishment, in my opinion, and at least a section of it figured that supporting an opaque system, and defending it in the name of national security, was the easiest way to minimise its own accountability.

Were other states not carrying out fake encounters? Why was Gujarat any different? This question needs to be answered. It is true that, across India, state police forces were engaging in fake encounters, custodial torture and other cruelties. However, in Gujarat, the state arm of a Central agency, according to multiple sources I have interviewed over the years, played a major role in orchestrating some of these encounters, especially in the Ishrat Jahan case.[29] Secondly, and more importantly, based on my extrapolation from various enquiry committee reports, including the Justice Bedi Committee report,[30] the encounters were all aimed at building the political image of the chief minister and his party, and stoked Islamophobia through fake claims.[31]

With the experience gained in Gujarat, when Modi rode into

New Delhi, one of the most visible impacts of his rule was on the security establishment. One often heard rumours that senior officers were seeking political favours for their postings far more than they did under the UPA regime. My own assessment is that amongst intelligence agencies, the paramilitary, the Delhi police and other arms of the security establishment, there was a palpable retreat of transparency and the rise of absurdity. Within weeks of the new prime minister taking over, the IB served a customised report to him.

The report, 'Impact of NGOs on Development', was delivered within weeks of Modi's swearing in. It claimed, based on no data, that India's GDP was negatively impacted by 2 to 3 per cent because of NGO activism.[32] It must be remembered here that Modi already firmly believed that civil society and the media had unfairly targeted him for his role in the Gujarat riots and encounter cases.[33] The report was a clever bureaucratic exercise in pleasing the master. It listed seven protests that it pointed to as anti-development—orchestrated efforts at taking down India's development. Where it talked about the protests against the Kudankulam Nuclear Power project in Tamil Nadu, it was careful to mention that the local leader S.P. Udayakuma was 'US-educated', a disqualification in a new regime that prefers 'hard work to Harvard'. Where it talked about anti-coal agitations, it said that Greenpeace provided financial support to the Tata Institute of Social Sciences to study the impact on health and pollution in the Mahaan power project area. It claimed that Greenpeace had received Rs 45 crore in foreign funding in seven years, and expanded its activities to oppose coal-fired power plants and coal mining. Also quoted were allegations by Sajjan Jindal, chairman and managing director of JSW Steel, that corporate rivalries are a reason for these protests. The report also listed Amnesty International as one of the offending NGOs.

The string of absurdities in the report would lay the foundation for a crackdown on civil society and activists at a scale that India had never before witnessed.[34]

This was followed by targeted raids on political rivals[35] and specific business houses and action against critics,[36] all of which have now become the norm. The wave of transparency that swept through Indian governance and establishment structures through the previous decade, thanks to laws like the Right to Information Act, was swiftly reversed. In 2021, the US think tank Freedom House downgraded India's status from 'Free' to 'Partly free'[37]—one indicator among many of the democratic slide that these developments have led to.

12

Chaos

There was heightened security cover in Ranchi. Prime Minister Narendra Modi was to land in the city on 21 August 2015. Hours before his visit, the Ranchi police received a call from the local military intelligence (MI) unit. They had been tracking a terrorist carrying a consignment of explosives coming in from Bangladesh. He was now on his way to Ranchi by train. The police and the MI swung into action. According to the MI's sources, the consignment was in the Burdwan–Hatia passenger train. The train left Burdwan in the morning, and was to wind its way via Bokaro and Dhanbad to Hatia by the evening, covering almost 400 kilometres in about twelve hours. The consignment was being followed by an MI informant. The explosives had been placed in the train at Burdwan by a person who got off at Jhalda station, whereupon another person took custody of the bag, the informant had said.

This was the second instance in recent days when the local MI, under a young and ambitious major, had made sensational intelligence breakthroughs. In the first instance, the same MI unit informed the police about a consignment of ammunition in a bus at Namkum. The police–MI team raided the bus on 12 August, just three days before Independence Day, and recovered the ammunition.

Despite live tracking the consignment from Bangladesh, the MI waited for hours before informing the police, and the consignment was recovered closer to Ranchi. As the train pulled into Kita railway station, the police–MI team swept in and recovered an airbag that contained two dozen gelatin sticks, RDX, six crude bombs, detonators and timers, chemicals like sulphur, urea and gunpowder, noisy sutli bombs, wires and the like. A white paper with a coded message was also retrieved. The man carrying the explosives was identified as Intezar Ali, a resident of Hindpirhi locality of Ranchi, a registered Unani medical practitioner. The son of an ex-serviceman, Ali ran a clinic near Moti Masjid in the locality and lived with his wife and three children. The local media was briefed extensively by the security agencies.

The coded note recovered with the explosives was kind of strange. It was neatly written, and used a certain abbreviation style common in the army. For example, it mentioned TGT, an abbreviation for 'target' used by the army, and it also listed 'NMO' and 'A.M.T.S.H' as the targets. These unusual scribbles raised the suspicions of an honest professional in the security establishment.

Further, the explosives that were supposed to have come from Bangladesh were wrapped in the Ranchi edition of the *Dainik Bhaskar* of 10 and 18 August, and some other explosives were in polythene bags from shops in Ranchi and Khunti. There were copies of the Holy Quran in the consignment, published by Alim Book Depot in Delhi.

An NIA team that landed in Ranchi to investigate the case was not given access to the MI officials. But the team figured out that what was recovered was not RDX but potassium chlorate.

Soon, the MI's carefully staged threat to the prime minister and Amit Shah was shown up as a phoney operation. The officials in Delhi and local police officers figured out what had really happened. Deepu Khan, a petty criminal who was also an informant for both the MI and the local police, made the bag containing the explosives in Ranchi, went to Burdwan and boarded the train. He was guided constantly over the phone by a subedar in the MI unit. When the army and police carried out the raid, the informant was still on the train. After the news broke, Deepu Khan vanished.

According to my own enquiries, there was no indication that what the young major in the local MI unit did was part of any larger conspiracy, nor that there was any political will behind it. However, he was latching on to a powerful new narrative: that the regime's image and popularity is linked to its tough stand on terrorism. In this worldview, right-wing Hindutva bombers never existed—that was only a fake narrative created by the United Progressive Alliance (UPA) government to discredit Hindus. On the other hand, in this new reality, there were Muslims plotting against the nation everywhere.

The Modi government depends on fake news and suppressed dissent to whip up nationalistic frenzy.[1] In recent years, I have had sources in the Indian security establishment—which has grown to mammoth proportions, on account of what is perceived to be India's inefficient and largely undemocratic battles with insurgencies and terrorism—repeatedly telling me that at least some sections of the intelligence agencies are playing a role in the Modi government's efforts at creating false narratives. I believe that past governments have not shown enough political will to ensure that the security and intelligence agencies do not end up behaving like the terrorists they fight. It, therefore, appears to me that, as a result, large sections of the various state police forces as well as federal investigation and intelligence agencies are all now fully deployed in the service of the political executive. The most noticeable slide, I think, has been in the youngest organisation in the security apparatus, the NIA.

The trauma of the Mumbai attacks began to fade as a more refined security architecture, one that was capable of tackling terrorists quickly, began to take shape. NSG commando hubs were created in major cities, a three-tier integrated system began to monitor the seas around the country and a federal investigation agency was created to investigate all cases of terrorism. The NIA hit the road running.

By 2011–12, it was investigating both the IM and Abhinav

Bharat. There were striking similarities between the two cases. Most terrorists in both groups were Indians, there was hard evidence on their activities, many of their key operatives were in custody, both had killed dozens of innocents across the country and neither had faith in Indian democracy. The IM's ferocity had waned after the Batla House encounter, and Abhinav Bharat was silent after it was exposed in 2008. But the threats they posed were real. Several key, hardened terrorists of both groups were still out there.

The NIA's big success against IM came in August 2013. Some say that the federal agency took the credit for the risky operation even though it had not been part of the actual exercise in Nepal. However, the arrest of Yasin Bhatkal, one of the founders of IM, was a powerful blow to the group's capabilities. According to reports that have emerged since his arrest, a group of Indian operatives crossed over to Nepal undercover, mounted a surveillance operation in Pokhara and the surrounding areas, and when they were sure of their target, got the Nepal police to assist them in nabbing Bhatkal. When the IM leader was arrested on 29 August 2013, he was wanted by the police of twelve Indian states, as well as by Central agencies. A key bomber in most IM attacks, he was like a ghost to the agencies. Bhatkal used several aliases and kept shifting his base. However, many of the group's leaders were in Pakistan still, and it continued to receive support from that country.

In contrast, the Abhinav Bharat investigation was far smoother. In November 2010, the CBI had made a major breakthrough by tracing Swami Aseemanand, a Gujarat-based RSS figure with an influential network and patrons. He had been missing ever since the right-wing conspiracy was exposed towards the end of 2008. When the CBI handed over the case to the NIA, it contained a very long confession by Aseemanand (born Naba Kumar Sarkar), recorded before a magistrate in Delhi. His statement was triggered by an unusual experience of compassion. After his arrest, Aseemanand was in Chanchalguda District Jail in Hyderabad as part of the investigations into the blast inside Mecca Masjid. There he met a young inmate, Kaleem. The young man brought him food and water, and generally looked after the elderly inmate. 'During my interaction with Kaleem, I learnt that he was previously arrested in the Mecca Masjid bomb blast case and he had to spend about one-and-a-half years in prison.' Kaleem's kindness had a massive impact on him. 'I was very moved by Kaleem's good conduct and my conscience asked me to do prayaschit [penance] by making a confession statement so that real culprits can be punished and no innocent has to suffer.'[2]

When Aseemanand first submitted to the magistrate on 16 December 2010 that he wanted to confess, the magistrate asked him to ponder over his decision and weigh its implications. He was sent to Tihar Jail to ensure that there was no pressure on him from the CBI or the police. After two days of contemplation, Aseemanand was back before Metropolitan Magistrate Deepak Dabas on 18 December 2010. Over five hours that day, Aseemanand spoke to the magistrate, unravelling the entire inner workings of Abhinav Bharat, the role of some senior RSS leaders in propping it up and the various attacks they had mounted.[3] The magistrate took extra care to ensure that the convict was doing this out of his free will, and even asked the court stenographer to leave the chamber while Aseemanand recorded the confession. In a forty-two-page document written in Hindi and signed by him, Aseemanand provided an unparalleled piece of evidence in India's war on terror. Never had a terror case seen such a detailed statement recorded under the requirements of the Criminal Procedure Code, Section 164, before a judicial magistrate and thus entirely admissible in a trial. This was not your usual forced confession obtained by police torture.[4]

Among the most startling claims in his statement was that senior RSS leader Indresh Kumar had a critical role in organising the terror group. Indresh Kumar has denied this claim, and the RSS has rubbished Aseemanand's confession. However, it is irrefutable that the Sangh cadres were part of the bombings: one of the key accused Devendra Gupta was RSS Vibagh Pracharak of Muzaffarnagar; another member, Lokesh Sharma, was the first to claim Indresh Kumar's involvement.

Aseemanand gave details of how the terror group operated—one group for finance and logistics, a second one for explosives and a third one to plant bombs. All three operated independently, on a need-to-know basis.

In December 2012, the NIA made its first breakthrough, arresting a person named Mohan, one of the bombers of Malegaon in 2006, in which at least thirty-five people were killed and nine innocent Muslims were wrongly framed and jailed by the Maharashtra police. The CBI later supported the false accusations against these Muslim men. It took years to undo even a part of that damage. However, the NIA was operating in a new dawn of professionalisation, and it, at least, had no past to defend or baggage to carry. There was an overall feeling in the security establishment at this moment in time that fake narratives and phoney investigations will come back to haunt them.

Y.S. Modi, the present DG of NIA, articulates this professionalisation in a message on its website: 'Investigation and prosecution of offences affecting sovereignty, security and integrity of India.' Modi is the IPS officer who oversaw the investigation into the murder of Haren Pandya in Gujarat.

The ideals of the NIA found revisionist new definitions after the BJP came to power in 2014. In June 2015, the first comprehensive articulation of this was evident in an interview published in the *Indian Express*. Rohini Salian, special public prosecutor in the Malegaon 2008 attack case, said that, since the new government came to power, she had been under pressure from the NIA to go soft on the Hindutva terrorists.[5] Just after the political change at the Centre, an NIA officer called her and asked for a meeting. 'He came and said to me that there is a message that I should go soft,' she said in the *Express* interview. But she continued to do her job. Almost a year later, on 12 June 2015, the same NIA officer told her that 'higher-ups' did not want her to appear in court. 'The meaning is very clear—don't get us favourable orders. Unfavourable orders are invited—that goes against the society,' she told the reporter Sunanda Mehta.

In 2016, NIA's real intentions became even clearer when it filed a supplementary report exonerating Pragya Singh Thakur. However, the court refused to entertain NIA's new narrative. It was on a motorcycle belonging to Thakur that the bomb had been planted, and the key bombers were Ramachandra Kalsangra and Sandeep Dange, both associates of Thakur and among the NIA's most wanted. The NIA, in fact, had a voluminous amount of evidence to prove Abhinav Bharat's role in the bombings—several recordings of their secret meetings, witness statements recorded before a magistrate detailing that Thakur had offered assistance in bombing Malegaon, phone intercepts, call details showing that Thakur was in constant touch with Kalsangra in the run-up to the blast of 2008, motorbike ownership details, recordings of phone calls of Lt Col Prasad Shrikant Purohit about Thakur's role, and more.[6] Yet, the NIA said that Abhinav Bharat was not a crime syndicate, and so they could not be booked under the Maharashtra Control of Organised Crime Act (MCOCA). It produced the statements of two Madhya Pradesh policemen who were original witnesses for the Mumbai ATS for a crucial recovery but had now refuted that claim. Most strikingly, the country's premier counterterrorism agency had new statements from two witnesses who had originally recorded statements before a magistrate that Thakur had offered manpower for carrying out the blasts. These witnesses were now refuting their own sworn statements. The NIA got the two witnesses to record their revised statements before a magistrate in Delhi.

There were more alarming actions on its part. The NIA had recorded two army witnesses who claimed that an assistant sub-inspector of police had planted RDX in the house of an accused. However, it did not bother to record the statement of the accused police officer. The NIA instead produced statements to discredit the investigations of the ATS, which showed that the Maharashtra police had used torture on witnesses.

When the defence began challenging the very authenticity of the blast and the resultant injuries, the NIA took a laborious route:

it produced ninety witnesses, including many who were injured in the blast, to prove that the blast had indeed taken place. Affidavits from witnesses would have sufficed, but the NIA seemed keen on prolonging the trial rather than concluding it. While the court agreed with some of the NIA's contentions, it did not agree with the agency's claim that Thakur was not part of the conspiracy. As of end March 2021, the trial is still underway.

Even as the agency actively scuttled any chances of punishing the Hindu terror-accused, it was aggressively creating a new narrative with fresh enemies.

Starting early 2018, the Pune police began arresting activists across India for their alleged role in instigating violence following an event on 31 December 2017 at Bhima Koregaon. Every one of the arrested sixteen is an activist who has dedicated his or her life to working for human rights.[7] The Maharashtra police filed a charge sheet, accusing them of a terror conspiracy.[8]

What were they conspiring to do? To assassinate Prime Minister Narendra Modi. It is plain to see, I believe, that apparently out-of-control security agencies appear to be scripting their own version of the truth. In the Bhima Koregaon case, the key evidence, a letter recovered from the laptop of activist Rona Wilson, was planted by someone with great resources who had carried out a cyberattack on his computer over several years, according to globally reputed forensic experts.[9]

The groundwork for the Bhima Koregaon case had begun earlier. On 29 December 2017, supporters of two Hindutva activists, Sambhaji Bhide and Milind Ekbote, desecrated the final resting place of a Dalit legend named Govind Gaikwad. According to local folklore, Gaikwad had performed the last rites of Emperor Shivaji's son, the only one who dared to face the wrath of the Mughals.[10]

Bhide is not your ordinary right-wing foot soldier, but an influential man, revered, among others, by the current prime minister. During the 2014 election campaign, in a speech in Raigad, Maharashtra, Modi said: 'I am extremely grateful to Bhide Guruji as he did not give me any invitation. He ordered me. And all of you are aware of his orders and to hear them and follow them. I know Bhide Guruji from many years now and when we were learning about public service, we were given Bhide Guruji's example.' The prime minister went on to call him a sage.

The desecration of Govind Gaikwad's tomb, not far from Bhima Koregaon, where thousands of Dalits were to gather in a few days, triggered violence that spread across the state. An FIR was filed against Sambhaji Bhide and Milind Ekbote on 2 January 2018.[11] A few weeks later, when they claimed that Ekbote was untraceable, the Supreme Court hauled up the state police for the slow progress of the investigation.[12] The BJP chief minister of the state at the time said that the police had raided several locations and examined more than a hundred call details to locate him. On 14 March, the police finally arrested Ekbote, and the Supreme Court cancelled his interim bail plea.

A few weeks later, a nineteen-year-old Dalit, whose house was burnt in the violence, was found dead in a well. Her family said she was under severe pressure to withdraw her statement to the police, and had been murdered. Meanwhile, her brother, also a witness, was arrested on charges of attempt to murder, filed by a policeman.

After this, the narrative changed dramatically. Maharashtra and Delhi police teams raided Rona Jacob Wilson's house in June 2018, and booked him under the UAPA. The case widened, and in August, five others, including Sudha Bharadwaj, were arrested. After the new Maharashtra government came to power, dethroning the BJP, it ordered an SIT to look into the case. Within three days, the NIA took over the case, without even waiting for Maharashtra's approval.[13] By October 2020, the agency had filed over 10,000 pages of a charge sheet, and named more people as part of the conspiracy.

Among the arrested was Rona Jacob Wilson, a founding member of the Committee for Release of Political Prisoners, an organisation that was founded after S.A.R. Geelani was released in the 2001 Parliament attack case. A major focus of Wilson's work has been on people booked under the draconian UAPA. In April 2018, the Pune police raided his house and took away his computer, a memory stick and other devices. He was arrested on 6 June 2018 from his Delhi home for being part of an alleged conspiracy to instigate violence at Bhima Koregaon. They said he was part of a banned Maoist group, and was also involved in a conspiracy to assassinate Prime Minister Modi and overthrow his government.

Arsenal Consulting, a US-based forensics team, in a report to the Bombay High Court,[14] said that they found that someone with 'extensive resources (including time)' had accessed Wilson's computer on 13 June 2016 and manipulated it for almost two years. 'Arsenal has connected the same attacker to a significant malware infrastructure which has been deployed over the course of approximately four years to not only attack and compromise Mr Wilson's computer for 22 months, but to attack his co-defendants in the Bhima Koregaon case and defendants in the high profile Indian cases as well,' its report said. Arsenal guides law enforcement and military institutions around the world in the development of digital forensic tools, and has also been involved in investigating terrorist organisations and military coups. In spite of its vast experience, the firm was struck by what it saw in India: 'It should be noted that this is one of the most serious cases involving evidence tampering that Arsenal has ever encountered.'

In operations that usually lasted from sometime in the afternoon to around 10 p.m., the attackers worked to compromise Wilson's computer, beginning with an email from someone using Varavara Rao's email address. The person using Rao's email made multiple efforts to get Wilson to open a particular document, and at 6.18 p.m., Wilson replied saying that he had managed to open it. The attacker then began a series of manipulations, including planting several documents and synchronising his computer with other devices attached to it.

The attacker left behind a great deal of evidence of this tampering. For instance, PDFs had been saved from Word 2010 or Word 2013, whereas Wilson's computer only had Word 2007. The Arsenal investigation found that Wilson had never even opened the top ten documents that the police, and later the NIA, used to frame the conspiracy. The documents had been delivered to a secret folder, and lay there until the computer was seized by the police and analysed. The last of the attacker's manipulations occurred a few hours before Pune police swooped down on Wilson's house.

That was not the end of the cyberattack on the Bhima Koregaon accused and their supporters. Citizen Lab, a Canada-based institution that examines such breaches, said that, between January and October 2019, nine human rights defenders were targeted with emails containing malicious links.[15] Three of the nine were also targeted by Pegasus spyware through WhatsApp in 2019. The NSO group, which manufactures Pegasus spyware, told the court that they only sell to government intelligence and law enforcement agencies.[16]

Who was responsible for this expensive, long-drawn-out manipulation of evidence and targeting of individuals? The only logical answer is that it has to have been one or more government agencies. Which ones though? There are numerous intelligence agencies and security forces that have intelligence operations. A conservative count puts at least twenty-two intelligence arms at the Union level, besides the police at the state level. All of them have some kind of cyber operations, while some of them, like NTRO, R&AW and even IB, have significant capabilities in that area.

Indian and international media have been asking a number of questions around this issue, especially after the Arsenal and Citizen Lab revelations. How did the police and NIA come to target a certain group of people who would go on to be called 'Urban Naxals', creating a very particular narrative? Did someone in the security or intelligence agencies show enterprise in pleasing the political executive? Or did the executive come up with the broad contours of the idea and leave it to the security establishment to stitch up a narrative?

Will any of those officials who were party to the cyber takeover of Wilson's computer ever be held accountable? And more urgently, as the police and NIA story unravels, how long will the Bhima Koregaon accused—among them the poet Varavara Rao, activist Stan Swamy, academic Anand Teltumbde, journalist and activist Gautam Navlakha—be denied bail and justice?

The scripting of political narratives by the security establishment appears to be gathering pace.

B.K. Bansal, a director general in the Ministry of Corporate Affairs, was arrested by the CBI on 16 July 2016. The agency said he had accepted a Rs 20 lakh bribe from a Mumbai-based pharmaceutical company that had duped thousands of investors. A week after the arrest, his wife, Satyabala, and daughter, Neha, committed suicide in their east Delhi apartment. Two months later, Bansal and his son, Yogesh, too killed themselves in the same house. An entire family was gone. However, Bansal left behind a detailed suicide note,[17] in which he named the CBI officers who had tortured him and harassed his family. Bansal claimed in the suicide note that DIG Sanjeev Gautam threatened him, saying that no one would touch him, i.e. Gautam, because he was Amit Shah's man.

A few months before the Bansal family committed suicide, a CBI team landed up in the office of Delhi Chief Minister Arvind Kejriwal. The primary target of the raid was Kejriwal's principal secretary, Rajendra Kumar, an IAS officer who was known for his integrity and had been awarded the Prime Minister's Medal for his outstanding services. As the CBI case dragged on, Kumar decided to opt for voluntary retirement from service, for which he put in a request in January 2017.

I met Kumar to interview him for the *Hindu*, where I worked then. During our conversation, he said the CBI officers offered to let him go free if he named his boss, Kejriwal. I quote from the interview:

JJ: You mean they wanted you to name Arvind Kejriwal? Who told you? Did they explicitly tell you to name Mr Kejriwal?

RK: Yes, yes. There is an inspector in the CBI. And the DIG himself.

JJ: Who is the DIG?

RK: DIG Sanjeev Gautam.

JJ: The same officer who was accused of harassment by Bansal in his suicide note?

RK: Yes, he told me that 'look if you want to get out of it, you will have to tell us things which can get him [Kejriwal] entangled legally'. Not only this case, there is another case of Sandeep Sailas, a railway officer. He has written about misbehaviour, misconduct and illegality conducted by the DIG. The point is, I don't understand in which scenario an officer of a DIG rank can be so important that the whole CBI is willing to get its name dragged, its prestige lowered, they are still defending him. Either there is something very seriously wrong with the organisation, or may be some individuals in the CBI are more powerful than the CBI itself.[18]

In another part of the interview, Kumar spoke about the Bansal case: 'How can a responsible democratic system force somebody to commit suicide in such a gruesome manner? His wife, daughter and son were forced to commit suicide. Let us assume that he was guilty, then it is only the law, the judicial process, which could have determined that he was guilty and punished. People entrusted with the difficult task of investigation have absolutely no business to harass someone . . . each time they harass or abuse or beat somebody, it is not only the abuse of the process of law, but a much bigger illegality committed which will have to be answered at a later day.'

Kumar is waiting for the trial to conclude, so he can move on with his life. Sadly, he is far from alone in this predicament. There is a strange pattern in some of these cases: the investigation agency prepares a massive charge sheet, running to thousands of pages, attaching all kinds of 'evidence' that no one will have the time or patience to go through in detail. When these cases go to trial, the accused may well be exonerated. But in the slow churn of the Indian judiciary, the process is the punishment.

Within a decade of its founding, the NIA was no longer the professional and hard-nosed agency it was devised to be.

In 2017, a special court convicted three RSS workers in the Ajmer dargah bombing of 2007. However, the judgement raised questions about the NIA's clean chit to Pragya Singh and Indresh Kumar without due process.

In April 2018, NIA judge Ravinder Reddy acquitted all accused in the Mecca Masjid blast because, he said, the prosecution could not prove its case. Sheikh Abdul Kaleem, the youngster who moved Aseemanand to confess his crime, said that he plans to write his memoir, but wondered if anyone would publish it. Kaleem completed his law degree in 2013, but was denied jobs by most law firms he applied to.

On 21 March 2019, in the Samjhauta Express blast case, the special NIA court found that the agency had failed to prove the conspiracy, and acquitted Aseemanand and his co-accused. The judicial confession and other related evidence was not enough to hold them.

On 17 April 2019, Home Minister Amit Shah rose to speak in the Rajya Sabha about a bill to extend the NIA's powers. He spoke of the Samjhauta Express blast case, and said the government had decided not to appeal against the acquittal verdict because the charge sheet did not have substantial proof. He claimed that seven people had been originally arrested, the real culprits, but that they were let go with a view to furthering the conspiracy that Hindu terror exists. Shah was lending credence to the original hypothesis that it was an Islamic terror attack—a theory that has repeatedly been proved wrong by investigation agencies. He accused the previous UPA government of linking the attack to the Hindu religion. In making these allegations, the home minister showed a clear lack of respect for the professional breakthroughs of several police forces, the CBI and the NIA.

And as this book endeavours to prove, these agencies, in turn, free of strong accountability mechanisms, are allowing at least a section of the establishment to run loose. The NIA is, of course, far from the only agency that the political executive has wielded to scuttle Indian democracy. The Delhi police, for instance, is another visible sign of the frightening rot that has set into the system.

On 23 February 2020, BJP rabble-rouser Kapil Mishra addressed a crowd of Citizenship (Amendment) Act (CAA) supporters. Bed Prakash Surya, the police chief of northeast Delhi district, quietly stood by as Mishra issued an ultimatum to the police to clear the streets of anti-CAA protestors. He tweeted a summary of his threat, ordering the Delhi police 'to clear the roads in Jaffrabad and Chand Bagh of protestors', and threatening them: 'Don't try to reason with us after this, because we won't listen.'[19] A video of his speech was also tweeted, where he said they will maintain peace for as long as US President Donald Trump was in India. 'After that we refuse to listen to even the police if the roads are not cleared.'

The police officer quietly walked out of the frame.

Then began the riots.

Notes

Prologue

1. Josy Joseph and Pradeep Thakur, 'Punjab cops hound whistleblower, family', 9 July 2010, https://timesofindia.indiatimes.com/india/punjab-cops-hound-whistleblower-family/articleshow/6144969.cms.
2. Powell, Jonathan and Clayton Thyne, 'Coups In The World, 1950-Present' (ongoing data project), https://www.jonathanmpowell.com/coup-detat-dataset.html.
3. Shah Commission of Inquiry: Interim Report Two, 26 April 1978.
4. Shah Commission of Inquiry: Third and Final Report, 6 August 1978.
5. Ibid.
6. Shah Commission of Inquiry: Interim Report Two, 26 April 1978.
7. Shah Commission of Inquiry: Third and Final Report, 6 August 1978.
8. Madan Lokur, 'From Emasculating Fundamental Rights To Selective FIRs: Need A Remedy Against Officers Of State', *LiveLaw.in*, 6 October 2020, https://www.livelaw.in/columns/from-emasculating-fundamental-rights-to-selective-firs-need-a-remedy-against-officers-of-state-writes-justice-madan-lokur-164016.
9. Anand Patel, 'Nearly 50 per cent MPs in new Lok Sabha have criminal records', *India Today*, 25 May 2019, https://www.indiatoday.in/elections/lok-sabha-2019/story/50-per-cent-mps-new-lok-sabha-criminal-records-1534465-2019-05-25.

1. A Distant Echo

1. Wahid's story has been constructed through interviews that the author conducted with him.
2. Writer's own conclusion based on extensive field reporting, and other public sources.

3. Writer's own conclusion based on extensive field reporting, and other public sources.
4. NHRC Annual Report, 2000–01.
5. Ibid.
6. National Crime Records Bureau, https://ncrb.gov.in/en/crime-in-india-table-addtional-table-and-chapter-contents?field_date_value[value][year]=2013&items_per_page=All.
7. Ibid.
8. Prime Minister's High-Level Committee for Preparation of Report on Social, Economic and Educational Status of the Muslim Community of India, November 2006.
9. Josy Joseph, 'The Cop Who Came in from the Cold', *Mumbai Mirror*, 19 January 2020, https://mumbaimirror.indiatimes.com/others/sunday-read/the-cop-who-came-in-from-the-cold/articleshow/73363152.cms.
10. Paramita Ghosh, 'Irshad Ali was a police informer. Until the police framed him', *Hindustan Times*, 27 February 2017, https://www.hindustantimes.com/india-news/irshad-ali-was-a-police-informer-until-the-police-framed-him/story-kZheoeNBckWIWuvkhXsZkK.html.
11. Ibid.
12. Josy Joseph, 'The Cop Who Came in from the Cold', *Mumbai Mirror*, 19 January 2020, https://mumbaimirror.indiatimes.com/others/sunday-read/the-cop-who-came-in-from-the-cold/articleshow/73363152.cms.
13. Vinod K. Jose, 'Mulakat Afzal', *The Caravan*, 2 February 2013, https://caravanmagazine.in/reportage/mulakat-afzal.
14. Afzal Guru, 'I Hope My Forced Silence Will Be Heard', *Outlook*, 21 October 2004, https://www.outlookindia.com/website/story/i-hope-my-forced-silence-will-be-heard/225472.
15. Bhartesh Singh Thakur, 'ACP Rajbir murder case: Life term sentenced to property dealer', *Hindustan Times*, 29 October 2015, https://www.hindustantimes.com/punjab/acp-rajbir-murder-case-life-term-sentenced-to-property-dealer/story-kkgd3BybmfgvW5uVdl63iN.html.
16. Correspondent, 'The rise and fall of ACP Rajbir Singh', *Hindustan Times*, 25 March 2008, https://www.hindustantimes.com/delhi/the-rise-and-fall-of-acp-rajbir-singh/story-Sk9JrdkdI61IaCUoutYrnJ.html.
17. Concerned Citizens' Tribunal, *Crime Against Humanity: Volume II: An inquiry into the carnage in Gujarat; Findings and recommendations*, https://cjp.org.in/justice-for-suresh/crime-against-humanity-vol-2/.

18. Ibid.
19. Ibid., Vol. II, p. 75.
20. Ibid.
21. Ibid.
22. IANS, '2002 Gujarat riots: Despite request to Narendra Modi, Army lost a crucial day waiting for vehicles, says Lt General Zameer Uddin', *The New Indian Express*, 6 October 2018, https://www.newindianexpress.com/nation/2018/oct/05/2002-gujarat-riots-despite-request-to-narendra-modi-army-lost-a-crucial-day-waiting-for-vehicles-1881533.html.
23. Neeraj Chauhan, 'In CBI FIR, complainant says he paid Rs 3 crore to special director Rakesh Asthana', *The Times of India*, 22 October 2018, https://timesofindia.indiatimes.com/india/cbi-fir-against-rakesh-asthana-nowhere-mentions-complainants-conversation-meeting-or-exchange-of-bribe/articleshow/66307995.cms.
24. Ibid.
25. Prabhash K. Dutta, 'Inside story of Alok Verma vs Rakesh Asthana fight in CBI', *India Today*, 23 October 2018, https://www.indiatoday.in/india/story/inside-story-of-alok-verma-vs-rakesh-asthana-fight-in-cbi-1373623-2018-10-23. Also see: Munish Chandra Pandey, 'Free food, hotel rooms at Rs 175 a night: Rakesh Asthana daughter's wedding on CBI radar', *India Today*, 24 October 2018, https://www.indiatoday.in/india/story/rakesh-asthana-daughter-wedding-1374619-2018-10-24.
26. Munish Pandey, 'Sterling Biotech case: ED summons Dino Morea, DJ Aqeel in Rs 15,000 crore scam', *Business Today*, 1 July 2019, https://www.businesstoday.in/current/economy-politics/sterling-biotech-case-ed-summons-dino-morea-dj-aqeel-rs-15000-crore-scam/story/360280.html.
27. Pradeep Thakur, 'In a boost to ED, court declares Sandesara brothers "fugitive economic offenders"', *The Times of India*, 29 September 2020, https://timesofindia.indiatimes.com/city/delhi/in-a-boost-to-ed-court-declares-sandesara-brothers-fugitive-economic-offenders/articleshow/78375493.cms.
28. Rahul Nair, 'He Rose to Power Too Soon: IPS Officers on Rakesh Asthana', *TheQuint.com*, 26 October 2018, https://www.thequint.com/news/india/cbi-rakesh-asthana-in-gujarat-cadre-ips-officers-speak.

29. Narender Pani, 'Many parallels between Indira, Modi regimes', *BusinessLine*, 24 February 2020, https://www.thehindubusinessline.com/opinion/columns/many-parallels-between-indira-modi-regimes/article30900536.ece.
30. ENS, 'Explained: What is Justice Bedi report on Gujarat fake encounters, why SC order could spell trouble for several policemen', 9 January 2019, https://indianexpress.com/article/explained/explained-justice-bedi-report-on-gujarat-fake-encounters-5530501/; 'Sohrab case IPS to head Gujarat police', *The Telegraph*, 5 April 2017, https://www.telegraphindia.com/odisha/sohrab-case-ips-to-head-gujarat-police/cid/1398297; 'The Man Who Would Not Bend', *Outlook*, https://magazine.outlookindia.com/story/the-man-who-would-not-bend/293302.
31. Manoj Mitta, '"Preplanned inhuman collective violent act of terrorism": What Modi got away with in the Godhra case', *Scroll.in*, 27 February 2017, https://scroll.in/article/830319/preplanned-inhuman-collective-violent-act-of-terrorism-what-modi-got-away-with-in-the-godhra-case.
32. Concerned Citizens' Tribunal, Crime Against Humanity: Volume II: An inquiry into the carnage in Gujarat; Findings and recommendations, https://cjp.org.in/justice-for-suresh/crime-against-humanity-vol-2/.
33. Ujjwal K. Chowdhury, 'Ten Reasons Modi is Just Like Indira Gandhi. And That's Not a Good Thing', *TheWire.in*, 3 June 2018, https://thewire.in/politics/ten-reasons-modi-is-just-like-indira-gandhi-and-thats-not-a-good-thing.
34. Uday Balakrishnan, 'Keeping the military apolitical', *The Hindu*, 31 October 2019, https://www.thehindu.com/opinion/op-ed/keeping-the-military-apolitical/article29835217.ece.
35. Concerned Citizens' Tribunal, Crime Against Humanity: Volume II: An inquiry into the carnage in Gujarat; Findings and recommendations, https://cjp.org.in/justice-for-suresh/crime-against-humanity-vol-2/.
36. Vinod K. Jose, 'Narendra Modi's shadow lies all over the Haren Pandya case', *The Caravan*, 6 July 2019, https://caravanmagazine.in/politics/haren-pandya-narendra-modi-murder-case-supreme-court.
37. Sanjoy Majumder, 'Narendra Modi "allowed" Gujarat 2002 anti-Muslim riots', *BBC.com*, 22 April 2011, https://www.bbc.com/news/world-south-asia-13170914. Also see: Garima Mishra, 'Ex-DGP Sreekumar launches "Gujarat Behind The Curtain"', *The Indian*

Express, 26 September 2016, https://indianexpress.com/article/india/india-news-india/ex-dgp-sreekumar-launches-gujarat-behind-the-curtain/.

38. Correspondent, 'Modi out of hospital, Pandya out of poll', *The Telegraph*, 24 November 2002, https://www.telegraphindia.com/india/modi-out-of-hospital-pandya-out-of-poll/cid/856003.
39. Shastri Ramachandran, 'The Many Questions Still Unanswered 15 Years After Haren Pandya's Killing', *TheWire.in*, 5 November 2018, https://thewire.in/rights/haren-pandya-killing-gujarat. Also see: Vidya Subrahmaniam, 'A whodunnit riddled with bullet holes', *The Hindu*, 30 September 2011, https://www.thehindu.com/opinion/op-ed/a-whodunnit-riddled-with-bullet-holes/article2497777.ece.
40. Dionne Bunsha, 'An ex-minister's murder', *Frontline*, 25 April 2003, https://frontline.thehindu.com/other/article30216602.ece.
41. Bureau, 'Denying ticket to Pandya was "big injustice": Advani', ZeeNews.com, 6 April 2003, https://zeenews.india.com/news/nation/denying-ticket-to-pandya-was-big-injustice-advani_90359.html.
42. Bureau, 'Did Vanzara kill Pandya too?', *Mail Today*, 9 September 2009, https://www.indiatoday.in/latest-headlines/story/did-vanzara-kill-pandya-too-56134-2009-09-09.
43. Vinod K. Jose, 'Narendra Modi's shadow lies all over the Haren Pandya case: an excerpt', *The Caravan*, 6 July 2019, https://caravanmagazine.in/politics/haren-pandya-narendra-modi-murder-case-supreme-court.
44. Ibid.
45. Wire Staff, 'The "Botched and Blinkered" Past of the NIA's Next Chief', *TheWire.in*, 19 September 2017, https://thewire.in/government/the-botched-and-blinkered-past-of-the-nias-next-chief.
46. *Central Bureau Of Investigation vs Mohd. Parvez Abdul Kayuum*, 5 July 2019, https://indiankanoon.org/doc/85115254/.
47. Krishnadas Rajagopal, 'SC refuses plea for fresh probe or reinvestigation into Haren Pandya killing', *The Hindu*, 5 July 2019, https://www.thehindu.com/news/national/sc-refuses-cpils-plea-for-fresh-probe-into-murder-of-haren-pandya/article28292324.ece.
48. Krishnadas Rajagopal, 'Prashant Bhushan held guilty of contempt for tweets against CJI', *The Hindu*, 14 August 2020, https://www.

thehindu.com/news/national/prashant-bhushan-held-guilty-of-contempt-for-tweets-against-cji/article32351999.ece.

49. Aparna Alluri and Anand Katakam, 'The Ishrat Jahan encounter case, explained', *Hindustan Times*, https://www.hindustantimes.com/static/ishratjahan/.
50. Metropolitan Magistrate Inquiry Number 1/2009, available at https://www.countercurrents.org/israt.pdf.
51. Aparna Alluri and Anand Katakam, 'The Ishrat Jahan encounter case, explained', *Hindustan Times*, https://www.hindustantimes.com/static/ishratjahan/.
52. Praveen Swami, 'I was nationalist, then Communist, but Babri and riots changed me: IM operative Sadiq Sheikh', *The Indian Express*, 1 October 2015, https://indianexpress.com/article/india/india-news-india/i-was-nationalist-then-communist-but-babri-and-riots-changed-me-says-im-operative-sadiq-sheikh/.

2. Ripped Apart

1. Menaka Rao (reporting by), 'Mumbai blasts 2006: India court finds 12 men guilty', BBC.com, 11 September 2015, https://www.bbc.com/news/world-asia-india-34218396.
2. The Newswire, 'Maharashtra ATS Chief KP Raghuvanshi Removed', *Outlook*, 25 March 2010, https://www.outlookindia.com/newswire/story/maharashtra-ats-chief-kp-raghuvanshi-removed/677767.
3. Examination-in-chief of Wahid by Adv. Sharif Shaikh h/f adv Shetty for A8 R.O (Y.D. Shinde), Special Judge, Spl. Judge under MCOC Act 99, Date 18/06/13 Mumbai.
4. National Campaign Against Torture, *India: Annual Report on Torture: 2019*, 26 June 2020, http://www.uncat.org/wp-content/uploads/2020/06/INDIATORTURE2019.pdf.
5. S. Ahmed and S.Balakrishnan, 'ATS officer may have committed suicide', *The Times of India*, 30 August 2006, https://timesofindia.indiatimes.com/city/mumbai/ats-officer-may-have-committed-suicide/articleshow/1937771.cms.
6. Dayanand Kamath and Anupam Dasgupta, 'Suicide or accident? ATS officer's death leaves cops in doubt', *DNA*, 29 August 2006, https://www.dnaindia.com/mumbai/report-suicide-or-accident-ats-officer-s-death-leaves-cops-in-doubt-1050037.

7. Neeraj Chauhan, 'Nearly 5 persons died every day in custody during FY19-20: MHA to Parliament', *Hindustan Times*, 16 September 2020, https://www.hindustantimes.com/india-news/nearly-5-persons-died-every-day-in-custody-during-fy19-20-mha-to-parliament/story-GNjgYoiutXfTMzkVn7nDTN.html.
8. Debashish Panigrahi, 'Raghuvanshi had a rocky ride as ATS chief', *Hindustan Times*, 26 March 2010, https://www.hindustantimes.com/mumbai/raghuvanshi-had-a-rocky-ride-as-ats-chief/story-oJNiAuvpLfHfZvJSWUkFEP.html.
9. Ibid.
10. Gurpreet Bal, 'Violence, migration and entrepreneurship: Punjab during the Khalistan movement', *Economic and Political Weekly*, Vol. 40, No. 36 (3–9 September 2005), pp. 3978–3986, https://www.jstor.org/stable/4417114?seq=1.
11. Author's interview with Abdul Wahid.
12. Ibid.
13. Josy Joseph, 'Malegaon blasts: It may not be the usual suspects', *DNA*, 9 September 2006, https://www.dnaindia.com/india/report-malegaon-blasts-it-may-not-be-the-usual-suspects-1051919.
14. Examination-in-chief of Wahid by Adv. Sharif Shaikh h/f adv. Shetty for A8 R.O (Y.D. Shinde) Special Judge, Spl. Judge under MCOC Act 99, Date 18/06/13 Mumbai.
15. NHRC, 'Guidelines on Administration of Lie Detector Test', https://nhrc.nic.in/press-release/guidelines-administration-lie-detector-test.
16. *Sr. Sephy V. Union of India*, https://caselaw.in/kerala/sr-sephy-v-union-of-india-b-a-no-7311-of-2008-ker/6063/.
17. 'Malini's trek to hall of shame', *The New Indian Express*, 28 February 2009, https://www.newindianexpress.com/cities/bengaluru/2009/feb/28/malinis-trek-to-hall-of-shame-29217.html.
18. Rakesh Prakash, 'Dr Narco and Ms Hide', *Bangalore Mirror*, 28 February 2009, https://bangaloremirror.indiatimes.com/opinion/sunday-read/dr-narco-and-ms-hide/articleshow/22204505.cms.
19. 'Narco Queen Disgraced', *Bangalore Mirror*, 27 February 2009, https://bangaloremirror.indiatimes.com/bangalore/others/narco-queen-disgraced/articleshow/22206542.cms
20. Manish Ranjan and Sahil Makkar, 'No narco analysis without consent, rules Supreme Court', *Mint*, 22 May 2010, https://www.livemint.

com/Home-Page/Xs1om9C5GeFvbmSgGoCSsM/No-narco-analysis-without-consent-rules-Supreme-Court.html.

21. *Chawl v. State of Maharashtra*, 21 July 2009, https://indiankanoon.org/doc/1970566/. The Supreme Court order is available here: *The State of Maharashtra & Ors v. Saeed Sohail Sheikh & Ors*, https://indiankanoon.org/doc/117760733/.
22. Ibid.
23. *Chawl v. State of Maharashtra*, 21 July 2009, https://indiankanoon.org/doc/1970566/
24. *The State of Maharashtra & Others v. Saeed Sohail Sheikh & Others*, 2 November 2012, https://indiankanoon.org/doc/117760733/.
25. Sabika Abbas, 'Manjula Shetye's Death in Byculla Jail: A Year on, Little has Changed', *TheWire.in*, 26 June 2018, https://thewire.in/government/manjula-shetyes-death-in-byculla-jail-a-year-on-little-has-changed.
26. She opposed and challenged the transfer from Pune to Nagpur (https://mat.maharashtra.gov.in/Site/Upload/Pdf/O.A.274-2020%20Transfer.pdf) and then did not resume duty, which led the prison department to order her suspension: Mateen Hafeez & Clara Lewis, 'Maharashtra: DIG may be suspended for neglecting duty', *The Times of India*, 30 August 2020, https://timesofindia.indiatimes.com/city/mumbai/maharashtra-dig-may-be-suspended-for-neglecting-duty/articleshow/77829575.cms.

3. Meet the Bombers

1. Rakesh Maria, *Let Me Say It Now*, Westland, Delhi, 2020, p. 330.
2. Ibid., p. 330.
3. 'Blast accused says he was in "D" Company of don's aide', *The Indian Express*, 27 September 2008, http://archive.indianexpress.com/news/blast-accused-says-he-was-in--d--company-of-don-s-aide/366517/.
4. Rakesh Maria, *Let Me Say It Now*, Westland, Delhi, 2020, p. 340.
5. Vijaita Singh, 'The Mumbai train blast mystery thickens', *The Hindu*, 22 January 2018, https://www.thehindu.com/news/national/the-mumbai-train-blast-mystery-thickens/article22492043.ece; IndianExpressOnline, 'Sadiq Sheikh: "We Planted Bombs" in 7/11 Mumbai Train Blasts | Police Interrogation Video', YouTube, https://www.youtube.com/watch?v=mqet4ezofkQ.

6. Praveen Swami, 'Post-script to 2006 Mumbai blasts verdict: A police video of IM's Sadiq Sheikh saying "we did it", *The Indian Express*, 1 October 2015, https://indianexpress.com/article/india/india-others/post-script-to-verdict-a-police-video-of-ims-sadiq-sheikh-saying-we-did-it/.
7. Rakesh Maria, *Let Me Say It Now*, Westland, Delhi, 2020, p. 348.
8. See this report from the Jamia Teachers' Solidarity Group for details of the discrepancies: '"Encounter" at Batla House: Unanswered Questions', https://revolutionarydemocracy.org/batla/batla.htm.
9. See para 7 in *Pragya Singh Chandrapalsingh v. The State of Maharashtra*, https://indiankanoon.org/doc/159691224/.
10. Ajoy Ashirwad Mahaprashasta, 'Here's Why Investigators Saw Clear Hindutva Link to Samjhauta Bombing', *TheWire.in*, 21 March 2019, https://thewire.in/communalism/2007-samjhauta-express-blast-case-vikash-narain-rai.
11. Ibid.
12. Ibid.
13. Rakesh Dixit and Ipsita Chakravarty, 'After a decade of investigations, it appears no one killed RSS pracharak Sunil Joshi', *Scroll.in*, 3 February 2017, https://scroll.in/article/828397/after-a-decade-of-investigations-it-appears-no-one-killed-rss-pracharak-sunil-joshi.
14. Ibid.
15. Deeptiman Tiwary, 'Explained: The case against BJP candidate Sadhvi Pragya Thakur', *The Indian Express*, 20 April 2019, https://indianexpress.com/article/explained/sadhvi-pragya-thakur-digvijaya-singh-bjp-bhopal-lok-sabha-elections-malegaon-case-ajmer-dargah-blast-5681180/.
16. Consider, for instance, the police looking at 'Love Jihad', a Hindu right-wing construct that has been repeatedly proven to be false: https://thewire.in/communalism/uttar-pradesh-love-jihad-police-yogi-adityanath-hindutva-vigilantes. Vibhuti Narayan Rai, a retired police officer, about the pressure of Hindutva forces on the police: https://indianexpress.com/article/opinion/columns/hindutva-mob-impunity-muslim-houses-attacked-7200038/. The *New York Times* reports on how India's police are accused of abusing Muslims: https://www.nytimes.com/2020/01/02/world/asia/india-protests-police-muslims.html. Maria Arena, the Chair of the European Parliament's

Subcommittee on Human Rights, expressed grave concern about India's deteriorating rule of law, and called for an investigation into the Delhi police's role in the February 2020 riots against Muslims: https://southasiamonitor.org/india/european-rights-body-calls-probe-human-rights-violations-india.

17. Ananya Bharadwaj, 'CBI, ED, IT probes against opposition politicians—on at election time, off after that', *ThePrint.in*, 16 April 2021, https://theprint.in/india/cbi-ed-it-probes-against-opposition-politicians-on-at-election-time-off-after-that/640596/. Also see: 'ED has become a political tool of BJP, says Thomas Isaac', *Mathrubhumi*, 28 November 2020, https://english.mathrubhumi.com/news/kerala/ed-has-become-a-political-tool-of-bjp-says-thomas-isaac-1.5240450.
18. PTI, 'ED raids multiple premises in money laundering case against GVK Group, MIAL', *Mint*, 28 July 2020, https://www.livemint.com/companies/news/ed-raids-multiple-premises-in-money-laundering-case-against-gvk-group-mial-11595918444000.html.
19. 'Judicial Harassment of Teesta Setalvad', https://www.frontlinedefenders.org/en/case/judicial-harassment-teesta-setalvad.
20. Geetika Mantri, '67 journalists arrested, detained, questioned in India in 2020 for their work', TheNewsMinute.com, 6 January 2021, https://www.thenewsminute.com/article/67-journalists-arrested-detained-questioned-india-2020-their-work-140963.
21. Kumar Anshuman & Jayant Sriram, 'Fear of CBI inquiries and arbitrary transfers grips the bureaucracy in the wake of the case against former coal secretary P.C. Parakh', *India Today*, 18 November 2013, https://www.indiatoday.in/magazine/the-big-story/story/20131118-coal-scam-2g-scam-pc-parakh-bureaucrats-cbi-trai-policy-paralysis-768463-1999-11-30.
22. The NIA's derailing of the Samjhauta Express case is an example of this: https://indianexpress.com/article/india/all-four-walk-free-in-samjhauta-express-attack-that-killed-68-aseemanand-5636716/. As is the Bhima Koregaon case, where forensic evidence was planted: https://www.washingtonpost.com/context/new-forensics-report-concludes-evidence-was-planted-in-case-against-indian-activists/1fb9874f-0f32-44fc-b9e9-0e59b69e9200/. Opposition leader Rahul Gandhi appears to have noticed too: https://scroll.in/latest/950193/rahul-gandhi-takes-dig-at-nia-chief-says-davinder-singhs-case-will-be-as-good-as-dead-under-him.

23. Rakesh Dixit and Ipsita Chakravarty, 'After a decade of investigations, it appears no one killed RSS pracharak Sunil Joshi', *Scroll.in*, 3 February 2017, https://scroll.in/article/828397/after-a-decade-of-investigations-it-appears-no-one-killed-rss-pracharak-sunil-joshi.
24. Nikita Saxena, 'Good Faith, Bad Faith', *The Caravan*, 15 May 2019, https://caravanmagazine.in/religion/elections-2019-hindu-terror-islamic-sikh-terrorism-mac-narendra-modi. Dnyanesh Jathar, 'Hindu terrorism only a narrative created by Congress: Fadnavis', *The Week*, 23 April 2019, https://www.theweek.in/news/india/2019/04/23/Hindu-terrorism-only-a-narrative-created-by-Congress-Fadnavis.html.
25. Ajoy Ashirwad Mahaprashasta, 'Here's Why Investigators Saw Clear Hindutva Link to Samjhauta Bombing', *TheWire.in*, https://thewire.in/communalism/2007-samjhauta-express-blast-case-vikash-narain-rai.
26. Suhasini Haidar, 'U.S., U.K., India had many leads but failed to stop 26/11', *The Hindu*, 22 December 2014, https://www.thehindu.com/news/national/deadly-nearmisses-in-spycraft-history-resulted-in-2611/article6715736.ece.
27. Wire Staff, 'Full Text: What the High Level Inquiry Committee on the 26/11 Attacks Had to Say', *TheWire.in*, 25 November 2018, https://thewire.in/security/26-11-mumbai-terror-attack-inquiry-committee.
28. Suhasini Haidar, 'U.S., U.K., India had many leads but failed to stop 26/11', *The Hindu*, 22 December 2014, https://www.thehindu.com/news/national/deadly-nearmisses-in-spycraft-history-resulted-in-2611/article6715736.ece.

4. Raiding Mumbai

1. Jason Burke, 'Mumbai's infamous police "encounter squad" dream of comeback', *The Guardian*, 6 March 2011, https://www.theguardian.com/world/2011/mar/06/mumbai-police-encounter-squad-return.
2. Wire Staff, 'Full Text: What the High Level Inquiry Committee on the 26/11 Attacks Had to Say', *TheWire.in*, 25 November 2018, https://thewire.in/security/26-11-mumbai-terror-attack-inquiry-committee.
3. HT Correspondent, 'Aerial strikes are Mumbai's next worry: Pradhan report', *Hindustan Times*, 27 December 2009, https://www.hindustantimes.com/mumbai/aerial-strikes-are-mumbai-s-next-worry-pradhan-report/story-CEDEkFI5MUvqXfUXSyMlFI.html.

4. Report of the High Level Enquiry Committee on 26/11, p. 7.
5. Central agencies such as CBI and ED, and state police forces have investigated dozens of arms procurement cases. Some details can be found here: https://sites.tufts.edu/corruptarmsdeals/tag/india/.
6. Shreya Raman, Shreehari Paliath, '14 Years On, No State/UT Has Fully Implemented SC-Mandated Police Reforms', *IndiaSpend.com*, 22 September 2020, https://www.indiaspend.com/14-years-on-no-state-ut-has-implemented-sc-mandated-police-reforms.
7. PTI, 'Mumbai constable survives terror attacks to recount horror', *The Times of India*, 29 November 2008, https://timesofindia.indiatimes.com/city/mumbai/mumbai-constable-survives-terror-attacks-to-recount-horror/articleshow/3772676.cms.
8. TT Bureau, 'When Modi Turned Up at Karkare's House', *The Telegraph*, 20 April 2019, https://www.telegraphindia.com/india/when-modi-turned-up-at-karkares-house/cid/1689083.
9. Anand Patel, 'Exclusive: Col Purohit was falsely implicated, UPA wanted to hasten probe, says ex-top military intelligence officer', *India Today*, 1 September 2017, https://www.indiatoday.in/india/delhi/story/lieutenant-colonel-shrikant-prasad-purohit-2008-malegaon-blast-case-upa-government-1035602-2017-09-01.

5. Free at Last

1. 'Sadiq Sheikh: "We Planted Bombs" in 7/11 Mumbai Train Blasts | Police Interrogation Video', https://www.youtube.com/watch?v=mqet4ezofkQ.
2. Ibid.
3. PTI, 'IM founder member Sadiq unlikely to be booked in 7/11 blast', *The Economic Times*, 17 March 2009, https://economictimes.indiatimes.com/news/politics-and-nation/im-founder-member-sadiq-unlikely-to-be-booked-in-7/11-blast/articleshow/4278325.cms.
4. Submissions to the review committee on POTA by Commonwealth Human Rights Initiative, 7 October 2003.
5. T.S. Subramanian, 'The arrest of Nedumaran', *Frontline*, 17 August 2002, https://frontline.thehindu.com/other/article30245808.ece.
6. V. Venkatesan, 'A reality check', *Frontline*, 13 August 2004, https://frontline.thehindu.com/the-nation/article30223881.ece.
7. Submissions to the review committee on POTA by Commonwealth Human Rights Initiative, 7 October 2003.

8. 'Impact of Anti-Terrorism Laws on the enjoyment of Human Rights in India', *Liberation*, https://www.upr-info.org/sites/default/files/document/india/session_1_-_april_2008/libinduprs12008liberationuprsubmission.pdf.
9. 'Parliamentary proceedings: 2.2 % of cases registered under the UAPA from 2016-2019 ended in court conviction", *The Hindu*, 10 February 2021, https://www.thehindu.com/news/national/22-of-cases-registered-under-the-uapa-from-2016-2019-ended-in-court-conviction/article33804099.ece.
10. Mahtab Alam, 'The Advocate Of The Terrorised: Remembering Shahid Azmi, On The Day He Was Murdered', YouthKiAwaaz.com, 11 February 2015, https://www.youthkiawaaz.com/2015/02/shahid-azmi-murder-case/.
11. 'Indefensible Murder', *ThePatriot.in*, 16 February 2020, http://thepatriot.in/2020/02/16/indefensible-murder/. Ajit Sahi, 'A Grain in My Bowl', *Tehelka*, 27 February 2010, https://swap.stanford.edu/20100402180206/http%3A//tehelka.com/story_main43.asp?filename%3DNe270210a_grain.asp.
12. These are part of the arguments captured in the final judgement: MCOC Special Case No.21 of 2006, decided on 30 September 2015 in the Special Court No. I of the Special Judge Under the Maharashtra Control of Organised Crime Act, 1999 and the National Investigative Agency Act, 2008 at Mumbai.
13. Ibid.
14. Aishwarya S. Iyer, 'Mumbai 7/11 Train Blasts: Status Check, Five Years After Verdict', *TheQuint.com*, 12 September 2020, https://www.thequint.com/news/india/mumbai-2006-bomb-blasts-711-status-check-5-years-since-high-court-verdict.
15. Bhavna Uchil, '2006 Mumbai serial train blast convict dies of COVID-19 in Nagpur hospital', *The Free Press Journal*, 20 April 2021, https://www.freepressjournal.in/mumbai/2006-mumbai-serial-train-blast-convict-dies-of-covid-19-in-nagpur-prison.
16. These are part of the arguments captured in the final judgement: MCOC Special Case No.21 of 2006, decided on 30 September 2015 in the Special Court No. I of the Special Judge Under the Maharashtra Control of Organised Crime Act, 1999 and the National Investigative Agency Act, 2008 at Mumbai.

17. Dipanjan Sinha, 'Innocence Network: After freedom, the fight for justice', *Hindustan Times*, 11 April 2019, https://www.hindustantimes.com/weekend/after-freedom-the-fight-for-justice/story-Gcg33k19seHL5ks0c3w5VL.html.

6. A Valley in Flames

1. Owen L. Sirrs, *Pakistan's Inter-Services Intelligence Directorate: Covert Action and Internal Operations*, Routledge, Delhi, 2017.
2. Muhammad Yusuf Saraf, *Kashmiris Fight for Freedom (1947–78): Vol-2*, Ferozsons Ltd, Lahore, 1979.
3. There are no official figures on the total number of India's security personnel in Kashmir, or the cost incurred there. Guesstimates put the number of army personnel, paramilitary and state police combined in the range of half a million. See, for instance: Mirza Waheed, 'India's illegal power grab is turning Kashmir into a colony', *The Guardian*, 14 August 2019, https://www.theguardian.com/commentisfree/2019/aug/14/narendra-modi-kashmir-hindu-first-india-autonomy.
4. https://undocs.org/S/RES/39(1948).
5. Josef Korbel, *Danger in Kashmir*, Princeton Legacy Library, Princeton, NJ, 2016 (originally published in 1954).
6. https://unmogip.unmissions.org/unmogip-facts-and-figures.
7. Naseer Ganai, 'Srinagar's dreaded interrogation centres get makeover', *India Today*, 20 February 2012, https://www.indiatoday.in/india/north/story/srinagar-dreaded-interrogation-centres-get-makeover-93597-2012-02-20.
8. Naseer Ganai, 'Srinagar's dreaded interrogation centres get makeover', *India Today*, 20 February 2012, https://www.indiatoday.in/india/north/story/srinagar-dreaded-interrogation-centres-get-makeover-93597-2012-02-20.
9. Ibid.
10. Ibid.
11. Lt Gen. H.S. Panag (Retd), 'Strengthen counter-infiltration grid by moving 10 RR battalions from terror operations', *ThePrint.in*, 14 May 2020, https://theprint.in/opinion/strengthen-counter-infiltration-grid-move-10-rr-battalion-from-terror-ops/421059/.
12. Zahid Rafiq, 'From Kashmir to California: In the footsteps of a wanted killer', *The Christian Science Monitor*, 12 June 2012, https://

www.csmonitor.com/World/Asia-South-Central/2012/0612/From-Kashmir-to-California-in-the-footsteps-of-a-wanted-killer.

13. Documents that Pramod shared with me as his frustration with the system mounted.
14. Prabhu Chawla, 'There is not even a single area in which Kashmir has not suffered: G.M. Shah', *India Today*, 31 July 1984, https://www.indiatoday.in/magazine/cover-story/story/19840731-there-is-not-even-a-single-area-in-which-kashmir-has-not-suffered-g.m.-shah-803176-1984-07-31.
15. Altaf Hussain, 'Kashmir's flawed elections', *BBC News*, 14 September 2002, http://news.bbc.co.uk/1/hi/world/south_asia/2223364.stm.
16. Saurabh Vaktania, 'Not relevant after 65 years: Congress on BJP claim that Nehru denied probe into Syama Prasad Mookerjee's death', *India Today*, 23 June 2019, https://www.indiatoday.in/india/story/congress-nehru-syama-prasad-mookerjee-jp-death-inquiry-1554722-2019-06-23.
17. Ravi Rohmetra, 'A tribute to Mookerjee', *Daily Excelsior*, 23 June 2013, https://www.dailyexcelsior.com/a-tribute-to-mookerjee/.
18. H.K. Dua, 'Vajpayee was democrat to the core', *Outlook*, 17 August 2018, https://www.outlookindia.com/newsscroll/vajpayee-was-democrat-to-the-core/1367124.
19. Suba Chandran, 'Limited War with Pakistan: Will It Secure India's Interests?', Program in Arms Control, Disarmament, and International Security, University of Illinois at Urbana-Champaign, August 2004, p. 18, https://core.ac.uk/download/pdf/161954175.pdf.
20. Josy Joseph, 'We will support any serious attempt to solve the Kashmir issue', Rediff.com, 6 April 2006, https://www.rediff.com/news/2001/apr/06inter.htm.
21. Hartosh Singh Bal, 'How the Congress propped up Bhindranwale', *The Caravan*, 8 June 2019, https://caravanmagazine.in/conflict/how-the-congress-propped-up-bhindranwale.
22. https://www.tribuneindia.com/2012/20120708/spectrum/main1.htm.
23. Sant Nirankaris, a Sikh sect that believed in a living guru, took out a procession in Amritsar to celebrate Baisakhi in 1978—an important day for Sikhs because Guru Gobind Singh founded the Khalsa order on Baisakhi day in 1699. The Nirankari procession was an act of

provocation to the orthodox Sikhs. A group of angry Sikhs assembled near the Golden Temple under the leadership of Bhindranwale, and with kirpans drawn, they marched towards the Nirankari procession. The Nirankaris were ready, and shot down thirteen men.

24. The Newswire, 'Former CM Bhajan Lal disqualified from Haryana assembly', *Outlook*, 25 March 2008, https://www.outlookindia.com/newswire/story/former-cm-bhajan-lal-disqualified-from-haryana-assembly/556719.
25. 'Decades of Terror: Exploring Human Rights Abuses in Kashmir and the Disputed Territories', 108th Congress, Second Session, 21 May 2004, https://www.govinfo.gov/content/pkg/CHRG-108hhrg96410/html/CHRG-108hhrg96410.htm.
26. Mark Tully & Satish Jacob, *Amritsar: Mrs Gandhi's Last Battle*, Rupa & Co, Delhi, 1985, p. 84.
27. Carol Off, 'A new battlefield for India's Sikhs', *Maclean's*, 6 December 1982, https://archive.macleans.ca/article/1982/12/6/a-new-battlefield-for-indias-sikhs.
28. 'Famous Sikhs: General Shabeg Singh', *AllAboutSikhs.com*, https://www.allaboutsikhs.com/biographies/1900/famous-sikhsgeneral-shabeg-singh/.
29. William Claiborne, 'Sikh Mutinies Spreading in India's Army', *The Washington Post*, 12 June 1984, https://www.washingtonpost.com/archive/politics/1984/06/12/sikh-mutinies-spreading-in-indias-army/5974cbaa-26f6-46d2-88e0-e7fc468779ed/.
30. 'Army Begins Court Martial Of Sikhs Who Mutinied After Temple Siege', APNews.com, 24 February 1985, https://apnews.com/article/70beac35e6f6a0aaac28edd33663d04d
31. Sanjoy Hazarika, 'Indians Say Exiles in Europe and U.S. Stirred Sikh Revolt', *The New York Times*, 11 July 1984, https://www.nytimes.com/1984/07/11/world/indians-say-exiles-in-europe-and-us-stirred-sikh-revolt.html.
32. 'Operation Blue Star: Chronology of Events', http://www.sikhmuseum.com/bluestar/chronology.html.
33. William K. Stevens, 'Punjab Raid: Unanswered Questions', *The New York Times*, 19 June 1984, https://www.nytimes.com/1984/06/19/world/punjab-raid-unanswered-questions.html.
34. Allistair Fitzgerald (ed.), *Air Crash Investigations: Mass Murder in the*

Sky—The Bombing of Air India Flight 182, Lulu Press, Morrisville, NC, 2011, p. 335.

35. Sumantra Bose, *Kashmir: Roots of Conflict, Paths to Peace*, Harvard University Press, 2009, Chapter 2: The Kashmir–India Debacle.
36. Ibid., p. 49.
37. G.N. Gauhar, *Elections in Jammu and Kashmir*, Manas Publications, Delhi, 2002, p. 120.
38. Sumantra Bose, *Kashmir: Roots of Conflict, Paths to Peace*, Harvard University Press, 2009, location 456 of the eBook on Kindle.
39. Ibid., location 456 to 479 of the eBook on Kindle.

7. Our Boys

1. Josy Joseph, 'Till the LTTE get Eelam, they won't stop: interview with Major General Harkirat Singh', Rediff.com, March 2000, https://www.rediff.com/news/2000/mar/30lanka.htm.
2. Depinder Singh, *Indian Peace Keeping Force in Sri Lanka*, Natraj Publishers, Delhi, 2001, p. X.
3. Vineet Khare, 'Return to Sri Lanka: Indian soldier revisits a brutal battlefield', *BBC News*, 18 October 2017, https://www.bbc.com/news/world-asia-india-41377725. Also see: Press Information Bureau (Defence Wing), 'Economic Burden by Sending IPKF in Sri Lanka', 15 December 1999, https://archive.pib.gov.in/archive/ArchiveSecondPhase/DEFENCE/1999-JULY-DEC-MIN-OF-DEFENCE/PDF/DEF-1999-12-15_300.pdf.
4. A.G. Noorani, 'Shocking Disclosures', *Frontline*, 21 September 2007, https://frontline.thehindu.com/other/article30192914.ece.
5. Josy Joseph, 'The day the elected government was in place, the military role of the IPKF was over: interview with Lieutenant General A.S. Kalkat', Rediff.com, March 2000, https://www.rediff.com/news/2000/mar/27lanka.htm.
6. Josy Joseph, 'Till the LTTE get Eelam, they won't stop: interview with Major General Harkirat Singh', Rediff.com, March 2000, https://www.rediff.com/news/2000/mar/31lanka.htm. Also see: 'Kumarappa, Pulendran Eighteenth anniversary held in Jaffna', TamilNet, 5 October 2005, https://www.tamilnet.com/art.html?catid=13&artid=16019.
7. Ibid.

8. Depinder Singh, *Indian Peace Keeping Force in Sri Lanka*, Natraj Publishers, Delhi, 2001, p. X.
9. Ibid., p. X.
10. Ibid., pp. 85–122.
11. Sushant Singh, 'On Indian military decisions of today, shadow of a pyrrhic victory yesterday', *The Indian Express*, 13 October 2017, https://indianexpress.com/article/explained/indian-army-sri-lanka-ltte-liberation-tigers-of-tamil-eelam-jaffna-indian-peace-keeping-force-ipkf-in-fact-on-indian-military-decisions-of-today-shadow-of-a-pyrrhic-victory-yesterday-4887671/.
12. Manoj Joshi, 'Jain Commission opens up old wounds India inflicted upon itself', *India Today*, 1 December 1997, https://www.indiatoday.in/magazine/cover-story/story/19971201-jain-commission-opens-up-old-wounds-india-inflicted-upon-itself-831009-1997-12-01. Also see: Josy Joseph, 'The intelligence agencies said, Don't worry about the LTTE, they are our boys, they will not fight us: J.N. Dixit', Rediff.com, March 2000, https://www.rediff.com/news/2000/mar/24lanka.htm.
13. Neena Gopal, *The Assassination of Rajiv Gandhi*, Viking, Delhi, 2016, p. 67.
14. Sachi Sri Kantha, 'Mannar Massacres Which Led to the "Anuradhapura Massacre" of May, 1985', *Sangam.org*, https://sangam.org/2007/05/Mannar_Massacres.php?uid=2395.
15. Mervyn De Silva, 'Holy Buddhist city of Anuradhapura witnesses one of the bloodiest day in Sri Lankan history', *India Today*, 15 June 1985, https://www.indiatoday.in/magazine/neighbours/story/19850615-holy-buddhist-city-of-anuradhapura-witnesses-one-of-the-bloodiest-day-in-sri-lankan-history-770149-2013-12-16.
16. Ana Pararajasingham, 'The Sri Lankan government's military solution', *Green Left Weekly*, No. 214, 6 December 1995, http://www.hartford-hwp.com/archives/52/075.html.
17. Upinder Singh, *A History of Ancient and Early Medieval India: From the Stone Age to the 12th Century*, Pearson, Delhi, 2008, p. 47.
18. Rohan Bastin, 'Ritual Games for Goddess Pattini', *Social Analysis: The International Journal of Anthropology*, Vol. 45, No. 2, November 2001, pp. 120–142, https://www.jstor.org/stable/23170115?seq=1.
19. Special Correspondent, 'Memorial planned for Velu Nachiyar', *The Hindu*, 3 November 2012, https://www.thehindu.com/news/national/tamil-nadu/memorial-planned-for-velu-nachiyar/article4059116.ece.

20. Samuel Ratnajeevan Herbert Hoole, 'Christian Reaction to the Ethnic Conflict in Sri Lanka', *Dharma Deepika*, December 1996, Vol. 2, No. 2, pp. 122–150, https://www.researchgate.net/publication/215831961_Christian_Reaction_to_the_Ethnic_Conflict_in_Sri_Lanka.
21. Sachi Sri Kantha, 'Black Tigers: A Review', Tamilnation.org, 22 June 2004, https://tamilnation.org/ltte/black_tigers/index.htm.
22. For more, read the interview: Josy Joseph, 'The most difficult part was managing the withdrawal', *Outlook*, March 2000, https://www.rediff.com/news/2000/mar/27lanka.htm.
23. J.N. Dixit, *Assignment Colombo*, Konark Pubishers, Delhi, 2002, p. X.
24. P.K. Balachandran, 'Sri Lankan navy man who struck Rajiv with rifle butt arrested for predicting death of Sirisena', *The New Indian Express*, 31 January 2017, https://www.newindianexpress.com/world/2017/jan/31/sri-lankan-navy-man-who-struck-rajiv-with-rifle-butt-arrested-for-predicting-death-of-sirisena-1565533.html.
25. A.P. Maheshwari, 'From a Policeman's Heart: Society which honours its heroes produces more heroes!', The Indian Police Journal, November–December 2018, https://bprd.nic.in/WriteReadData/CMS/Spl.%20issue%20of%20IPJ.pdf.
26. 'The Fight Goes On For India's War Widows', *Qrius.com*, 13 August 2020, https://qrius.com/the-fight-goes-on-for-indias-war-widows/.

8. The Militancy Enterprise

1. Rahul Pandita, *Our Moon Has Blood Clots: A Memoir of a Lost Home in Kashmir*, Penguin Random House, Delhi, 2014, p. 63–64.
2. Basharat Peer, *Curfewed Night*, Random House India, Delhi, 2009, p. 16.
3. News Desk, '"Worst massacre in Kashmir's history": What happened on Gaw Kadal on this day in 1990', *TheKashmirWalla.com*, 21 January 2021, https://thekashmirwalla.com/2021/01/worst-massacre-in-kashmirs-history-what-happened-on-gaw-kadal-on-this-day-in-1990/.
4. 'Protection Aspects of UNHCR Activities on Behalf of Internally Displaced Persons', *Refugee Survey Quarterly*, Vol. 14, Issue 1–2, Spring 1995, pp. 176–191, https://doi.org/10.1093/rsq/14.1-2.176.
5. Mohammad Yousaf & Mark Adkin, *The Bear Trap—Afghanistan's Untold Story*, Jang Publishers, 1992, p. 29.
6. Ibid., p. 31.

7. 'Afghanistan's refugees: forty years of dispossession', *Amnesty.org*, 20 June 2019, https://www.amnesty.org/en/latest/news/2019/06/afghanistan-refugees-forty-years/.
8. Directorate of Intelligence, 'The Costs of Soviet Involvement in Afghanistan', https://www.cia.gov/readingroom/docs/DOC_0000499320.pdf.
9. Noor Ahmad Khalidi, 'Afghanistan: Demographic Consequences of War, 1978–1987', *Central Asian Survey*, Vol. 10, No. 9, 1991, pp. 101–126, http://www.nonel.pu.ru/erdferkel/khalidi.pdf.
10. Steve Coll, *Directorate S: The C.I.A. and America's Secret Wars in Afghanistan and Pakistan*, Penguin Press, USA, 2018, p. 47.
11. Ibid.
12. Ibid., p. 45.
13. Harinder Baweja, 'Mufti Sayeed's dark hour: Militants released for abducted daughter', *Hindustan Times*, 8 January 2016, https://www.hindustantimes.com/india/mufti-saeed-s-dark-hour-militants-released-for-abducted-daughter/story-527VIWsrLi2F3kiQ1hTT4O.html.
14. Nirupama Subramanian, 'Explained: The Kashmir Pandit tragedy', https://indianexpress.com/article/explained/exodus-of-kashmiri-pandits-from-valley-6232410/.
15. Sumegha Gulati, 'Why Kashmiris are using the hashtag #JagmohanTheMurderer after the Padma award announcement', *Scroll.in*, 29 June 2019, https://scroll.in/article/802579/why-kashmiris-are-recalling-jagmohanthemurderer-after-the-padma-award-announcement.
16. DH Web Desk, 'Who is Masood Azhar?', *Deccan Herald*, 1 May 2019, https://www.deccanherald.com/national/who-is-masood-azhar-731596.html.
17. Heather Timmons, 'In 'The Meadow,' a Chilling Alternate View of the 1995 Kashmiri Kidnappings', *The New York Times*, 13 April 2012, https://india.blogs.nytimes.com/2012/04/13/in-the-meadow-a-chilling-alternate-view-of-the-1995-kashmiri-kidnappings/.
18. Junaid Kathju, 'Civilian Killings in Kashmir: Probe After Probe, But No Justice', *TheQuint.com*, 2 May 2019, https://www.thequint.com/news/india/civilian-killings-security-forces-jammu-kashmir-investigations-no-justice.

19. Mohammad Umar, '26 Years After Kunan Poshpora, Army Still Enjoys Immunity For Sexual Violence', *TheWire.in*, 23 February 2017, https://thewire.in/rights/26-years-after-kunan-poshpora-army-still-enjoys-immunity-for-sexual-violence.
20. Iftikhar Gilani, 'Genesis of Insurgency in Kashmir: 1947–1989', unpublished; used with permission.
21. Safwat Zargar, 'Why did it take Kashmir police 23 years to make the first arrest in the Saderkoot massacre case?', *Scroll.in*, 20 May 2019, https://scroll.in/article/923696/why-did-it-take-kashmir-police-23-years-to-make-the-first-arrest-in-the-saderkoot-massacre-case.
22. Ibid.
23. Ibid.
24. Ibid.
25. Irfan Mehraj and Freny Manecksha, 'The Life and Death of a Pro-Government Militant in Kashmir', *TheWire.in*, 5 May 2017, https://thewire.in/politics/rashid-billa-kashmir-ikhwan.
26. Mukhtar Ahmad and Seema Guha, 'Dance of death on bloody Saturday—Kuka Parray shot in third weekend hit', *The Telegraph*, 13 September 2003, https://www.telegraphindia.com/india/dance-of-death-on-bloody-saturday-kuka-parray-shot-in-third-weekend-hit/cid/799635.
27. 'Fact Sheet on Jammu & Kashmir', Ministry of External Affairs, 20 May 2002, https://mea.gov.in/in-focus-article.htm?18987/Fact+Sheet+on+Jammu+amp+Kashmir.

9. The Hijack and its Aftermath

1. Vijay Sakhare, 'To what extent is the Kargil War a case of intelligence failure?', Takshashila, July 2020, https://takshashila.org.in/to-what-extent-is-the-kargil-war-a-case-of-intelligence-failure/.
2. Praveen Swami, 'The sacking of a Brigadier', *Frontline*, 23 June 2001, https://frontline.thehindu.com/the-nation/article30251027.ece.
3. Peerzada Ashiq, 'Three, including Army captain, chargesheeted in Shopian "fake encounter" in July', *The Hindu*, 27 December 2020, https://www.thehindu.com/news/national/other-states/three-including-army-captain-chargesheeted-in-shopian-fake-encounter-in-july/article33427265.ece.
4. A.S. Dulat with Aditya Sinha, *Kashmir: The Vajpayee Years*, HarperCollins, Delhi, 2015, p. 52.

5. Ibid.
6. Ibid., p. 58.
7. Javed M. Ansari, 'IC-814 hijacking still haunts Jaswant Singh', *India Today*, 31 October 2013, https://www.indiatoday.in/india/story/ic-814-hijacking-still-haunts-jaswant-singh-216125-2013-10-31.
8. Josy Joseph, *A Feast of Vultures: The Hidden Business of Democracy in India*, HarperCollins, Noida, p. 147–168.
9. Josy Joseph, 'Kandahar hijacked Kashmiri lives in Nepal', *DNA*, 8 May 2007, https://www.dnaindia.com/india/report-kandahar-hijacked-kashmiri-lives-in-nepal-1095403.
10. Aamir Ali Bhat, '"Names of killers still reverberate in my ears": 19 years after Chittisinghpora massacre, lone survivor recounts night that killed 35 Sikhs', *Firstpost.com*, 21 March 2019, https://www.firstpost.com/india/names-of-killers-still-reverberate-in-my-ears-19-years-after-chittisinghpora-massacre-lone-survivor-recounts-night-that-killed-35-sikhs-6299441.html.
11. Praveen Swami, 'The massacre at Chattisinghpora', *Frontline*, 1 April 2000, https://frontline.thehindu.com/other/article30253665.ece.
12. Ibid.
13. Ibid.
14. Muzamil Jaleel, 'Why justice eludes the victims of Pathribal fake encounter?', *The Indian Express*, 20 August 2017, https://indianexpress.com/article/india/why-justice-eludes-the-victims-of-pathribal-fake-encounter-4804985/.
15. The Newswire, 'Pathribal incident: IPS officer reinstated after clean chit', *Outlook*, 15 September 2005, https://www.outlookindia.com/newswire/story/pathribal-incident-ips-officer-reinstated-after-clean-chit/323020.
16. Muzamil Jaleel, 'Why justice eludes the victims of Pathribal fake encounter?', *The Indian Express*, 20 August 2017, https://indianexpress.com/article/india/why-justice-eludes-the-victims-of-pathribal-fake-encounter-4804985/.
17. Ravi Nair, 'Akshardham Judgment—The Law at Work', *Kractivist.com*, 21 June 2014, https://www.kractivist.org/akshardham-judgment-the-law-at-work/.
18. 'Fiction Must Make Sense', *Outlook*, 3 June 2014, https://www.outlookindia.com/blog/story/fiction-must-make-sense/3283.

19. Ibid.
20. Adambhai Sulemanbhai Ajmeri & Ors vs State of Gujarat, 16 May 1947, https://indiankanoon.org/doc/129620993/.
21. The Newswire, 'SC Acquits 6 Convicts in Gujarat Akshardham Attack Case', *Outlook*, 16 May 2014, https://www.outlookindia.com/newswire/story/sc-acquits-6-convicts-in-gujarat-akshardham-attack-case/841068.

10. Our Brutal Existence

1. Josy Joseph and Pradeep Thakur, 'Punjab cops hound whistleblower, family', *The Times of India*, 8 July 2010, https://timesofindia.indiatimes.com/india/punjab-cops-hound-whistleblower-family/articleshow/6144969.cms.
2. Ibid.
3. Ibid.
4. Kanwar Sandhu, 'J.F. Ribeiro's reign as Punjab director-general of police under severe critical scrutiny', *India Today*, 31 October 1989, https://www.indiatoday.in/magazine/special-report/story/19891031-j.f.-ribeiro-reign-as-punjab-director-general-of-police-under-severe-critical-scrutiny-816649-1989-10-31.
5. Ibid.
6. There are numerous examples of this. For example: Neha Dixit, 'A Chronicle of the Crime Fiction That is Adityanath's Encounter Raj', *TheWire.in*, 24 February 2018, https://thewire.in/rights/chronicle-crime-fiction-adityanaths-encounter-raj; '"Informer will be rewarded": J&K Police release list of 9 wanted terrorists, announce cash reward', TimesNowNew.com, 14 March 2021, https://www.timesnownews.com/india/article/informer-will-be-rewarded-jk-police-release-list-of-9-wanted-terrorists-announce-cash-reward/732244.
7. Ram Narayan Kumar with Amrik Singh, Ashok Agrwaal and Jaskaran Kaur, *Reduced to Ashes: The Insurgency and Human Rights in Punjab; Final Report: Volume One*, South Asia Forum for Human Rights, Kathmandu, p. 52.
8. Ibid., p. 5.
9. Ibid., p. 6.
10. Ibid. p. 55.
11. Ibid. p. 56.

12. Ibid., p. 56.
13. Ibid., p. 57.
14. Ibid., p. 59
15. Ibid., p. 6.
16. Ibid., p. x.
17. Ibid., pp. 9, 10.
18. Ibid., p. 161.
19. Ibid., p. 52.
20. Ibid.
21. Ibid.
22. Ibid.
23. Ibid.
24. Ibid., p. 53.
25. Asmita Bakshi, 'In Punjab, families of the "disappeared" await justice', *Mint*, 21 December 2020, https://lifestyle.livemint.com/news/big-story/in-punjab-families-of-the-disappeared-await-justice-111608471391872.html.
26. *'These Fellows Must Be Eliminated': Relentless Violence and Impunity in Manipur*, Human Rights Watch, 29 September 2008, https://www.hrw.org/report/2008/09/29/these-fellows-must-be-eliminated/relentless-violence-and-impunity-manipur.
27. Ibid.
28. Teresa Rehman, 'Murder in Plain Sight', *Tehelka*, 8 August 2009, http://old.tehelka.com/murder-in-plain-sight/.
29. PTI, 'Army officer Major Vijay Singh Balhara booked by CBI in Manipur extra-judicial killing case', *Financial Express*, 2 August 2018, https://www.financialexpress.com/india-news/army-officer-major-vijay-singh-balhara-booked-by-cbi-in-manipur-extra-judicial-killing-case/1267456/.
30. Hegde Commission Report on AFSPA, https://www.scribd.com/document/488932965/Hegde-Committee-Reports-pdf.
31. Ibid.
32. Ibid.
33. Gargi Verma, 'Chhattisgarh: NHRC accuses state officials of 'abetting' crimes of Salwa Judum', *The Indian Express*, 11 February 2020, https://indianexpress.com/article/india/chhattisgarh-nhrc-accuses-state-officials-of-abetting-crimes-of-salwa-judum-6261396/.

34. V. Venkatesan, 'A verdict and some questions', *Frontline*, 11 March 2005, https://frontline.thehindu.com/social-issues/article30203804.ece.
35. Josy Joseph & Pradeep Thakur, 'Punjab cops hound whistleblower, family', *The Times of India*, 9 July 2010, https://timesofindia.indiatimes.com/india/punjab-cops-hound-whistleblower-family/articleshow/6144969.cms.
36. Harish V. Nair, 'Supreme Court clamps down on "bench hunting"', *India Today*, 20 December 2014, https://www.indiatoday.in/india/north/story/supreme-court-bench-hunting-forum-shopping-favourable-order-bail-applications-lawyer-dushyant-dave-232036-2014-12-20.
37. Based on Samdeep Mohan Varghese's claims.
38. Correspondent, 'CBI books Delhi company in Rs 1,800-crore bank fraud case', Hindustan Times, 4 December 2020, https://www.hindustantimes.com/india-news/cbi-books-delhi-company-in-rs-1-800-crore-bank-fraud-case/story-VnZcd2m7NYQzogoVCbTxzN.html.

11. Gujarat Model

1. Pradip Kumar Maitra, 'RSS miffed with PM's "autocratic style"', *Hindustan Times*, 7 March 2015, https://www.hindustantimes.com/india/rss-miffed-with-pm-s-autocratic-style/story-YBCDifuM66asURHJ8opWHK.html.
2. Josy Joseph, 'Top generals, babus & netas in land-grab', *The Times of India*, 24 October 2010, https://timesofindia.indiatimes.com/india/Top-generals-babus-netas-in-land-grab/articleshow/6805880.cms.
3. 'Full text of DG Vanzara's letter slamming Amit Shah, Modi', *FirstPost.com*, 4 September 2013, https://www.firstpost.com/politics/read-full-text-of-dg-vanzaras-letter-slamming-amit-shah-modi-1083311.html.
4. Various enquiry reports read together, such as Krishnadas Rajagopal, 'Youth out to "kill Modi" died in fake encounter: report', *The Hindu*, 12 Januaru 2019, https://www.thehindu.com/news/national/youth-out-to-kill-modi-died-in-fake-encounter-report/article25974444.ece); 'Kauser Bi killed, body burnt; Gujarat govt to SC', Rediff.com, 30 April 2007, https://www.rediff.com/news/2007/apr/30fake.htm; 'Ishrat Jahan killed in fake police encounter: Probe', *The Times of*

India, 7 September 2009, http://timesofindia.indiatimes.com/articleshow/4983183.cms.

5. PTI, 'Justice Bedi panel indicts 9 cops, says 3 out of 17 Gujarat encounters fake', *Hindustan Times*, 12 January 2019, https://www.hindustantimes.com/india-news/justice-bedi-panel-indicts-9-cops-says-3-out-of-17-gujarat-encounters-fake/story-suLPKhReRcnfFEmPfp1cPN.html.
6. Krishnadas Rajagopal, 'Youth out to "kill Modi" died in fake encounter: report', *The Hindu*, 12 January 2019, https://www.thehindu.com/news/national/youth-out-to-kill-modi-died-in-fake-encounter-report/article25974444.ece.
7. 'Centre for CBI enquiry into Gujarat encounters', Rediff.com, 26 April 2007, https://in.rediff.com/news/2007/apr/26fake.htm.
8. *Central Bureau of Investigation v. Amitbhai Anil Chandra Shah And Anr*, 27 September 2017, https://indiankanoon.org/doc/48179074/.
9. Rebecca Samervel, 'Sohrabuddin said Vanzara ordered hit on Haren Pandya, gangster tells court', *The Times of India*, 4 November 2018, https://timesofindia.indiatimes.com/india/sohrab-said-vanzara-ordered-hit-on-haren-pandya-gangster-tells-court/articleshow/66494293.cms.
10. IANS, 'Prajapati killing: Trial against former Gujarat minister Amit Shah stayed', NDTV.com, 18 October 2012, https://www.ndtv.com/india-news/prajapati-killing-trial-against-former-gujarat-minister-amit-shah-stayed-502160.
11. 'Charge sheet has proof against Amit Shah: CBI', *Hindustan Times*, 16 December 2014, https://www.hindustantimes.com/india/charge-sheet-has-proof-against-amit-shah-cbi/story-svg1G4p88L2NN09Z8K2rHJ.html.
12. ENS, 'Days after he pulled up Amit Shah, CBI judge shifted', *The Indian Express*, 26 June 2014, https://indianexpress.com/article/india/india-others/days-after-he-pulled-up-shah-judge-shifted/.
13. Prem Shankar Jha, 'The Last Pillar of Indian Democracy Weakens Itself', *TheWire.in*, 5 May 2018, https://thewire.in/law/the-last-pillar-of-indian-democracy-has-crumbled.
14. Rohan Venkataramakrishnan, 'New reports tell us more about Sohrabuddin judge's death – and bring up fresh questions', *Scroll.in*, 27 November 2017, https://scroll.in/article/859391/new-

reports-tell-us-more-about-sohrabuddin-judges-death-and-bring-up-fresh-questions.

15. Niranjan Takle, 'A Family Breaks Its Silence: Shocking details emerge in death of judge presiding over Sohrabuddin trial', *The Caravan*, 20 November 2017, https://caravanmagazine.in/vantage/shocking-details-emerge-in-death-of-judge-presiding-over-sohrabuddin-trial-family-breaks-silence.
16. Ibid.
17. Niranjan Takle, 'Chief Justice Mohit Shah offered Rs 100 crore to my brother for a favourable judgment in the Sohrabuddin case: Late Judge Loya's sister', *The Caravan*, 21 November 2017, https://caravanmagazine.in/vantage/loya-chief-justice-mohit-shah-offer-100-crore-favourable-judgment-sohrabuddin-case.
18. Rohan Venkataramakrishnan, 'New reports tell us more about Sohrabuddin judge's death – and bring up fresh questions', *Scroll.in*, 27 November 2017, https://scroll.in/article/859391/new-reports-tell-us-more-about-sohrabuddin-judges-death-and-bring-up-fresh-questions.
19. 'Kapil Sibal claims Loya came to him to be taken off case', *DNA*, 1 February 2018, https://www.dnaindia.com/india/report-kapil-sibal-claims-loya-came-to-him-to-be-taken-off-case-2580185.
20. s.saurabh1998, 'Democracy Will Not Survive Without a Free Judiciary', LegalBites.in, 14 January 2018, https://www.legalbites.in/democracy-will-not-survive-without-a-free-judiciary/.
21. 'Loya Case the Tipping Point, Four SC Judges Say Democracy Is in Danger', *TheWire.in*, 12 January 2018, https://thewire.in/law/sc-justices-hold-historic-press-conference-triggered-judge-loya-case. Also see: Vakasha Sachdev, '"Most Inappropriate": Judges Slam Justice Mishra's PM Modi Praise', *TheQuint.com*, 23 February 2020, https://www.thequint.com/news/law/retired-judges-criticise-justice-arun-mishra-versatile-genius-comment-pm-modi-ap-shah-rs-sodhi-sawant.
22. 'Sohrabuddin fake encounter case: Court drops all charges against Amit Shah', *FirstPost.com*, 30 December 2014, https://www.firstpost.com/india/sohrabuddin-fake-encounter-case-court-drops-all-charges-against-amit-shah-2022637.html.
23. Vijay Hiremath and Anubha Rastogi, 'We were Rubabuddin's lawyers once; here's our account of what we saw happen with the

Sohrabuddin Sheikh fake encounter case', *TheLeaflet.in*, 4 January 2019, https://www.theleaflet.in/rubabuddins-former-lawyers-on-how-the-sohrabuddin-sheikh-fake-encounter-case-was-compromised/#.

24. Sukanya Shantha, 'All 22 Accused Acquitted in Sohrabuddin Shaikh Fake Encounter Case', *TheWire.in*, 21 December 2018, https://thewire.in/rights/all-22-accused-acquitted-in-sohrabuddin-shaikh-fake-encounter-case.
25. Ibid.
26. Dushyant Dave, 'Sohrabuddin Judgment: A Blot on Independence of Judiciary', BarAndBench.com, 7 January 2019, https://www.barandbench.com/columns/sohrabuddin-judgment-blot-independence-judiciary.
27. Sharmeem Hakim and Sunil Baghel, 'Judgment negates theory of police-politician nexus', *Mumbai Mirror*, 1 January 2019, https://mumbaimirror.indiatimes.com/mumbai/crime/judgment-negates-theory-of-police-politician-nexus/articleshow/67330829.cms.
28. '"Premeditated probe": Judge's brutal takedown of CBI in Sohrabuddin case', *Hindustan Times*, 28 December 2018, https://www.hindustantimes.com/india-news/premeditated-probe-judge-s-brutal-takedown-of-cbi-in-sohrabuddin-case/story-8kaz6vySswaiQIHtocEPNI.html.
29. Devesh K. Pandey and Darshan Desai, 'CBI charges four IB officers in Ishrat Jahan case', *The Hindu*, 6 February 2014, https://www.thehindu.com/news/national/CBI-charges-four-IB-officers-in-Ishrat-Jahan-case/article14073546.ece.
30. PTI, 'Justice Bedi panel indicts 9 cops, says 3 out of 17 Gujarat encounters fake', *Hindustan Times*, 12 January 2019, https://www.hindustantimes.com/india-news/justice-bedi-panel-indicts-9-cops-says-3-out-of-17-gujarat-encounters-fake/story-suLPKhReRcnfFEmPfp1cPN.html.
31. Author's conclusions, based on various inquiry reports, including the Justice Bedi Commission report.
32. PTI, 'NGOs stance on several development projects to hit economic growth: IB', *Hindustan Times*, 11 June 2014, https://www.hindustantimes.com/india/ngos-stance-on-several-development-projects-to-hit-economic-growth-ib/story-srwS2TLNdJwWiEwCWc3XXM.html.

33. Meera Mohanty, 'PM Narendra Modi says he is victim of NGOs' conspiracy', *The Economic Times,* 21 February 2016, https://economictimes.indiatimes.com/news/politics-and-nation/pm-narendra-modi-says-he-is-victim-of-ngos-conspiracy/articleshow/51081446.cms?from=mdr.
34. Sumit Ganguly, 'The Death of Human Rights in India?', *Foreign Policy,* 2 October 2020, https://foreignpolicy.com/2020/10/02/the-death-of-human-rights-in-india/.
35. Shoaib Daniyal, 'Modi's "raid raj" could easily become a tool to target political opponents', *Scroll.in,* 28 December 2016, https://scroll.in/article/825302/the-daily-fix-modis-raid-raj-could-easily-become-a-tool-to-target-political-opponents.
36. Sheikh Saaliq, 'Critics of India's Modi government face sedition charges', *Associated Press,* 6 March 2020, https://apnews.com/article/8c675cc2b23c5c83b0df523b09fa23f8.
37. 'Freedom in the World 2021', https://freedomhouse.org/country/india/freedom-world/2021.

12. Chaos

1. Meenakshi Ganguly, 'Dissent Is "Anti-National" in Modi's India', *Scroll.in,* 13 December 2019, https://scroll.in/article/946488/dissent-is-anti-national-in-modis-india-no-matter-where-it-comes-from; Regina Mihindukulasuriya, 'Nearly 18,000 Twitter accounts spread "fake news" for BJP, 147 do it for Congress: Study', *ThePrint.in,* 31 January 2020, https://theprint.in/politics/nearly-18000-twitter-accounts-spread-fake-news-for-bjp-147-do-it-for-congress-study/356876/.
2. Ashish Khetan, 'In the words of a zealot…', *Tehelka,* 18 December 2010, http://old.tehelka.com/in-the-words-of-a-zealot/.
3. Ibid.
4. Vijaita Singh, 'Had enough proof against Aseemanand', *The Hindu,* 9 March 2017, https://www.thehindu.com/news/national/had-enough-proof-against-aseemanand/article17436792.ece.
5. Sunanda Mehta, 'Since this new govt came, I have been told to go soft on accused (Hindu extremists): Special Public Prosecutor Rohini Salian', *The Indian Express,* 25 June 2015, https://indianexpress.com/

article/india/india-others/since-this-new-govt-came-i-have-been-told-to-go-soft-on-accused-hindu-extremists-special-public-prosecutor/.

6. Deeptiman Tiwary, 'Explained: The case against BJP candidate Sadhvi Pragya Thakur', *The Indian Express*, 20 April 2019, https://indianexpress.com/article/explained/sadhvi-pragya-thakur-digvijaya-singh-bjp-bhopal-lok-sabha-elections-malegaon-case-ajmer-dargah-blast-5681180/.
7. The Bhima Koregaon 16 are: Surendra Gadling, Sudhir Dhawale, Rona Wilson, Shoma Sen, Mahesh Raut, Varavara Rao, Sudha Bharadwaj, Arun Ferreira, Gautam Navlakha, Vernon Gonsalves, Anand Teltumbde, Stan Swamy, Hany Babu, Sagar Gorkhe, Ramesh Ghaichor and Jyoti Jagtap.
8. 'Bhima Koregaon case: Pune Police claim assassination plot against prime minister in chargesheet', *Scroll.in*, 15 November 2018, https://scroll.in/latest/902278/bhima-koregaon-case-pune-police-file-chargesheet-against-five-accused-who-were-arrested-in-june.
9. Niha Masih and Joanna Slater, 'They were accused of plotting to overthrow the Modi government. The evidence was planted, a new report says', *The Washington Post*, 10 February 2020, https://www.washingtonpost.com/world/asia_pacific/india-bhima-koregaon-activists-jailed/2021/02/10/8087f172-61e0-11eb-a177-7765f29a9524_story.html.
10. Nihalsing B. Rathod, 'One year of Bhima-Koregaon case: Part II | Why Elgar Parishad spooked Sambhaji Bhide and Milind Ekbote, the alleged architects of January 1, 2018 anti-Dalit violence', *TheLeaflet.in*, 6 January 2019, https://www.theleaflet.in/one-year-of-bhima-koregaon-case-part-ii-why-elgar-parishad-spooked-sambhaji-bhide-milind-ekbote/.
11. Sukanya Shantha, 'Case Against Hindutva Leaders Ignored, No Justice in Sight for Bhima Koregaon Violence Victims', *TheWire.in*, 26 September 2020, https://thewire.in/caste/bhima-koregaon-violence-hindutva-leaders-case\.
12. 'SC admonishes Maharashtra Police for not doing enough to arrest Hindutva leader Milind Ekbote', *Scroll.in*, 21 February 2018, https://scroll.in/latest/869465/sc-admonishes-maharashtra-police-for-not-doing-enough-to-arrest-hindutva-leader-milind-ekbote.
13. Somendranath Sharma and Shruti Ganapatye, 'NIA takes over

Bhima-Koregaon probe', *Mumbai Mirror*, 25 January 2020, https://mumbaimirror.indiatimes.com/mumbai/crime/nia-takes-over-bhima-koregaon-probe/articleshow/73599127.cms.

14. Sukanya Shantha, 'Incriminating Letters Were 'Planted' on Rona Wilson's Laptop: US Digital Forensics Firm', *TheWire.in*, 10 February 2021, https://thewire.in/tech/rona-wilson-elgar-parishad-letters-planted-us-firm.
15. Miles Kenyon, 'Citizen Lab and Amnesty International Uncover Spyware Operation Against Indian Human Rights Defenders', The Citizen Lab, 15 June 2020, https://citizenlab.ca/2020/06/citizen-lab-amnesty-international-uncover-spyware-operation-against-indian-human-rights-defenders/.
16. Seema Chishti and Dipankar Ghose, 'Surveillance via WhatsApp: On snoop target list—Rights lawyers to activists, DU prof to Defence journalist', *The Indian Express*, 1 November 2019, https://indianexpress.com/article/india/whatsapp-spyware-pegasus-surveillance-india-targets-6097093/.
17. IANS, 'Bansal's suicide note names DIG who bragged about being "Amit Shah's man"', *Business Standard*, 28 September 2016, https://www.business-standard.com/article/news-ians/bansal-s-suicide-note-names-dig-who-bragged-about-being-amit-shah-s-man-116092801280_1.html.
18. Josy Joseph, 'Ex-Principal Secretary to Delhi CM recounts his recent ordeal', *The Hindu*, 14 January 2017, https://www.thehindu.com/news/cities/Delhi/Ex-Principal-Secretary-to-Delhi-CM-recounts-his-recent-ordeal/article17036457.ece.
19. ANI, 'Arrest BJP's Kapil Mishra for Delhi riots: Brinda Karat writes to Amit Shah', *The New Indian Express*, 26 February 2020, https://www.newindianexpress.com/nation/2020/feb/26/arrest-bjps-kapil-mishra-for-delhi-riots-brinda-karat-writes-to-amit-shah-2108727.html.

Index

Acknowledgements

Thousands of officials, numerous spies, an innumerable number of whistle-blowers, and a string of dishonest bureaucrats, bullying tax inspectors and blackmailing investigators have all helped me understand the complex realities of India's security establishment and its permanent executive. I can thank none of them in public. They made this book possible.

Writing this book became my way of finding sanity before the workday filled up with the chaos of establishing Confluence Media as a platform-agnostic investigative journalism outfit. There are far too many kind and courageous individuals to thank for in this new phase—Binny, Jim, Subrata, Sailesh, Vishal, Niyaz, Shomik, Mahesh, Anisa, Gautam, Sasidharan, Rajeev, Adrian, Chindu, Sonal, Abhishek, Ushinor, Joyal, Aalif and others. If I have missed thanking anyone here, it is not deliberate.

Samir Bangara left on an early morning ride in June 2020, never to return. By then he had given me a crash course in start-ups, even as he created an impressive legacy of his own. This is my requiem for Samir.

In writing this book, Anand Mangnale, a restless and bright young colleague whom it is difficult to bracket into any one profession, and Nishtha Sood, a diligent researcher, provided immense assistance.

This book, and everything else I do in my life, reflects a bit of my boarding-school days and the many opinions of my schoolmates and my three siblings. I am grateful to all of them.

My professional pursuits come at a huge cost to the family. My wife, Priya Solomon, a far better writer than I am, gave up much of her own career to look after our family. Our daughter, Supriya, is now a compassionate, beautiful young woman starting her college life, and often my intellectual sparring partner. All my professional efforts, I believe, are in the hope of making the world a better place for her generation.

I am indebted to Kanishka Gupta, a dear friend and my agent, editor Amish Raj Mulmi, both of whom have been part of this book's journey from the very first step. My editors at Westland—Karthika, Ajitha, Dipanjali—have been, as usual, supportive, indulgent with time and patient.

Ultimately, this book is because of the everyday frustrations of fellow Indians, for whom the democracy they experience is mostly corrupt, lazy and intimidating. The terror must end. Every Indian must walk, and sleep, in the assurance that the state is in their service. The state is not a mafia operation.